WORDS MADE FLESH

THE ADEODATUS SERIES ON CATHOLIC EDUCATION & CULTURE

*General Editors: Alex E. Lessard & R. Jared Staudt*

The Adeodatus Series on Catholic Education & Culture offers books and essay collections dedicated to the retrieval, renewal, and refinement of the Catholic educational tradition. In covering Catholic educational figures, principles, themes, pedagogies, curricula, and culture, this series provides rich, practical resources to support Catholic leaders, teachers, and laity.

# WORDS MADE FLESH

## The Sacramental Mission of Catholic Education

R. Jared Staudt

FOREWORD BY *Patrick Reilly*

Catholic Education Press
Washington, D.C.

The paper used in this publication meets the minimum requirements of
American National Standards for Information Science—Permanence of
Paper for Printed Library Materials, ANSI Z39.48-1992.

∞

Cataloging-in-Publication Data is available at the Library of Congress
ISBN: 978-1-949822-44-1
eISBN: 978-1-949822-45-8

# TABLE OF CONTENTS

*Come, Holy Spirit,*
*fill the hearts of your faithful and kindle in them the fire of your love.*
*Send forth your Spirit and they shall be created.*
*And you shall renew the face of the earth.*


I dedicate this book to all my friends in Colorado,
especially those from the Augustine Institute,
Our Lady of Lourdes School,
the Archdiocese of Denver, and the Chesterton Academy of
Our Lady of Victory.

# Acknowledgments

Catholic education has shaped my life. I am greatly indebted to many mentors, teachers, friends, collaborators, and students through the years. My conversion occured when a Catholic school gave me a second chance in seventh grade, drawing me into the life of the Church and its educational mission. This book expresses the fruit of fifteen years of work in support of the renewal of Catholic education. It weaves together insights and material from talks, trainings, courses, prior articles, especially from the *Denver Catholic* (used with permission), and new content.

I first experienced the vision for a sacramental approach to education, rooted in the Dawsonian vision of the Study of Christian Culture, within the Catholic Studies Program at the University of St. Thomas. I'm grateful for the mentorship of the late Don Briel, who guided my undergraduate thesis on Christopher Dawson and my master's thesis on St. John Henry Newman. In 2018, I connected with another of his students, Dr. Alex Lessard, and our collaboration through Adeodatus has provided new impetus for the next stage of my service in Catholic education. I also simply cannot imagine my educational work without the theological mentorship of Dr. Matthew Levering and the late Fr. Matthew Lamb at Ave Maria University.

I'm grateful to many other friends who have shaped my approach to education. Dr. Joseph Burns and Dr. Sean Innerst guided me through my first years teaching catechetics and theology at the Augustine Institute. During this time, one of my students, Rosemary Vander Weele, invited me to offer formation for her teachers at Our Lady of Lourdes, which deepened my thinking and experience of Catholic liberal education. John O'Brien first introduced me to poetic knowledge and the influence of John Senior, which has proved pivotal in coalescing my vision of education. While at the University of Mary, I collaborated closely with Dr. Joshua Hren of Wiseblood Books, who enhanced my appreciation for the sacramental vision of literature. At the Archdiocese of Denver, Dr. Scott Elmer offered a model of pastoral ministry, and my colleagues in the Office of Catholic Schools, Elias Moo, Abriana Chilelli, and Toni Vaeth, exemplified educational leadership. I'm still in awe of Dave Holman and Ash Lessard for taking an enormous leap of faith in collaborating on founding the Chesterton Academy of Our Lady of Victory. Arriving in the Carolinas last year, I am also grateful for the unexpected friendship and collaboration with Dr. Michael Shick, the founding President of Rosary College.

# Foreword

Learning should be filled with revelations—those wondrous moments when a text, or a sermon, or a lecture opens our understanding to something that was there all along, but in the shadows. I believe Dr. Staudt's book will be a revelation for many of its readers, especially teachers and school leaders who know in their hearts the special value of Catholic education but need a master to pull aside the curtain and fully reveal its splendor.

For me, this book pulls together so much of the wisdom about education that I have encountered in my own studies, mostly by reading the great masters: Aristotle, St. Augustine, St. Thomas Aquinas, St. John Henry Newman, Mortimer Adler, Sr. Miriam Joseph, Luigi Giussani, Ronald McArthur, Stratford Caldecott, and so many more. Here Dr. Staudt articulates so much of what I and my team at The Cardinal Newman Society have been striving toward, together with many other partners like the vitally important Adeodatus apostlate, in the renewal of faithful Catholic education.

Dr. Staudt is appropriately creative in his application of this wisdom to the contemporary Church and culture, but it is by synthesizing and presenting the divine order of what the Church already knows about education—too often neglected and even forgotten in recent decades—that his book is truly a welcome revelation to all those who are engaged in the great task of renewal.

Such revelations are especially important to Catholics today, emerging from the confusion in Catholic education over the last few decades. Few adults under the age of 60 have ever experienced Catholic education as it ought to be, and many have been heartbroken by the immorality and apostasy of their children who were entrusted to Catholic schools and colleges. But this only heightens our desire for something much better and our determination to ensure that future generations receive the complete formation in truth and virtue that is promised by an authentic Catholic education.

In my few decades of wrestling with this problem, I have experienced many enlightening revelations of the nature of Catholic education, especially when reading the masters I listed above—and two other experiences stand out as especially influential. The first was in 1990 when, as a 20-year old student, I was greatly disappointed with my Jesuit university's infidelities. As editor of my college newspaper, I wrote frequently in opposition to campus scandals and advocated Catholic teaching, and for this I was scorned by my fellow students, professors, and university leaders.

Like most young Catholics of my generation, I was ignorant of Newman's *Idea of a University* and unable to draw upon the deep well of the Church's guidance for Catholic schools. I was also unfamiliar with the budding renewal of faithful Catholic education at a rising number of schools, homeschools, and colleges across America. Only recently have these achieved the stature they deserve among faithful Catholic families, and we are glad to recognize them in The Newman Guide.

Just as I was growing discouraged by my university's intransigent secularization and my limited ability to explain the problem, Pope Saint John Paul II issued his apostolic constitution, *Ex corde Ecclesiae*, on Catholic higher education. The constitution was a great gift to the Church. For too long, young people had been subjected to the nonsense and even malformation of wayward colleges advertised as "Catholic education." The Holy Father's eloquent defense of the Catholic university, according to principles of human nature and knowledge that apply across all levels of education, brought tears to my eyes. I better understood what it was that I yearned for, and what I later discovered was being put into practice at the faithful Newman Guide colleges. I was enamored of the vision.

The beauty of authentic Catholic education was also compellingly revealed to me through the experience of classroom teaching—which for me began much later than most school teachers. As the parents of five kids, my wife Rosario and I had done our best to form them in truth, goodness, and beauty, the most natural Catholic education. Then Rosario asked me to teach logic to 7th–9th graders in her Aquinas Learning hybrid program.

For nearly two decades, I had devoted myself and The Cardinal Newman Society to the reform and renewal of faithful Catholic education, speaking frankly about its failings while celebrating those educators for whom Christ was truly master and perfect *rabbi*. But I didn't think I was called to teaching in a classroom. I worked regularly with educators, but I had never worked in a school.

Yet after all my years of poring through the writings of Newman and other great masters to contemplate the nature of Catholic education, it was in the act of teaching young people that I gained new appreciation for the great value of Catholic education. What a blessing it is to teach, especially in the light of the Catholic Church and the hope of Christ, Word and Wisdom! There's nothing like planting knowledge and seeing it blossom in the fertile souls of young people. It's by engaging in Catholic education that one truly gets to know it—by experiencing its sacramental mission, as Dr. Staudt describes it, a communion of creature and Creator.

And what an awesome responsibility it is! Newman prayed for his students: "May I engage in them . . . remembering the worth of souls and that I shall have to answer for the opportunities given me of benefiting those who are under my care."[1]

In a similar way, I believe this book will be a revelation to the reader who perhaps senses the form and worth of Catholic education but cannot adequately explain it. Dr. Staudt's insights into the sacramental mission of Catholic education are precious. Just as when I first read Newman or *Ex corde Ecclesiae*, or when I experienced the joy of teaching, this book reveals everything I knew in my heart about Catholic education in a clear, organized, and very useful manner.

---

1. Quoted in Anne Mozely, ed., *Letters and Correspondence of John Henry Newman during His Life in the English Church with a Brief Autography* (London: Longman, Green, and Co., 1903), 132. Accessed at newmanreader.org

What Dr. Staudt captures so well is the fundamentally human nature of education, which in most instances today has neglected human nature for the purpose of forming workers, which ultimately results in less valuable workers because of their inability to reason and to rise to the contemplation of God and the order of creation. Man is both creature and spirit, and an education that forms students to be more fully human must tend to the soul—intellect, will, and passion—through a healthy body and complete respect for human dignity. That dignity is not, as commonly assumed today, rooted in liberty but found in man's unique and supernatural calling to full communion with God—to which every aspect of education must be ordered. A human education does not accumulate information but ascends above knowledge—to borrow a phrase from Newman—to the contemplation of God.

Catholic education is, as our expert author argues so well, sacramental. And every person is called to this sacramental experience of using man's unique gift of reason to know God's handiwork and thereby know something of Him. Moreover, we do this not as pagans but as Christians united to the Word, Jesus Christ, through whom we better understand everything we can possibly learn in every branch of knowledge.

This book appears amid a nationwide movement toward classical education—a movement of which Dr. Staudt is a prominent leader. Even before Pope St. John Paul II sought the reunification of faith and reason, the decline of Catholic identity and fidelity in many Catholic schools and colleges was frequently lamented, and now the classical movement is also reminding Catholic educators of the importance of forming young people in the skills of reasoning and the contemplation of higher truths. Most education today lacks sufficient attention to both reason and faith.

Of course, recovering what has been lost in liberal education is just one important step in the renewal, which must also recover the inspired developments of Catholic education across the centuries. The best classical educators recognize that the wisdom of the Greeks and Romans was fully incorporated in the best Catholic education for many centuries, and so we ought not look back to pagan education (as has been the emphasis of the Protestant classical movement) but to what Catholic educators were doing so well not very long ago. The footsteps are still fresh in the garden.

It is also worthy of note that Dr. Staudt makes this gift of his knowledge just as the Church in the U.S. is in the midst of its urgently needed Eucharistic Revival, renewing devotion to the Real Presence in the Eucharist. The Cardinal Newman Society has been making the argument that, as Catholic education is the most effective means of evangelization, it must be prioritized as key to the recovery of understanding of the Eucharist and its importance to our worship, our formation, our living, and our salvation. Like the happy trend of restoring the tabernacle to the center of the altars in churches across the country, Dr. Staudt clearly situates the Eucharist at the center of Catholic education, where it has always belonged.

So be prepared: this is one of those books you'll hold onto, whether or not you're a "professional" educator. With every chapter, you will yearn to be part of the excitement within one of the growing numbers of schools, homeschools, and colleges where authentic, faithful, Eucharistic education is alive and under the loving care of the Master Teacher, Jesus Christ. I hope, for you and many Catholics, this book is a revelation that increases both understanding and the desire for the complete Catholic formation of every young Catholic. Adeodatus, under the leadership of Alex Lessard and in partnership with great minds like Jared Staudt, is devoted to this full recovery of true Catholic education—for which this book is a valuable tool.

PATRICK J. REILLY
*President and founder, The Cardinal Newman Society*

# Introduction

## The Sacramental Mission of Catholic Education

Forming souls and building culture together form the sacramental mission of Catholic education. These two goals, laid out by the Church for Catholic education, are profoundly related. Catholic education follows the same principle of sacramentality that permeates the whole of Catholic life. Its internal form flows from conformity to the *Logos*, the divine mind, that shapes the way disciples think, imagine, and pray. As sacramental, it also leads to a concrete embodiment in the life of the Christian community and the daily actions of the disciple. As expressed in this book, a sacramental approach to education draws together the inner and outer life: mind and body, soul and culture, prayer and work, salvation and mission, the individual and community. We need nothing less than a reintegration of the person and our communities through a renewal of education.

The Catholic Church has an unparalleled history of education, inheriting the legacy of the Greco-Roman world, building upon it through the scholastic studies of Christendom, and transmitting it in a new and transformed way to the modern world. In fact, the whole model of "school" embraced through the world today flows from the tradition of the liberal arts and the university preserved by the Church. Although the Catholic Church remains a major force in education, it no longer serves as the driving force of educational theory and practice.

The task for Catholics, then, is one both of looking back and forward at the same time. There is much to rediscover and reappropriate from the Church's two-thousand-year history. At the same time, new challenges emerge with the saturation of technology and confusion about the very nature of the human person. Given the Church's robust sapiential tradition, she can address these new challenges better than any other institution. This will be a task both of forming the souls of new generations and guiding them in living in modern culture according to what they learn from the Church.

## How to Make Catholic Education More Robustly Catholic

In order to fulfill this lofty goal, Catholic schools first must rediscover the purpose of their very existence. Why does the Church run schools? In its mission to spread the Good News to all nations, Christians have always recognized education, the vital task of forming the mind and soul, as central in this effort. With profound changes in both Church and culture over the last sixty years, it is certainly time to ask this question again, "Why does the Church run schools?" To effectively fulfill their mission, schools must understand their purpose anew and commit to following it, despite the many obstacles facing them.

Once schools ask this question and begin to reflect on their mission, many find themselves asking another question, "How can we make our school more Catholic?" Schools begin looking at their curriculum, how they teach the faith, whom they hire, and how often they celebrate Mass. There is no single solution, although one thing is clear: the school's Catholic identity and mission must provide the central *raison d'être* for the school and all that it does. Too often we conceive of Catholic schools like any other school, with certain "add-ons" that make it distinctive, such as Mass and religion class. This reduction arises when a majority of teachers, administrators, and parents have been formed in a secular model of education and do not recognize the distinctive Catholic approach to formation.

Catholics schools need nothing less than a spiritual and intellectual renewal, one that radiates from its very center and gives new life to all that happens within its walls. No amount of bureaucratic maneuverings, technological add-ons, or flashy textbooks will suffice to make substantial changes. Likewise, adding a few accidental elements related to the faith, however important they may be, will not transform a school to be more robustly Catholic. Moving beyond extrinsic changes, the faith has to permeate the whole, shaping the school's approach to formation and education in an organic way.

There are two general ways of conceiving how this can occur. First, the way the school conceives of its pedagogy and curriculum must flow from and lead to a Catholic worldview, which shapes a Christian way of thinking. Second, the school should cultivate a distinctively Catholic culture, which forms its teachers and students in a Christian way of living. This draws together the two fundamental tasks of the school: forming souls and building culture. Explaining this reality, Pope Benedict XVI made clear that "Catholic schools should therefore seek to foster that unity between faith, culture, and life which is the fundamental goal of Christian education."[1] As he articulates it, education does not find its *telos* in employment or practical skills, but in a way of life. Catholic education teaches its students how to live in an integrated and holistic way to guide its graduate to a mature Christian adulthood, and which secondarily will lead graduates to do well in the world.

To explicate this vision of the unity of faith and culture, we could start with ten simple and practical points to make a school more Catholic. These points will be explained in more detail throughout the remainder of this book.

First, just as the *Eucharist* "is the source and summit of the whole Christian life,"[2] so it must be the heart of the school. The cul-

1. Benedict XVI, Address to the Participants in the Convention of the Diocese of Rome, June 11, 2007, https://www.vatican.va/content/benedict-xvi/en/speeches/2007/june/documents/hf_ben-xvi_spe_20070611_convegno-roma.html.

2. Second Vatican Council, *Lumen Gentium*, 11, https://www.vatican.va/ archive/hist_councils/ii_vatican_council/documents/vat-ii_const_19641121_lumen-gentium_en.html.

ture of the school should form around the rhythm of the liturgy. At a minimum the school should have Mass weekly, but daily Mass more than anything else should be the priority in Catholic formation, because it draws students to the true Teacher, the Word of God. Eucharistic adoration should also occur on a weekly basis, teaching the students how to adore and honor Jesus in the Eucharist. Although it is hard at first, it is amazing how the students learn to appreciate this silent time with Jesus.

The next most important element consists in the *witness of teachers and administrators*. They embody the faith in their example and way of teaching and leading. Pope Benedict explained that teachers "must also be ready to lead the commitment made by the entire school community to assist our young people, and their families, to experience the harmony between faith, life, and culture."[3] Hiring teachers must include mission fit and dedication to forming children in the faith. Formation for current teachers is essential to help them grow in their relationship with God and knowledge of the Catholic tradition. In addition to teachers, we need the witness of *clergy and religious* as an active presence in the school. Their role will make clear that the school exists as part of the Church's mission of evangelization. Their presence also will plant seeds for vocations and help ensure that the school remains faithful to its task of formation.

Even secular people expect that a faith-based school will provide strong *human formation*. If our graduates are not more virtuous and mature than students graduating from the public schools, we have fundamentally failed. Without this formation, how else will students be able to navigate the challenges of our culture, let alone exercise leadership? Students also need to experience Jesus in a living way, not only in prayer, but also by encountering the poor. Human formation

---

3. Benedict XVI, Address at a Meeting with Catholic Educators at The Catholic University of America, April 17, 2008, https://www.vatican.va/content/benedict-xvi/en/speeches/2008/april/documents/hf_ben-xvi_spe_20080417_cath-univ-washington.html.

and service should make the teaching of the faith concrete. If it is just words in a book, it will be quickly discarded, as too often occurs.

Continuing this point, another crucial way of making the faith come alive entails teaching our students how to *pray*. Prayer is where we meet God most directly. Pope Benedict made this point very clearly at the beginning of *Deus caritas est*: "Being Christian is not the result of an ethical choice or a lofty idea, but the encounter with an event, a person, which gives life a new horizon and a decisive direction."[4] Faith cannot remain an abstract academic discipline, evaluated by a written test, because it must flow from a living encounter with Christ. We have to teach our students to pray, especially through *lectio divina*, where they learn to enter into a conversation with God, listening to his voice in Scripture and responding to him.

Catholic education flows from a long *tradition*. The Church boasts two thousand years of an educational tradition that encompasses great works of literature, scientific breakthroughs, and a great synthesis of faith and reason. Saints have led the way as the Church's greatest teachers, reformers, and witnesses. And yet, many Catholic school students learn information in the abstract and not as part of an ongoing, living tradition of Catholic culture. They remain ignorant of the greatest cultural achievements of the Church. As Christopher Dawson argues in *The Crisis of Western Education*, we have to immerse our students in the living legacy of Christian culture so they can be formed by it, live it, and pass it on to the next generation.[5]

Education is largely a matter of language, which we use to communicate and express ideas (this is true even outside the liberal arts). *Latin* is the Church's own language, and learning it opens a doorway to Catholic history, tradition, and liturgy. It helps to impart a distinct

---

4. Benedict XVI, encyclical letter *Deus caritas est*, 1, https://www.vatican.va/content/benedict-xvi/en/encyclicals/documents/hf_ben-xvi_enc_20051225_deus-caritas-est.html.

5. Christopher Dawson, *The Crisis of Western Education* (Washington, D.C.: The Catholic University of America Press, 2003).

identity, including being able to pray in common with other Catholics throughout the world. Practically speaking, it sheds light on the English language as at least thirty percent of its vocabulary comes from Latin and another thirty from French (which itself originates in Latin). Also, Latin helps us to grasp the basics of grammar more easily than through English (due to English's simpler grammar).

The *arts* provide immersion into the Catholic tradition. The Church has an unrivaled literary, musical, and artistic tradition. As we emphasize the technical elements of education, it is important to remember that computers can never replace deep thinking and creative expression. The arts will be more relevant than ever with the rise of robotics! Literature helps situate students within the story of the Church and to explore moral and spiritual themes in an embodied way. Building on Latin, Gregorian Chant provides a simple and beautiful way to help form a contemplative mind, and it also laid the foundation for the development of classical music. The visual arts are essential for cultivating an imagination informed by faith. Students should be familiar with the great Catholic artists and their works.

Immersion in the beauty of Catholic tradition should overflow to *school Masses*. School Masses are not known for their reverence or beauty, especially in music. If students learn to be prayerful in school, this should express itself primarily at Mass, as the students will come to know how to enter into its mysteries to meet God there. The homily should confidently lead the students into the mystery of the liturgy and its readings, reserving a conversation and Q&As for the classroom. Kneeling before the altar, students can encounter the transcendent mystery of God, coming into contact with the one who is Truth, Goodness, and Beauty himself.

Finally, the school should look and feel Catholic. The *environment* should be enriched by Catholic symbols and the beauty of Catholic art. Archbishop Michael Miller, CSB, in *The Holy See's Teaching on Catholic Schools*, expresses this point persuasively:

If Catholic schools are to be true to their identity, they should try to suffuse their environment with this delight in the sacramental. Therefore they should express physically and visibly the external signs of Catholic culture through images, symbols, icons and other objects of traditional devotion. A chapel, classroom crucifixes and statues, signage, celebrations and other sacramental reminders of Catholic ecclesial life, including good art which is not explicitly religious in its subject matter, should be evident.[6]

The visual environment will remind everyone of the spiritual community of which they are a part.

Robustly Catholic schools will arise as a combination of people who are committed to its mission, a curriculum and program of formation that imparts a Catholic vision, and an environment or culture that embodies this vision in its daily life. Schools can rediscover their mission and identity in simple and concrete ways, embracing aspects of this vision one step at a time.

## A Crisis of Conviction

For this work of renewal to happen, there must first be a strong commitment to the Church's vision of Catholic education. This cannot arise without a conviction rooted in faith. The supernatural and infused virtue of faith provides a divine vision of life and what matters most. It is not possible to appreciate the distinctive task of Christian formation without faith. Simply through our own efforts, we will always take a pragmatic view that prioritizes the immediate human needs of a community. Elevated into a participation in God's own knowledge, faith provides new priorities that put God and the eternal stakes of human life first. Faith does not simply add additional knowledge to reason. It "turns the world

---

6. Michael J. Miller, *The Holy See's Teaching on Catholic Schools* (Manchester, N.H.: Sophia Institute Press, 2006), 40.

upside down" (Acts 17:6) by changing how we view and value all
things in light of God.

When searching for the cause of decline in any Catholic community, whether it be a school, parish, university, or charitable organization, we should begin by probing conviction. All too often,
Catholic communities lose their supernatural conviction, grounded
in faith, and become institutions focused on performing human
tasks. Education, health care, and service to the poor are, of course,
human tasks that flow from the concrete needs of people, which the
Church is called to address. We must respond to these human needs,
however, with more than our own efforts. Faith inspires us to act in
a Christian manner, and charity responds, although not with human
effort alone, but impelled by God's love working through us.

Too often today, Catholic organizations claim they must remain
neutral in the public sphere if they are performing general services,
including education. The Church, however, does not run schools
simply to teach children how to read and write. Even though these
are essential skills in education, they fall within a much broader task
of formation. Catholic schools have struggled to integrate all of their
activities within one clear and integrated vision. The conviction of
faith leads also to a conviction regarding reason—that it can come
to know the truth of things and that even faith builds upon this
capacity for truth. The Church teaches reading, beyond its own
intrinsic value, so that we can receive the truth of God's revelation
through it. In building up the mind, through faith and reason both,
schools help students to become more alive by entering into the truth.

For this reason, everything in the school flows from the fundamental conviction of faith: that the one true God, the Holy Trinity,
has created the world and made humanity in his image to be able to
perceive the truth of this world. The Son of God has entered into
the world to redeem fallen humanity, leading us to truth in a higher
way through faith. Together faith and reason draw us to the Word
of God because there is one truth rooted in the God who is Truth.

To approach truth from only one perspective would fall short of a vision of the whole. Teaching in a Catholic school, even the basics of reading, writing, and arithmetic, requires a supernatural conviction in the truth of God, creation, humanity, and redemption. The Supreme Court has recognized this fundamental truth about Catholic education. In its July 8, 2020, ruling, *Our Lady of Guadalupe School v. Agnes Morrissey-Berru,* the court recognized that Catholic school teachers are ministers carrying out a distinctively religious mission. For instance, the ruling relates: "What matters, at bottom, is what an employee does. . . . Educating young people in their faith, inculcating its teachings, and training them to live their faith are responsibilities that lie at the very core of the mission of a private religious school." The ruling also recognizes the canonical oversight of bishops: "In the Catholic tradition, religious education is 'intimately bound up with the whole of the Church's life.' Under canon law, local bishops must satisfy themselves that 'those who are designated teachers of religious instruction in schools . . . are outstanding in correct doctrine, the witness of a Christian life, and teaching skill.'"[7] The Supreme Court recognizes the freedom of the Catholic school to hire faith-filled teachers, *so long as* these teachers truly carry out a distinctively religious mission in their teaching.

If we cannot recognize Catholic schools as faith-driven communities offering distinctively Catholic formation, the protections of the court would no longer apply. Above and beyond that, they would fall short of their God-given mission. As culture becomes more secular, the temptation to conform to the culture becomes stronger. At the same time, if schools follow the cultural trends, the very purpose for their existence erodes, because they do not offer anything distinct from other schools. We will need more than the protection of the courts to survive, drawing upon a conviction that

---

7. *Our Lady of Guadalupe School v. Agnes Morrissey-Berru,* 591 U.S. (2020), 18, 19, quoting *Catechism of the Catholic Church,* 8; and *Code of Canon Law,* can. 804§2.

unites all the members of our communities in common action. Every teacher and employee must be able to communicate the distinctive identity and mission of Catholic schools. As time goes on, the surrounding culture will become more unable to understand the decisions of a truly Catholic community. Can we provide compelling answers for why we approach education the way that we do?

Catholic schools require a critical mass of employees who share the conviction rooted in faith in the supernatural mission of Catholic education. Helen Alvaré describes this dynamic astutely in her book *Religious Freedom after the Sexual Revolution: A Catholic Guide.*[8] First of all, no teacher should be rowing in the wrong direction, because "employees who *publicly* reject an institution's Catholic beliefs, are, by definition, unable to help it be all that it is called to be."[9] Teachers, in particular, drive the mission of a Catholic school by instantiating it and delivering it to students. In addition, teachers influence one another, creating a community of either conviction or lukewarmness within the school. Alvaré further points out that, in line with social influence theory, the "opinions commanding majority assent can significantly move the opinions of others in a group."[10] The greater the conviction of administrators, teachers, and parents, the more normative and influential the living of the faith will be within the school.

Rather than enforcing the bare minimum, Alvaré points to the need for institutional revival for the future health of our schools (and other institutions). Especially when challenged about beliefs, Catholic communities "should stop implying that 'the bishop made me do it.' Instead, they should communicate first a thicker and more *integrated* religious description of a Catholic institution as a community of 'all-in' service to Christ."[11] Our schools carry a mission

---

8. Helen Alvaré, *Religious Freedom after the Sexual Revolution: A Catholic Guide* (Washington, D.C.: The Catholic University of America Press, 2022).
9. Alvaré, 88.
10. Alvaré, 103.
11. Alvaré, 69.

on behalf of Christ to manifest in words and actions his loving presence. This requires, of course, hiring for mission and ensuring that all those who work in Catholic schools are willing to live and represent the faith and to communicate it to others. Alvaré also encourages us to be clear and confident in how we communicate. Our countercultural positions are well founded and even backed up empirically.[12] Clear communication flows from a stronger Christian community: both need to be strongly Christ-centered.

Conviction points the way forward: embracing the truth that God has entrusted to us, sharing it with love, and living it with confidence. If our institutions put faith first and remain rooted in the conviction of the truth, they can withstand many obstacles. The school community should exist as a place that embodies faith, building a Christian way of life (or culture) for its members, and becoming a place of refuge within a hostile culture.

## Rooted in the Soil, Made for the Stars: Recovering an Imaginative Vision

Conviction roots us in what is highest, but we also face a crisis threatening the very foundation of our humanity—a sickness of our imagination. Catholic education cannot simply remain on its current trajectory of competing according to academic standards and expectations of the culture. It requires greater inspiration to thrive, needing to be infused with a divine fire of life and love. A vivified imagination will rely on the beauty of the arts and nature, just as much, if not more than, many traditional disciplines. Our students will not care to learn the truth without inspiration and love. They

---

12. Chapter seven, for instance, "provides language and evidence to help Catholic institutions demonstrate that their teachings are loving, and argues that Catholic sexual expression norms are more likely to promote the outcomes that lawmakers claim they are seeking to realize via contemporary sexual expression laws: health, freedom, equality, and human dignity" (Alvaré, 13).

need their hearts and then their minds to be captured by the God who is truth, goodness, beauty, and love.

We are too far removed not only from God, but also his creation. A sacramental approach to education takes the body and creation seriously as the starting point for the contemplation of higher truths. Nature provides the foundation upon which grace and faith build, and this stable rock has worn thin in our lives. Simply looking at the stars each night would produce more philosophers—thoughtful and inspired people—and less atheists. The desire to know, the foundation for philosophical thinking, springs from wonder, the awe that arises from the overwhelming beauty of creation.

Without wonder, life becomes tedious. Descending into boredom and ennui exposes us to domination by destructive desires that enter into the vacuum of an untethered mind and heart. It's a problem rising up from the bottom and cutting us off from the top. We become too good for our roots, the dirt from which we were made, and have no interest in our true destiny, manifested by the splendor of the night sky. The great educator John Senior noted that "there is something destructive—destructive of the human itself—in cutting us off from the earth from whence we come and the stars, the angels, and God himself to whom we go."[13] We can decipher a link between the two: the soil that God used to make us literally derives from stardust—everything in the universe does. But the stars stand for something more than the building blocks of the universe, they are a witness and call to the reality that we are more than simply dirt: we are made for a transcendent purpose that alone will make us happy.

"Made for the stars but rooted in the soil" is how Fr. Francis Bethel, OSB, captures the arc of Senior's thought in his biography, *John Senior and the Restoration of Realism:* "He realized by his own experience that the human plant, in order to tend to the stars, must be nourished in

---

13. John Senior, *The Restoration of Christian Culture* (Norfolk, Va.: IHS Press, 2008), chap. 7.

the soil of this world. His turnabout and then his work with students deeply impressed on him that we must ground all intellectual and affective life on the experiential and imaginative level."[14] Educators somehow must capture both elements. The grit of earthly reality offers a needed foundation, getting our hands dirty and experiencing the goodness of God's creation. This dirt, *humus*, humbly reminds us of who we are, not bodiless angels, or worse, ghosts living in machines, as Descartes described us, surrounded by a bunch of other machines. Those who do not look down at the soil are not likely to look up either, because they are too busy, or too distracted, living in an artificial world. Education can offer a turning back, a conversion to the world God created in both its dirtiness and beauty. That is where we can find our identity as dust bound for heaven.

Stars remind us of our call in Catholic education to transcend the confines of our immediate experience. The stars point us to God, which is why we would have less atheists if we spent more time stargazing. Looking at a fully illuminated night sky is humbling, when we think of our own littleness before the great vastness of the universe. And yet, stars are also exhilarating and inspiring, because they remind us that we are called to something greater. God, the one who created the stars, and knows each one, calls us beyond this earth and beyond the cosmos into his own life. Psalm 8 captures the humility and exhilaration inspired by the heavens:

> When I look at thy heavens, the work of thy fingers,
>> the moon and the stars which thou hast established;
> what is man that thou art mindful of him,
>> and the son of man that thou dost care for him?

---

14. Francis Bethel, *John Senior and the Restoration of Realism* (Merrimack, N.H.: Thomas More College Press, 2017), 8. This soil could also be a rich cultural experience, as Senior found in the Catholic literary revival of the twentieth century with its "Catholicism grounded in human soil—in songs and stories and mirth, in customs and manners" (120).

Yet thou hast made him little less than God,
    and dost crown him with glory and honor.
Thou hast given him dominion over the works of thy hands;
    thou hast put all things under his feet,
all sheep and oxen,
    and also the beasts of the field,
the birds of the air, and the fish of the sea,
    whatever passes along the paths of the sea.
O Lord, our Lord,
    how majestic is thy name in all the earth! (vv. 4–9)

Though the Lord made us out of dust, he calls us to share his dominion over the earth. Even in our littleness, the stars teach us our greatness because they witness to the call that God gives us as stewards over his creation. In taking up this work, we become cooperators with God, offering him true praise, recognizing his majesty and love.

Getting out and looking at the stars will do young students much good, setting a tone for the wonder needed for education as a whole. Following St. Augustine, we can allow the stars to teach them, listening to them speak of their Creator:

Consider the beauty of the heavens, the order of the stars and the sun illuminating the day with its brilliance. Consider the moon, whose glow softens the shadows at the coming of night. . . . Consider all of these and they will proclaim to you: Behold us and gaze upon us, for we are beautiful. This beauty is their confession. Who made this ever-changing beauty, unless it is He, whose beauty is changeless?[15]

The stars are more riveting than any video game, inspiring a silence that opens the soul to truth and goodness.

---

15. Augustine, *Selected Sermons*, ed. Q. Howe Jr. (New York: Holt, Rinehard and Winston, 1966), 102–3.

The effort to observe a real night sky could prove pivotal for our students. As we strive to educate healthy and holy children, we would be greatly served by simply getting out and looking at the stars together. We will feel more human and will be inspired to become more than human. Just think of all that our students are missing because they cannot see the sky that God intended us to witness each night! There is much that we cannot fix in our culture, but we can repair that absence. Heading out into the country or wilderness to stargaze will help us to get back to the soil and to look up at the same time. This would follow Gerard Manley Hopkins's command in his great poem "The Starlit Night."

> Look at the stars! look, look up at the skies!
> O look at all the fire-folk sitting in the air!
> The bright boroughs, the circle-citadels there!
> Down in dim woods the diamond delves! the elves'-eyes!
> The grey lawns cold where gold, where quickgold lies!
> Wind-beat whitebeam! airy abeles set on a flare!
> Flake-doves sent floating forth at a farmyard scare!
> Ah well! it is all a purchase, all is a prize.

With so much attention on academic progress and career readiness, the stars remind us that most fundamentally our students need to become human by rediscovering their rootedness in God's creation, the foundation for their eternal destiny in heaven. Our students can be reborn in wonder, awakening their imaginations to the truth, goodness, and beauty that Catholic education should offer.

### Words Made Flesh: The Vision of This Book

A sacramental approach to education flows from the Incarnation: "The Word became flesh" (Jn 1:14). The Word (the *Logos*) is the Truth itself, the one spoken forth by the Father in eternity and through whom all that is made comes into being. Made in the image and likeness of God, human beings have a mind (a *logos*) like the

Word, capable of receiving his truth and expressing our own words in response. Human beings are called to an everlasting dialogue with the Father through the Word made flesh, and Catholic education should be considered from this eternal vantage point. The Church educates because God has called us to know him, to love him, to receive his Word, and to respond. The Word does not speak to us only through written or spoken words, however, as he himself has become flesh, manifesting God to us tangibly in the world. He continues to offer his flesh to us in the Eucharist, drawing us into his body as his members in the world.

Catholic education must be sacramental in this deepest sense of drawing students into the reality of the Incarnation, helping them to encounter the Word made flesh and to live in communion with him. This requires a lived experience of the Word in his community, the Church, which continues Christ's incarnate presence in the world. Learning the truth is not enough, as it must be lived as a sacramental reality in the world, becoming the center of the Christian life, and a culture, a shared way of life with others. The "words" of Catholic education must become flesh in the lived experience of the student, becoming a response to God's movement toward them in the Incarnation. Just as the created world has been given to us as a gift from God, so the life of Catholic students should order these gifts back to God, sanctifying the world. Like the Word, our own words should express the truth of God and translate them into our work, giving them concrete expression.

A sacramental approach, therefore, takes the outward expressions of education just as seriously as the inward attention to the mind. The liberal arts focus on the cultivation and perfection of the intellect, but education as a whole seeks to form the entire person according to the model of the Word made flesh. The typical utilitarian approach to education has lost sight of the formation of the mind, but it also does not engage the body seriously enough. Catholic education can teach the ideas and books that matter most, while also helping students to act upon them, learning to live in accord with the truth. A sacramental approach can recover what we have lost in leaving the liberal arts behind while also achieving what a utilitarian approach tries to accomplish. In fostering the application of study, it can incorporate a hands-on approach through the arts, tangible work experience, and fostering relationships within a community. A Catholic approach, universal and holistic, can form the whole person, communicating truth, inspiring through beauty, and leading students into a life in accord with what is truly good.

This book proposes a sacramental vision of renewal, uniting interior formation with the building of a strong faith-based culture. Chapter one begins by looking at why we need Catholic schools in light of the challenges in the public schools and the limits of charter schools. Only Catholic schools can guide students to their true goal of human happiness in light of both faith and reason. Chapter two looks at how Catholic schools can form disciples more effectively, helping its students to come to faith, grow in maturity, and embrace mission. Chapter three examines the essential role of parents, who have the primary influence on the faith life of their children and can partner with schools more effectively. Chapter four lays out a vision for the entire curriculum united with a Catholic worldview, which imparts a way of viewing reality as a whole. Chapter five examines how books should be chosen and taught in the Catholic school in light of its mission to open students to the truth and to inspire the imagination. Chapter six, which lays out the heart of this book's pedagogical approach, explores the failed principles of progressive education, and how, nonetheless, some of their aims could be better fulfilled through a poetic pedagogy. Chapter seven presents the role of the Catholic school in recovering Catholic history, including a deeper literacy of essential Catholic figures, events, achievements, and places. Chapter eight looks at how the universal Catholic tradition respects the diversity of human cultures throughout the world while uniting them in a shared narrative of salvation history. Chapter nine makes a case for using Latin to increase literacy, both in a grammatical and a cultural sense. Chapter ten speaks of how beauty can inspire students in their learning by drawing upon the great achievements of the Catholic tradition. Chapter eleven examines the challenges presented by technology and how schools can respond by fostering silent contemplation. Chapter twelve offers practical suggestions for renewal, especially through formation for leaders and teachers and the renewal of schools and diocesan structures. Finally, the conclusion explores the way in which culture takes shape in the school, most significantly through the centrality of the Eucharist in Catholic education.

Before we begin, I want to respond to a possible objection: "Is your vision of renewal simply imposing classical education?" The word "classical" implies that we are emphasizing classical thought, language, and culture. The Church has always been dialoguing with classical culture as a continuing source of inspiration, but the "classical" element is not essential to the liberal arts. We do not need our schools to teach classical languages or to root the liberal arts primarily in classical culture or thought. It is not necessary to require Latin (although I will make a case for its study), Euclidean geometry, Homer, or Plato. We should, however, teach Greek and Roman history as part of the larger story of Western civilization, though not as the primary anchor. What is the focus, then, of a Catholic vision of renewal for education? Rather than "classical," our focus should be on the Christian tradition following the Church's own educational vision. The goal should be to teach from a Catholic worldview, rooted within the great Catholic heritage of thought and culture.

# 1 Why We Need Catholic Education:
## Pursuing True Happiness

We take education for granted today, even considering it as a human right. Formal education was rare throughout history, although everyone had to be educated into a culture and society, learning to take their place within a people's customs and life. In that broader sense, every human being needs education. Unlike animals, we must learn how to be human beings. Animals simply know what to do by instinct; we, however, have to discover the meaning and purpose of our lives. This requires a life-long pursuit of truth and goodness.

The word "school" stems from the Greek *skole*, meaning leisure. The length of time children spend in school still points to this root, with a large amount of time dedicated to their maturity and initiation into society. In this sense, education is a privilege, even if many children would not see it this way, especially with the drudgery and pressure of modern schools. We might go so far as to say that schools squander these years without really pursuing what education is truly about: moving toward the *telos*, the goal of human life. Or to go even further, modern schools frequently take children away from the pursuit of their true good in wisdom and virtue, leading them to focus on pragmatic concerns apart from the pursuit of truth.

For this reason alone, Catholic schools are necessary, if they are willing to recover what education is really about. Every school, regardless of its particularities, seems to have three major goals: (1) the imparting of information, (2) formation in discipline and skills, and (3) preparation for the future. We could summarize this as: instruction of the mind, formation of the will, and preparation for life. Each school attempts to do these three things in distinct ways. A Catholic school can fulfill them most deeply by (1) imparting a comprehensive view of reality through faith and reason; (2) forming students in virtue, aided by God's grace; and (3) preparing them for their eternal future, in addition to success in society. This chapter will reflect more deeply on the goals of Catholic education and how its approach differs from the major alternatives of public and charter schools.

## The Goal of Catholic Education

Catholic Schools Week coincides with the feast day of Catholic education's patron saint, St. Thomas Aquinas, on January 27th. In Catholic schools, we often ask the question, what is education for? Although we normally value education for its material benefits—academic achievement ordered toward career success—Catholic schools exist for a more fundamental purpose. They are called to spur on our young Catholics to the goal of life: true happiness in God.

Aquinas, in his great *Summa theologiae*, reflects on the nature of happiness, pointing out that only an infinite good, God himself, could ever fully satisfy us: "It is impossible for any created good to constitute man's happiness. For happiness is the perfect good, which lulls the appetite altogether; else it would not be the last end, if something yet remained to be desired."[1] If we aim at wealth, success, and pleasure, when these goods pass away (and they will), we will be left empty handed. We need a happiness that exceeds them, not only in intensity but also in duration, enduring beyond death.

Happiness should serve as our litmus test for Catholic schools. If our students can come to know the truth and then really live it, they will be on the path to happiness. True happiness is not a feeling or an accomplishment. It is the realization of our being, our potential as thinking and loving beings made in the image and likeness of God.

---

1. Thomas Aquinas, *Summa theologiae*, I-II, q. 2, a. 8.

God put us on this earth with a mission that is not focused simply on oneself. We realize our deepest longings through communion, moving outside of ourselves and into the life of God, sacrificing ourselves for the good of others. This is what brings happiness.

We would never say that we do not want our students to do well in school or in their careers. Yes, our schools teach skills, form dispositions, and impart the content that our students need to live a good life and to do well in the world. Yet, especially within our secular culture, forming a deeper sense of vocation and mission is instrumental to real success. If we cannot see that our earthly goods are meant for serving others, we will be trapped in seeking false happiness.

Pope Benedict XVI, while addressing Catholic educators in Washington, D.C., in 2008, challenged us to lead our students to the truth, and he urged us not to stop there. He said we have often neglected the will (or free choice) of our students, giving them information but not calling them into a life transformed by the good. Teaching the truth should not remain an intellectual exercise as it should lead necessarily to what it means to live a good life. We teach the truth because that in itself is good for students, and, in turn, should lead them to give of themselves within the great adventure of life, impelled by hope in the highest goods.

These harmful developments point to the particular urgency of what we might call "intellectual charity." This aspect of charity calls the educator to recognize that the profound responsibility to lead the young to truth is nothing less than an act of love. Indeed, the dignity of education lies in fostering the true perfection and happiness of those to be educated. In practice, "intellectual charity" upholds the essential unity of knowledge against the fragmentation which ensues when reason is detached from the pursuit of truth. It guides the young towards the deep satisfaction of exercising freedom in relation to truth, and it strives to articulate the relationship between faith and all aspects of family and civic life. Once their passion for the fullness and unity of truth has been awakened, young people will surely relish the discovery that the question of what they can know opens up the vast adventure of what they ought to do. Here they will experience "in what" and "in whom" it is possible to hope, and be inspired to contribute to society in a way that engenders hope in others.[2]

Forming students for their happiness breaks them out of isolation, drawing them into a mission. When their minds are opened to the truth and their wills inflamed by the good, they will be able to give hope to others, giving our society what it needs most.

Education should teach the art of living. Students who receive a genuinely Catholic education will know what matters most and how to order everything else to that ultimate goal. This gives deeper meaning to our lives because every choice can be ordered to God, drawing us deeper into communion with him and others. For schools to point students toward this true goal, we will have to be willing to be countercultural, to go against the current that so often distorts the truth and our freedom. The community itself becomes a means of formation by embodying a Christian way of life for its members, building a Christian culture in miniature. Culture is a way of life, the social fabric that weaves the interior and exterior threads of our life into a coherent whole. Unlike the goods of nature, culture arises as an artificial and cumulative creation of humanity over time. We inherit cultural norms and practices, which shape our life, as we continue and advance collectively in return.

When it comes to Catholic education, we do not simply form students within the culture of our nation but seek to impart a way of life centered on our faith, which gives light and life to all elements of culture. The Second Vatican Council's Declaration on Christian Education, *Gravissimum educationis*, presents this goal of cultural formation to the Church:

---

2. Benedict XVI, Address at a Meeting with Catholic Educators.

No less than other schools does the Catholic school pursue cultural goals and the human formation of youth. But its proper
function is to create for the school community a special
atmosphere animated by the Gospel spirit of freedom and charity,
to help youth grow according to the new creatures they were
made through baptism as they develop their own personalities,
and finally to order the whole of human culture to the news of
salvation so that the knowledge the students gradually acquire of
the world, life and man is illumined by faith.[3]

Not only does the Catholic school form culture within its walls,
it should also serve as a source of cultural renewal in the world
through its graduates. Pope Benedict XVI sought to reawaken
Catholic educators to the connection between education and culture,
stating that "Catholic schools should therefore seek to foster that
unity between faith, culture, and life which is the fundamental goal
of Christian education."[4] Essentially, this means that our schools
should serve as a "school for life," learning how to be a Christian in
the world and to change the world.

All education inculturates—teaching values and forming a
worldview. Stratford Caldecott explains that "the way we educate is
the way we pass on or transform our culture. It carries with it a message about our values, priorities, and the way we structure the

---

3. Second Vatican Council, *Gravissimum educationis* (Declaration on Christian
Education), 8, https://www.vatican.va/archive/hist_councils/ii_vatican_council/
documents/vat-ii_decl_19651028_gravissimum-educationis_en.html. Previously
in number 5, it integrates the handing on of a cultural inheritance within the
broader tasks of education: "Among all educational instruments the school has a
special importance. It is designed not only to develop with special care the intellectual faculties but also to form the ability to judge rightly, to hand on the cultural
legacy of previous generations, to foster a sense of values, to prepare for professional
life."
4. Benedict XVI, Address to the Participants in the Convention of the Diocese of
Rome.

world."[5] This is one reason why public schools teach secularism implicitly: if God is absent from instruction, they imply he is absent from life, because he is left out of the bulk of the child's formation. Children today have been formed to be moral and metaphysical relativists, which is why these traits now shape our culture. Catholic schools, as oases of culture, can point them in the right direction to pursue their true *telos* in God.

Happiness and culture relate to one another within the whole paradigm of forming souls and building culture. Happiness cannot be pursued in isolation. It requires a community focusing on the good together and assisting one another in pursuing this good in common. Virtue is acquired through repeated action, with the prompting, witness, and support of others. The school forms its students first by teaching them their goal, and then by embodying the pursuit of this goal within the life of the community.

## Get Out of Public Schools

Catholic immigrants within the United States built up the largest private school system in the world. They made enormous sacrifices, scraping pennies together for the formation of their children. Why were they so committed to giving their children a Catholic education? They understood the goal of education, that it provides the foundation for how to live—how to think, what to value, and how to contribute to the world. Catholic schools were formed to give children a complete formation, setting them up for both success and their eternal happiness. At the Third Plenary Council of Baltimore in 1884, the United States bishops sought to establish a parochial school at every parish, establishing that "parents must send their children to such schools unless the bishop should judge the reason

---

5. Stratford Caldecott, *Beauty for Truth's Sake* (Grand Rapids, Mich.: Brazos, 2009), 17.

for sending them elsewhere to be sufficient. Ways and means are also considered for making the parochial schools more efficient. It is desirable that these schools be free. Every effort must be made to have suitable schools of higher education for Catholic youth."[6] The bishops of the United States saw Catholic schools as *essential* to the formation of Catholic children.

Public education was viewed as a threat for being too Protestant. Catholic children would have to read the King James version of the Bible at these schools, which also bore a generally anti-Catholic disposition, viewing Catholics as unwelcome immigrants. States were also largely hostile to Catholic schools, wanting to form children according to their own maxims. The state of Oregon for instance, banned private schools in 1922 in its Compulsory Education Act, though this was overturned by the Supreme Court in 1925. Pope Pius XI even quoted the Oregon school decision in his encyclical *Divini illius magistri* in 1929: "The fundamental theory of liberty upon which all governments in this Union repose excludes any general power of the State to standardize its children by forcing them to accept instruction from public teachers only. The child is not the mere creature of the State; those who nurture him and direct his destiny have the right coupled with the high duty, to recognize, and prepare him for additional duties."[7] Catholic schools created an entire alternative school system throughout the country, peaking with over five million students in the 1960s, though down to under two million today (despite a significant increase in the Catholic population of the United States over these decades).[8]

---

6. Third Plenary Council of Baltimore (1884), Title 6, "Of the Education of Catholic Youth," https://www.newadvent.org/cathen/02235a.htm.

7. *Pierce v. Society of Sisters*, 269 U.S. 510 (1925), quoted in Pius XI, *Divini illius magistri* (1929), 37n28, https://www.vatican.va/content/pius-xi/en/encyclicals/documents/hf_p-xi_enc_31121929_divini-illius-magistri.html.

8. National Catholic Educational Association (NCEA), "2022–2023 Highlights," https://www.ncea.org/NCEA/NCEA/Who_We_Are/About_Catholic_Schools

It was only in the twentieth century that public schools took on a secularist agenda, focusing more on the utilitarian function of education rather than its inner, formative power. This new secular bent sought to engineer social change. One recent study by Lyman Stone has noted that "the decline in religiosity in America is not the product of a natural change in preferences, but an engineered outcome of clearly identifiable policy choices in the past." Public education spearheaded this decline, because, over the past few decades, youth "spent much of their life in schools that were far more secularized, and these are the generations during which religiosity has declined."[9]

Since the 1960s Catholic education likewise witnessed consistent decline and now an overwhelming majority of Catholic children are formed by public schools, giving the State outsized influence over the future of the Church. Authors Mary Rice Hasson and Theresa Farnan make a poignant and pressing case against public education in *Get Out Now: Why You Should Pull You Child from Public School Before It's Too Late*.[10] Here are their reasons for why public education has become untenable: (1) Public schools are now committed to spreading gender ideology, despite the findings of science; (2) Meant originally to form citizens, they have eroded patriotism and indoctrinated socialism; (3) The absence of engagement with religion combined with scientism has led to practical atheism and relativism; (4) School systems have been eroding parental rights and

/Catholic_School_Data/Highlights.aspx. For the 2022–23 school year, see NCEA, "Data Brief: 2022–2023 Catholic School Enrollment," https:// nceatalk.org/wp-content/uploads/2023/02/23_NCEA_Data_Brief_FINAL_ 2022-2023_Catholic_School_Enrollment_v9.pdf.

9. Quoted in CNA Staff, "Research Aims to Quantify and Explain Drop in US Religiosity," *Catholic News Agency*, May 26, 2020, https://www.catholicnews agency.com/news/44641/research-aims-to-quantify-and-explain-drop-in-us-religiosity.

10. Mary Rice Hasson and Theresa Farnan, *Get Out Now: Why You Should Pull You Child from Public School Before It's Too Late* (Washington, D.C.: Regnery Gateway, 2018).

marginalizing parents' role in their child's education; and (5) The steady decline in academic achievement has been furthered by the Common Core State Standards initiative.

Rather than recognizing any goal of human life, the public schools have embraced an ideology of absolute freedom that sees religion, the past, and even human nature as barriers to this freedom. Public education is conducting a mass experiment on children, not only by providing contraceptives and even abortion transport (in some cases without any parental notification), but also by pushing an aggressive sexual and gender ideology. As many now recognize, public schools deliberately groom children for the schools' ideological positions. Hasson and Farnan, therefore, state the case to leave the public schools with urgency: "The risk of harm to a child's moral and human formation in the public schools today is serious and nearly certain. Few children are intellectually adept enough to detect the illusion being passed off as truth or wise enough to avoid the moral pitfalls that accompany an immersion in 'sexual health' or gender ideology."[11] Children should never be placed in such a morally harmful environment.

We must reverse the decline of our Catholic schools as we need them now more than ever before! Rather than calling the identity of our children into question, Catholic schools can help them to discover and embrace their God-given identity as children of God, adopted into his divine life. Our schools can call them to live as disciples (or students) of Christ, from whom they will gain wisdom to see what matters most in the world, who will enter their vocation and work with the courage necessary to thrive in a secular world. The formation of disciples is holistic: entering into a relationship with God, knowing the truth, pursuing what is good by forming virtue, and developing the skills to succeed. Our children need a community of faith and love to reach their full potential, as only God

---

11. Hasson and Farnan, 148.

will lead them into the fullness of life and happiness. Any education without Christ fails fundamentally in imparting a truly human and complete formation.

The Church recognizes that parents are the primary educators of their children.[12] The challenges in education today require cooperation to give our children the best education possible. Our Catholic schools are becoming more committed to renewal and growth in the midst of greater need, but parents also must be more involved than in the past. Hasson and Farnan argue that it is time to "look for alternatives. . . . If you are concerned about your child's faith, intellectual formation, and patriotism, public schools are working against you. It's time to get out, now."[13] And where should families turn? Pius XI, in his encyclical *Divini illius magistri*, points to the Church as the family's true partner: "So admirable too is the harmony which she maintains with the Christian family, that the Church and the family may be said to constitute together one and the same temple of Christian education."[14] It is worth the financial sacrifice to give children what they need most for their education by pointing them to their true fulfillment, while protecting them from spiritual harm.

## Why Charter Schools Are Not Enough

As a father of six, I appreciate the difficulty of balancing family priorities. Attending to everyone's needs—emotionally, spiritually, materially, and socially—while managing the demands of family life, school, extracurricular activities, and work definitely takes its toll! It can be hard to stay focused on what matters most—getting our chil-

---

12. See CCC, nos. 2221–26, 2229. See also Second Vatican Council, *Gravissimum educationis*, 3, 6; John Paul II, apostolic exhortation *Familiaris consortio* (1981), 36; Second Vatican Council, *Lumen gentium*, 11.

13. Hasson and Farnan, *Get Out Now*, 177.

14. Pius XI, *Divini illius magistri*, 76.

dren to heaven. Education forms a large part of parents' strategy, navigating finances, prospects of future success, and religious formation. If we rule out public schools, how do we pick the right school? In my mind, deciding on a school requires an understanding of the purpose of education itself. Aristotle begins the *Nicomachean Ethics* by stating that to understand anything we need to know its purpose: "Every art and every inquiry, and similarly every action and pursuit, is thought to aim at some good."[15] What is the good sought by education? Without answering that question it is hard to make judgments about the worth or quality of any educational program. If we do not know the goal, how can we make a good choice?

The classical education movement arose to counteract the progressive agenda of the public schools, spearheaded by John Dewey, looking back, rather, to the great Christian tradition of education. Although the Catholic Church created classical education in the Middle Ages, the modern classical movement began in the Protestant world, inspired by Dorothy Sayers's "The Lost Tools of Learning," and grew to influence homeschooling as well.[16] Inspired by its success, classical education was taken up by charter schools, leaving the Christian tradition behind while continuing to focus on the trivium and quadrivium, as well as classical languages and literature. Ironically, Catholic schools have taken the longest to consider returning to classical methods, intrigued by its popularity and demonstrable success over modern, mainstream models.

With a range of classical options, particularly free charter schools, however, many wonder why we need Catholic schools at all. Catholic education requires sacrifice; and, with more affordable alternatives available, we have to ask, is it worth it? This is where we

15. Aristotle, *Nicomachean Ethics*, trans. W. D. Ross, I, 1, https://classics.mit.edu/Aristotle/nicomachaen.html.
16. Dorothy Sayers, "The Lost Tools of Learning" (1948), https://www.pccs.org/wp-content/uploads/2016/06/LostToolsOfLearning-DorothySayers.pdf.

need Aristotle's help again as he prods us to consider the nature of education. Until recently, the goal had always been identified as the formation of the person, initiation into a culture, and preparing for service in society. Education focused first on becoming "someone" and only after on doing things. Aristotle, quoting his own teacher, points to the end of education as an interior reality: "We ought to have been brought up in a particular way from our very youth, as Plato says, so as both to delight in and to be pained by the things that we ought; for this is the right education."[17] It is not about functionality but creating the right sensibility and refinement of desire: learning what is most worthwhile in life and conforming to it.

In fact, education, as we have seen, should lead us toward the true goal of life, our happiness, found in obtaining what is most worthy. Aristotle also points to this highest good: "Happiness seems, however, even if it is not god-sent but comes as a result of virtue and some process of learning or training, to be among the most godlike things; for that which is the prize and end of virtue seems to be the best thing in the world, and something godlike and blessed."[18] Although we could find irony in turning to a pagan to make the case for Catholic education, it is clear, however, that only Christian education can accomplish what Aristotle prescribes—leading students to the ultimate good—while an avowedly secular education cannot.

Education misses the mark if it leaves out what is most important. Once again, Aristotle shows us how pleasure, wealth, and honor cannot constitute our true happiness, because rather than giving us ultimate fulfillment, "we pursue these also for the sake of something else."[19] An education that focuses on these secondary goods teaches a way of life that will not lead to lasting happiness. How could we tell our children on Sunday that God is most impor-

---

17. Aristotle, *Nicomachean Ethics*, II, 3.
18. *Nicomachean Ethics*, I, 9.
19. *Nicomachean Ethics*, I, 6.

tant and then have them spend the largest block of their waking time in a system that deliberately excludes him? Within a secular education, our children are implicitly taught to think and live for these intermediate goals, making of them something absolute. Yet, the skills and facts that are imparted cannot reach their real purpose of supporting the meaning of our existence.

In talking to friends who teach in classical charter schools, they all describe having to "stop short" in their teaching, introducing great thinkers and ideas but not being able to fully impart their meaning. It is absolutely true that classical charters schools are preferable to standard public education, but "stopping short" cannot give young people the full picture of what it means to be a human being and how to live a fulfilled life. Furthermore, it is not possible to present the Western tradition without imparting an understanding of the Christian vision that preserved classical learning and transmitted it to Europe and the New World. Classical is not enough. It is only in the Christian tradition that notions of human dignity, freedom, and happiness reach their full meaning. Seeking to form good citizens, as many charter schools state is their aim, without the force that built Western civilization, leaves a huge, moral hole in the curriculum.

Many parents say that they will supplement a secular education with religious formation at home and church. That is good, of course, but it falls into the latent secularism of charter schools by separating education from the goal of true happiness and the deepest formation of the person. The family should not have to work to counteract the school environment, as there should be a partnership between them. Parents say, "I can add faith in myself," but faith cannot exist as an add-on, even if made an important one. It is the organizing principle of the whole of life and guides everything we do to its goal. To make faith supplemental does not allow for its primary importance and will make it more likely to continue as an add-on in the future. In a secular environment, students have to conduct learning and live "as if God does not exist," as Pope Benedict XVI defined secularism, a sort of practical atheism.[20]

Catholic education seeks to impart an education for life, one that integrates the wisdom of the great tradition with personal formation: not only talking about virtue but also forming it through a life of discipleship. Students have to learn how to live as Christians in the world, integrating the intellectual, moral, spiritual, and social life into a coherent whole. Catholic schools form good citizens, but also draw students into the City of God, which will last when this world collapses (sooner or later). Education finds its deepest expression in the Church, the institution that preserved classical learning after the fall of Rome, that built the first universities, inspired the greatest art, and also formed saintly scholars, such as St. Thomas Aquinas.

Education is one of the most important things we can give our children. We cannot settle for second best for them or give them a partial expression of what they need. We want to teach them how to be truly happy and how to integrate all aspects of their life through faith; to be successful, but, more importantly, to be holy. By integrating faith and reason in Catholic education, we impart the full vision of reality, uniting the formation of mind and soul. Only this will form the basis of true happiness—not only the goal of education, but also of life itself.

We can end where we began, with "the Philosopher" (as Thomas Aquinas called him), Aristotle: "And so the man who has been educated in a subject is a good judge of that subject, and the man who has received an all-round education is a good judge in general."[21] And to him, we can add the Apostle: "Do you not know that the saints will judge the world? ... Do you not know that we are to judge

---

20. Benedict XVI, apostolic exhortation *Sacramentum caritatis* (February 22, 2007), 77, https://www.vatican.va/content/benedict-xvi/en/apost_exhortations/documents/hf_ben-xvi_exh_20070222_sacramentum-caritatis.html.
21. Aristotle, *Nicomachean Ethics*, I, 3.

angels?" (1 Cor 6:2–3). Let us prepare our children to fulfill the supernatural vocation God intends for them!

## Putting It All Together: The Goals within the One Goal

God is the true goal and purpose of human life. He does not take away other goods; on the contrary, he enables us to appreciate them more deeply when ordered properly to him. Education has the same goal as human life itself: finding happiness in God. A more utilitarian or pragmatic approach seeks genuine goods of initiation into society and preparation for a career. Catholic education does not deny these goods, even as it situates them within a proper context. It recognizes them as means to a further end and, therefore, can approach them more successfully because it positions them within a broader and deeper vision of reality. Catholic education prepares for success better because it knows what success really means.

The interior and exterior goals of education can be integrated within a sacramental approach. Returning to the three overarching goals of instruction, formation, and preparation, we can see how Catholic schools fulfill these goals in light of our ordering to God. Here is a progression, though not strictly chronological, of the major goals of Catholic education.

### 1. Encounter the God Who Is Truth

This is the fundamental goal of the Catholic school. Pope Benedict articulated this to Catholic educators in the United States: "First and foremost every Catholic educational institution is a place to encounter the living God who in Jesus Christ reveals his transforming love and truth."[22] Although the school cannot control the personal spiritual experiences of its students, it must propose this encounter. The school does not teach truth as abstract information but seeks to

---

22. Benedict XVI, Address at a Meeting with Catholic Educators.

inspire the student to come to know the Truth in a personal way by coming to know the Word, Christ. This enables the Catholic school student to live as a disciple (literally, a student) of Jesus Christ. Jesus teaches his students how to think and how to live, inspiring them to want to know the truth and to seek what is good.

### 2. Form the Mind in Truth

Students encounter the Word of God both in coming to know his creation and the revelation of his work of redemption. Catholic education helps students to discover the one truth in two ways, uniting faith and reason in a single vision of reality. Jesus helps us to see rightly, in line with the traditional Catholic definition of truth: conformity or adequation of the mind to reality. Catholic education helps students to think soundly and express thoughts coherently and elegantly, forming habits of mind and the skills needed for learning.

### 3. Form the Will in the Good

Knowing the truth leads us to recognize what is truly good, making correct judgments about what should be pursued and what should be avoided. Education shapes desires by directing freedom and guiding it through virtue and self-control. Pope Benedict XVI rightly pointed out that "while we have sought diligently to engage the intellect of our young, perhaps we have neglected the will. Subsequently we observe, with distress, the notion of freedom being distorted."[23] We cannot stop at the mind, but must engage the heart, inspiring our students to shape and fulfil their potential in the proper way.

### 4. Integrate Faith and Life

Catholic schools teach students how to live. This education for life must be embodied in the community of the family, school com-

---

23. Benedict XVI, Address at a Meeting with Catholic Educators.

munity, and parish to build lasting habits and relationships. The principles imparted by Catholic education should find expression in recreation, friendship, and life outside the classroom, as students live to follow Christ in their daily life. Ultimately parents need to own the formation of their children in the home, with the school complementing the influence of parents in faith, learning, and virtue.

### 5. Service in Society

Catholic schools certainly prepare their students for the future, imparting practical preparation for career and space to discern a vocation. Their graduates should be the best prepared to work for the common good of society in cooperation with others. They certainly should be leaders in the Church and nation, expressing the Church's mission to proclaim the Gospel and transform society in Christ. Catholic education should impart a burning sense of mission.

### 6. Eternal Happiness

Happiness is not an emotion but a realization of the full potential of the human person through the highest and most important actions of our nature. Catholic education should prepare students for their true happiness in God, building habits of moral virtue, contemplation, and the life of the theological virtues. This goal is not extraneous to the others, as all the previous goals ultimately aim at happiness and find their fulfillment in God. All of human life should flow from God, be lived in God, and be for God. Catholic schools educate for eternal life.

# 2 Students of Jesus Christ:
## The Centrality of Discipleship and Prayer

Catholic schools exist for students. We can take that for granted but in the context of Catholic education, we do not engage students merely within an academic context. We want them to be students, that is "disciples," of Jesus Christ in a way that embraces their entire lives. This is what Jesus told us to do in the great commission: "Go therefore and make disciples of all nations, baptizing them in the name of the Father and of the Son and of the Holy Spirit, teaching them to observe all that I have commanded you; and lo, I am with you always, to the close of the age" (Mt 28:19–20). Catholic schools offer one response to this great commission. What better place to form students for Jesus Christ and teach them than in a school? The great commission truly comprises the mission statement of the Catholic school.

In a sacramental approach to education, the inner life of the soul and mind must be expressed in exterior elements. "Disciple" takes us to the heart of the interior reality of Catholic education, but even here we must look to the necessary external components of forming disciples through the concrete elements of communal life. This chapter will explore why and how Catholic schools need to form disciples of Jesus Christ. These insights flow from my work as Associate Superintendent for Mission and Formation in the Archdiocese of Denver where I helped to create and implement a framework for forming disciples in Catholic schools, "School of the Lord's Service."[1]

---

1. Archdiocese of Denver, *School of the Lord's Service: A Framework for Forming Disciples*, ed. R. Jared Staudt (2020), http://archden.uberflip.com/i/1312720-school-of-the-lord-s-service/0?.

## Why Schools Can and Should Form Disciples

Catholic schools should not teach religion as an academic discipline, but, rather, offer catechesis, the method the Church developed for helping Christians to grow in faith. Catechesis does not simply teach information; it aims to draw those being catechized into deeper relationship with the person of Jesus Christ. This does involve knowledge, coming to know who he is, including learning Christian doctrine, but it must also involve meeting Jesus in prayer. The work of catechesis is not done until the recipient is prepared to live the Christian life, following the virtues and dedicated to prayer and service. Catechesis aims at nothing less than a complete transformation of life in Christ. St. John Paul II makes this clear: "Catechesis aims therefore at developing understanding of the mystery of Christ in the light of God's word, so that the whole of a person's humanity is impregnated by that word."[2] We come to know Christ so that he can shape the way that we live concretely and as a whole.

Although it may seem that talk of discipleship in the Church is just the latest ecclesial fad, forming committed followers of Jesus Christ is the great task that God has given us. It can be hard for Catholics to comprehend the need for discipleship since we focus so heavily on the external. Our sacramental life and doctrine are great gifts, yet they have to be internalized to take root within us. We might be tempted to say that we are Catholic simply because we have received the sacraments or have attended a Catholic school, even if we never came to know God in a personal way. Discipleship puts forth the call to make a commitment to follow Jesus and to share in the mission to proclaim the Good News to others.

The Church's mission could be taken for granted more readily in the past when the surrounding culture supported Christian

---

2. John Paul II, apostolic exhortation *Catechesi tradendae* (1979), 20, https://www.vatican.va/content/john-paul-ii/en/apost_exhortations/documents/hf_jp-ii_exh_16101979_catechesi-tradendae.html.

morality. As we all know, those days are long gone. To form disciples now, we must paddle against a raging current. Even if more difficult, the mission to form disciples is more necessary than ever—as a rescue mission to save our children from a deeply inhuman way of life. In the past, Catholic schools had much more support for their mission, including from the surrounding culture. Today we can no longer presuppose knowledge of the Gospel. We have to propose it explicitly, sharing the kerygma (the message of salvation in Jesus) and inviting teachers, students, and parents to a deeper faith, one that is internalized and lived out. We can say with confidence that only friendship with Christ can help us through the minefield of our culture. This friendship blossoms most naturally in the family, with the support of the parish and the school.

How can we help our children to thrive in this brave new world with everything seemingly up for grabs? They need to think and live like Christians, committing to follow Jesus before all else, even when countercultural. To support them, first, we must help them to recognize the joy of life, appreciating it as a great gift that we have received from God. Second, we have to help them to face the challenges of life head on with courage, seeing life as an adventure, full of danger and risk, it is true, but also one that invites us to do great things for God. Third, we must teach them not only to be Christians, but also how to be human—to think and love rightly, rooted in healthy relationships and a commitment to what is greater than themselves as the only true path to happiness.

Our goal, therefore, has to be to teach our children how to live as faithful Christians in the modern world. To do so, we must serve as catechists of the Christian life, showing them how to make faith the center of their lives. If we do not teach our children how to live their faith in an integrated way every day, they will naturally follow the way of the world, floating with the stream. They need an apprenticeship in how to be a Christian today. Classes about the faith provide a foundation but are not enough to draw our children into a

Christian way of life, because following Jesus requires mentorship, with the role of parents by far the most influential. Living the faith together in daily life makes it come alive to our children, shaping everything that they do in tangible ways.

Forming disciples constitutes the most important service we can offer our students, even if families do not come to the school looking for this. Many people may come simply to escape the negative influences of the culture or the ideology permeating public schools. Even so, when they arrive, they should find a mission-focused community of disciples living out an apostolic mandate to share the Good News of Jesus Christ. Even if enrollment at a Catholic school cannot make the negative influences of the culture disappear, as places where Jesus is encountered, however, they can offer healing, transformation, and hope.

Archbishop Samuel Aquila has identified discipleship as a central task for Catholic education, writing within the Archdiocese of Denver's framework *School of the Lord's Service*:

> Jesus truly is the reason for the existence of our Catholics schools, and he wants to guide us in everything that we do. . . . Our schools must be places to encounter Jesus; nothing is more important. What does it mean to become a disciple of Jesus Christ? It means that we have truly encountered and met Jesus as the Son of God, experienced his love and mercy personally, and have accepted him as our Lord, living in a committed and daily relationship with him.[3]

A Catholic school graduate should have the opportunity to meet Jesus and be given regular opportunities to grow in friendship with him.

The school does not exist in a vacuum, and it is only by close cooperation with the parish and family that it can form student-disciples who will practice their faith into adulthood. The school depends upon the parish for its sacramental life and for the spiritual

---

3. Archdiocese of Denver, *School of the Lord's Service*, 1.

leadership of the pastor. In turn, it provides an important way of forming disciples who are ready to serve and live their faith through the parish. Even more fundamentally, the Catholic school supports parents in their role as primary educators. Schools are not simply drop-off services so that parents can outsource their religious responsibilities. In fact, parents have by far the most influence on the religious life of their children, as they soak up what they see, hear, and experience in the home. Schools support parents and help them in the task of educating, but for religious formation to take root parents must maintain the lead role.

The sociologist Christian Smith offers a vision for what works, drawing on his own extensive study of the religious practices of young adult Catholics throughout the United States. His book, *Young Catholic America: Emerging Adults in, out of, and Gone from the Church*, shows us how the parish, school, and family must work together for discipleship to take root in the life of our young people. He describes three approaches that together do work in handing on the faith:

> First, Catholic youth who have *strong relational bonds* with highly religious parents, other adults, and friends are more likely to maintain or increase their religious faith. . . . Second, developing an *internalized belief* system involving a faith that is personally important . . . helps teens to sustain religious faith. . . . Finally, Catholic teenagers who *live out their faith* through certain religious practices, especially reading the Bible and frequently attending Sunday school, are more likely to become highly religious emerging adults.[4]

An apostolic school cannot solve all of the problems of our society or the family, but it should take seriously its call to help its students live in friendship with Jesus, the one who can solve our problems. Catholic education offers the one thing that is necessary

---

4. Christian Smith, *Young Catholic America: Emerging Adults in, out of, and Gone from the Church* (New York: Oxford University Press, 2014), 178.

(Lk 10:42), that when possessed will help everything else to fall into place. Putting Jesus first strengthens everything that is done in the school: instruction, by drawing students to the Word who made the universe; character formation through the grace that he gives; preparation for the future by being ready to serve; and building a community united in faith and charity. An apostolic school has much to offer the world, giving it what it truly needs most.

## How to Form Disciples

Discipleship stands at the heart of the Church's mission because it is what Jesus has asked us to do. Catholics, however, have not been thinking explicitly in terms of forming disciples through personal engagement. Some may even assert that this effort is Protestant in nature, even though the Church has been doing it for two thousand years. In fact, the Church subsists as a communion of disciples in Christ, members joined to the Body in faith and charity. We are Catholics only because the apostles formed new disciples and those disciples have formed others down to us today. We are called to take our place as links in a great chain and pass our faith down to new generations.

Discipleship does include learning, although it must also extend beyond an academic context. In a talk, "Discipleship Beyond the First Encounter," Archbishop Samuel Aquila asks, "What is lacking in our efforts to form life-long Catholics?" After pointing out a renewal in catechesis stemming from the new *Catechism* in 1992, he relates that

> there is a second aspect of discipleship that is an indispensable companion to intellectual formation: the mentoring or modeling component. In the time of Christ, this handing on of a way of life—the art of Jewish living, so to speak—occurred through the rabbi-disciple relationship. The disciple would imitate the rabbi in everything, even down to how he walked, talked and dressed. The thought was that by imitating even the smallest details, the disciple would acquire the rabbi's virtues.

But this dimension of handing on the faith is becoming harder to find, especially as fewer families remain intact.[5]

Mentorship forms an essential part of forming disciples, and so if it is lacking our efforts will fall short. We could even call discipleship an apprenticeship in the Christian life. No one can become a Christian in isolation from others or simply by reading a book or taking a class. To be a disciple is to be rooted in relationship and community with others, praying together, learning from one another, and living out a mission together. A stronger approach to discipleship can help Catholic schools to form lifelong, practicing Catholics. Unfortunately, we too often hear of the terrible attrition rate of Catholics in young adulthood. Fortunately, we are able to identify things that do work in the formation of young Catholics and make a lasting impact.

The Barna Group, for instance, did a study of what kept millennials coming to church. The three highest indicators point us in the right direction for formation. 68 percent of young-adult, practicing Christians reported that "Jesus speaks to me in a personal and relevant way." Fifty-nine percent said they "had a close personal friend who was an adult at church or parish." Forty-five percent reported that they "better understood" their "purpose in life through church," expressed by how they can "positively contribute to society" and use their own "gifts and passions as part of God's calling."[6] These three elements—hearing the voice of Jesus, forming relationships, and serving others—are the three major aspects of discipleship that will help us to form lifelong Christians in Catholic education.

Discipleship flows precisely from these three realities: encountering Christ, growing to a greater conformity to Christ in relation

5. Archbishop Samuel Aquila, "Discipleship Beyond the First Encounter," Catholic Foundation Networking & Speaker Series, February 9, 2017.
6. Barna Group, "5 Reasons Millennials Stay Connected to Church," September 17, 2013, https://www.barna.com/research/5-reasons-millennials-stay-connected-to-church/.

to other Christians, and living out the mission of Christ in our lives. We could describe the stages of discipleship as coming to know Christ, becoming more like Christ, and bringing Christ to the world. If these are the stages through which children become disciples, we could then ask how to bring them about in the context of the Catholic school. We know from experience that book learning alone will not work. It will require spiritual experiences, where students can come to know Jesus in a personal way and interact with others to receive mentorship, to grow in friendship, and to live out the faith in a more active way.

Jesus, the true teacher, models how to form his student-disciples. It begins with an invitation: "*Come, follow me*" (Mt 4:19). Jesus calls each one of us to be his disciple, although parents, teachers, and friends are now the ones who have to make this invitation on his behalf. We can never presuppose faith but must propose it, inviting our students to have faith in Jesus and to make the choice to follow him. As the next step, the school creates opportunities to listen to Jesus' voice in prayer as well, giving him space to confirm this call within the heart. A disciple responds to this call, committing to follow Jesus and to put him first in his or her life. This begins a process of learning from Jesus how to live: "*Learn from me*" (Mt 11:29). Jesus invested time—three years—to mentor his own disciples, teaching them by modeling how to live. Likewise, we need mentors and friends to model the Christian life for our students and to support them through difficulties. Finally, Jesus sent his disciples on mission: "*Go . . . and make disciples*" (Mt 28:19). After learning how to live in the Kingdom of God, he sends his disciples to make other disciples—to bring his truth, healing, forgiveness, and peace to the world. This is the way the Church works: disciples gather more disciples around Jesus to abide in communion with him.

Disciples form other disciples by sharing what Jesus has done in their lives, giving testimony and witness to how he has changed them. There is then a further invitation to "come and see," to experience Jesus in some way in the community of the Church. Disciples invite others to share their life with them, and even to go on mission with them. Mentorship works by doing things together: praying, sharing meals, recreating, and serving others. Most people do not know how to pray, so an important element of leading others to Christ is praying with them so that they can learn how to vocalize prayer, listen to God speaking in Scripture, and meditate on the faith. Disciples also discover their deepest identity in Christ and find a sense of mission and vocation in him.

The school forms disciples by making its students aware that Jesus invites them to be disciples. It gives them space to hear his call and models a response in silent prayer and through the testimony of teachers and fellow students. Retreats can also provide longer moments of prayer and reflection for this response. The school provides opportunities for growing in the sacramental life through regular Mass, confession, adoration, and strong sacramental prep. It provides a context of mentorship and friendship within the community, giving a regular opportunity for discussing the implications of faith in life in small groups and providing consistent encouragement from others. Forming habits of virtue helps us to live in Christ-like fashion, to "lead a life worthy of the calling to which you have been called . . . until we all attain to the unity of the faith and of the knowledge of the Son of God, to mature manhood, to the measure of the stature of the fullness of Christ" (Eph 4:1, 13). The school community provides its students with opportunities to grow in virtuous action and to live out the mission of serving others and sharing the faith.

Children can be disciples, learn how to pray, grow in virtue, and share their faith with others. The school can help them to do all of these things, truly becoming a school of the Lord's service, a place that initiates the mission that Jesus entrusted to his Church. The school should not just teach about this mission but should also actively live it as a communion of disciples, including its administrators, teachers, students, and parents.

## Growing in the Truth of Christ

Jesus teaches us, as his students, the truth of who we are and of reality as a whole. He reveals our identity to us, made in his image and likeness and reborn as sons in the Son. We find our true happiness only in Jesus, who imparts to us a participation in his own divine nature. Only he can teach the whole of reality because he is the Word who made all things and he has entered into his creation to redeem it from within. He is the Truth of all things and he leads his disciples to think in line with this Truth: the Word of God, the *Logos*. As a result, disciples see and think in accord with the Word.

We see this vision of the whole of reality most clearly in the prologue of John's Gospel. "In the beginning was the *Word*, and the Word was with God, and the Word was God. He was in the beginning with God; *all things were made* through him, and without him was not anything made that was made. In him was *life*, and the life was the *light of men*. The light shines in the *darkness*, and the darkness has not overcome it" (Jn 1:1–5, emphasis added). Reality is defined by the Word, who speaks and reveals the Father and the whole truth of God. He is communication and communion, manifesting the Father through his oneness with him. This speaking extends to bring forth all of creation. "He spoke and it came to be" (Ps 33:9), meaning that all created things point back to the mind and truth of God. Human beings have not only life but also light, meaning they can see with their own "*logos*," or "mind," that participates in the truth of the Word. And yet, men still live in darkness, refusing to live according to the light given by the Word.

To overcome this darkness, God sends witnesses. "There was a man sent from God, whose name was John. He came for testimony, to *bear witness to the light*, that all might *believe* through him. He was not the light, but came to bear witness to the light" (Jn 1:6–8, emphasis added). When the light enlightens the mind, this reflected light can shine onto others. Every disciple is called to be like John the Baptist and give testimony to the light so that others may believe. Yet, the Word wants even greater intimacy with us.

> The true light that enlightens every man was *coming into the world*. He was in the world, and the world was made through him, yet the world knew him not. He came to his own home, and his own people received him not. But to all *who received him*, who believed in his name, he gave power to *become children of God*; who were born, not of blood nor of the will of the flesh nor of the will of man, but of God. (Jn 1:9–13, emphasis added)

The Word of God descended from heaven into his own creation. His goal in this rescue mission was nothing short of a re-creation, giving more than a reflected light by drawing into the Uncreated Light itself through the gift of adoption.

What does Jesus desire for his disciples? He brings two things in particular to them: grace and truth. "And the Word became flesh and dwelt among us, *full of grace and truth*; we have beheld his *glory*, glory as of the only Son from the Father. . . . And from his fullness have we all received, *grace upon grace*. For the law was given through Moses; grace and truth came through Jesus Christ. No one has ever seen God; the only Son, who is in the bosom of the Father, he has *made him known*" (Jn 1:14, 16–18, emphasis added). He wants his disciple-students to come to know the truth about God, themselves, and all things. He also offers them a share in his divine life by giving them his Holy Spirit to live in them and to lead them into the good. Ultimately, he reveals his glory to them so that they themselves can share in this glory, living as children of God in this life and the next.

We are saved by coming to know Jesus, and through him we come to know the Father. The Catholic school should not shy away from this reality, because its students are coming to learn from Jesus. These students must not be deprived of God's saving truth. We too often act as if the Church teaches bad news rather than the Good News of salvation. The truth sets us free (Jn 8:32), enabling us to live in the light and to pursue what is truly good. We should not act like we know for ourselves what is true and false, or what is good and evil (as Eve sought to do in grasping after the fruit of the tree of knowledge of good and evil). We need to learn these things from the Word. The obedience of the disciple frees us from the tyranny of the self and the lies of the serpent who wants us to believe that we can define good and evil for ourselves, to reshape our lives according to our own image.

Discipleship does not mitigate the necessity of teaching doctrine, but it places it within the context of a personal relationship with the Word. Rather than blind obedience, we can help students to see that belief opens up true freedom by helping them to see clearly and to live with greater joy and peace. Faith helps us to know that we are beloved sons and daughters of the Father. He created us in love and calls us to eternal happiness with him. He has a plan for our lives and knows what will lead us to happiness. The Church's teaching is a call to greater trust in God, who will lead us to the fullness of life in communion with him and others.

So many young people are lost today. Catholic schools should have confidence that we offer what is most needed. We can only overcome overwhelming difficulties with God and by living in the truth. We think that obedience to God will eliminate our freedom, while in reality he teaches us how to be free, how to discipline ourselves to experience what matters most. Love, as a choice to will the good of another, rather than a feeling, provides the real answer. Jesus shows us that we find our life only by losing it, by offering it in sacrifice for others. We are made to be a gift, not to fulfill our own self-focused desires. This is what Jesus seeks to teach us.

The Church is on a rescue mission, proclaiming Jesus' truth and bestowing his grace to the world. As Christians, we have to be faithful to the mission of Christ and continue to abide in communion with him. We do not know better than he does! Rather, we have to increase our faith in God, placing our trust in him and his plan for us. We have to trust in the power of the truth, which overcomes every obstacle in the end. Cardinal Gerhard Müller reminds us:

> Truth is not an abstract theory in the heads of a few individuals, but rather the ground on which everyone finds stability and strength, and the source from which all can quench their thirst for God and eternal life (Jn 4:14). Only the unambiguous character of the doctrine of the faith makes possible the breadth of the pastoral perspective and an orientation toward the goals, and this is so from every starting point. For God wills the salvation of all mankind and also that everyone should come to the knowledge of God and of the truth of his revelation. (1 Tim 2:4)[7]

The Catholic school is poised to share this knowledge and truth with its students.

Not only must we come to this knowledge of the truth, but we also must live it. Faith provides us with a relationship that sheds light on the meaning of our life and calls us into a communion of love. Cardinal Müller explains how truth and love are related:

> By faith, then, we see the transcendent horizon—of human history, and of the personal destiny of each human being made in God's image and destined for his household—that can motivate us to uphold human dignity without exceptions, even in the hardest cases. By faith, we gain the possibility of redeeming the suffering that the just must endure in a fallen world. And by faith, we add intimate love of God himself to the natural loves that motivate our perseverance.[8]

God opens up to us a whole new horizon for life, no longer entrenched simply in the immediate and our own limited views.

---

7. Cardinal Gerhard Müller, *The Power of Truth: Challenges to Catholic Doctrine and Morals Today* (San Francisco: Ignatius Press, 2019), 9.
8. Müller, 149.

Sharing the truth, what Pope Benedict called "intellectual charity," constitutes one of the Catholic school's greatest services to its students.[9] Contemporary culture attempts to paint the common-sense truth of the natural law and the truth of God's revelation as "hate." The culture will push ideology on Catholic school students, and so they need a space to think through these challenges, using faith and reason together, building common sense and the truth of God's revelation. The ideology of the subjective self, so aptly described by Carl Trueman, which not only "sees inner feelings as authoritative" but "also largely rejects the idea that human nature has any intrinsic moral structure or significance," will try to turn them against even the possibility of thinking through the truth.[10] The culture attempts to shut down thinking, while genuine education draws students out of their own feelings to guide and govern them in accord with reality.

A disciple, however, has the right to the whole truth. The Catholic school provides the best setting to receive this gift and to think through it. The school has a mission to defend its students against lies and ideology and to help them to cherish the gift of truth. The truth is a gift entrusted to the Church and, through her, offered to each one of us. The disciple receives the truth and lives in accord with it. The Catholic school must maintain this gift faithfully, and we all must abide within it. Where else will young Catholics find a place to encounter the God who is Truth and to be freed from threats to the truth? The school, a place to encounter the Word, can reflect the light that, despite all darkness, can keep our students sheltered in the Word, the one who is Truth itself.

---

9. Benedict XVI, Address at a Meeting with Catholic Educators.

10. Carl R. Trueman, *Strange New World: How Thinkers and Activists Redefined Identity and Sparked the Sexual Revolution* (Wheaton, Ill.: Crossway, 2022), 51. Trueman looks at the implications of this view on education in light of the sexual revolution, which views the "authentic person" as "the sexual being, the one guided by the inner voice of (sexualized) nature, and the role of education is not to repress that for the purpose of personal formation but to liberate it for the purpose of self-expression" (84).

# 3 Education as Initiation:
## Parents' Essential Role

Among the many different paths to discipleship, one stands out in its primacy and effectiveness. Although there are students who come to know Jesus primarily through school (and I am one of them) and there are others who come to know Jesus only after leaving the school, parents have been shown consistently to have the most influence by far on the faith life of their children. Christian Smith and Justin Bartkus make this abundantly clear in their report on American Catholic religious parenting: "Thus parents represent not simply *an* influence on the development of children's religious worldviews, but the arch-influence over it. Their efforts at religious formation are capable of overcoming the many cultural currents which flow in the direction of the secular."[1] They describe parents further as "definitive causal agents" through "day-to-day religious practices of the family and the ways parents model their faith and share it in conversation, collaboration, and exposure to outside religious opportunities."[2] Although it is common to hear this, for efforts to form disciples to take root, Catholic schools will need to act upon this reality much more intentionally.

This chapter examines the dynamics of parents' primary role in the formation of faith. Their role largely unfolds in an embodied way, instantiating faith within the practices of the home and the family's shared life. Even more than schools, families embody education's initiatory character, handing on the beliefs and practices of

---

1. Christian Smith and Justin Bartkus, *A Report on American Catholic Religious Parenting* (Notre Dame, Ind.: University of Notre Dame, 2018), https://churchlife-info.nd.edu/a-report-on-american-catholic-religious-parenting.
2. Smith and Bartkus, 8, 7.

the Christian community through their daily habits. The sacramental mission of Catholic education depends upon the support of families to live out the principles it seeks to instill.

## Learning Faith and Life at Home

If education really just entailed learning how to read or how to do addition, then you could conceive of the school as a sufficient entity to accomplish these goals. If education entails a formation for life—learning how to live—it requires initiation into a community that includes learning how to think, what to desire and value, how to relate to others, and how to discover one's own role within this community. Modern society, by emphasizing individual freedom to the extreme, has made it appear that children simply need to learn skills within an institution and then can guide themselves into life on their own. More than anything else, this false, autonomous conception of life has led to a crisis in education that touches the family more than anything else.

Education certainly encompasses more than reading, writing, and arithmetic. As preparation for life, it touches every aspect of one's intellectual, emotional, social, and spiritual life. When conceived of in this way, parents cannot be displaced in favor of practical training led by the State. In the Church's conception of education, parents stand at the very center of the child's development, including the spiritual life. The Second Vatican Council sees their role in education as "so important that only with difficulty can it be supplied where it is lacking."[3] Although the document recognizes that the family needs the support of the community, it articulates the foundational and general role of the parents in the formation of children:

> Parents are the ones who must create a family atmosphere animated by love and respect for God and man, in which the well-

---

3. Second Vatican Council, *Gravissimum educationis*, 3.

rounded personal and social education of children is fostered. Hence the family is the first school of the social virtues that every society needs. It is particularly in the Christian family, enriched by the grace and office of the sacrament of matrimony, that children should be taught from their early years to have a knowledge of God according to the faith received in Baptism, to worship him, and to love their neighbor.[4]

These elements ensure the success or failure of the school's educational efforts.

Parents have the responsibility of handing on the faith to their children. Even though they often feel inadequate on a doctrinal level, their influence happens most through the normal interactions of the home. Do parents talk about God, pray, live a Christian way of life, and prioritize going to church? Whether they do or do not, either way will have a profound impact on children. The primary educational role of parents can be seen in the fact that only they can translate the faith into everyday life in the home, making family catechesis more than simple instruction but formation into a culture—a Christian way of life. This makes our faith to be something real and alive to our children, something that shapes everything that they do and that takes on a tangible presence in their lives.

The domestic church is the place to learn how to live as a Christian on a daily basis in a comprehensive way. Learning the Christian life includes prayer, work, character formation, and overcoming daily difficulties. Parents teach their children a way of living within the culture of the family, which is meant to prepare children to live within the surrounding culture. Smith and Bartkus's study lays this out persuasively:

> We believe that any parent who wishes to pass on their Catholic faith must understand their home as a miniature *culture*, a project

---

4. *Gravissimum educationis*, 3.

which initiates children into certain core values, practices, and modes of experience, all of whose validity is constantly tested by what parents do and say in interpretive reinforcement of those core convictions. In the home, children receive wisdom about what matters in life, what commitments demand investment of time, energy, and emotion, and generally what a viable adult existence should look like. This idea of parenting as the building of a *culture* is often underappreciated.[5]

Parenting intrinsically involves educating children in how to think and live.

Once again, parents often overlook how this educational task happens in ordinary ways. Most importantly, if parents pray every day with their children, this will reinforce the centrality of God in family life, rather than simply seeing prayer as something that occurs occasionally or only at church. This prayer will bind the family together in a common approach to God, creating natural opportunities to talk about faith. Christian Smith, in another work co-authored with Amy Adamczyk, found that simply *talking* about God made a significant impact on faith life: "Parents routinely conversing with children about religious matters during the week exerts such a crucial influence on successful religious transmission."[6] Just by talking about it at least once a week shows that religion should not be confined to church and has an impact on life more broadly. When these conversations are marked by "openness, warmth, and mutuality," they give youth the opportunity to be self-reflective and make their own personal connections, though in relation to their parents.[7] In a time of cultural confusion, this space for conversation

---

5. Smith and Bartkus, *Report on American Catholic Religious Parenting*, 12.
6. Christian Smith and Amy Adamczyk, *Handing Down the Faith: How Parents Pass Their Religion to the Next Generation* (New York: Oxford University Press, 2021), 83.
7. Smith and Adamczyk, 43.

helps young people to figure out their path with the assistance of faith and family.

Talking together, praying, eating, and playing together—these are the essential ways that parents invest time in their children's formation. The home should be a sanctuary of love, providing an anchor in an unsettled world, providing guidance through talking, telling stories, and living life together. And in a busy world, time becomes a precious gift—just being together and showing love through our presence. The family table should be the center of family life, taking precedence over sports and other activities. We could add to Fr. Payton's traditional saying, "the family that prays together stays together," that "the family that eats together stays together." The family meal is a kind of sacrament of family life, breaking bread together each day.

Taking time to unplug so that we can eat and talk together sends a major signal on the priority of the family and strengthens relationships and trust. If we do this, we can share the faith in a natural way, as conversations will arise more readily. And with this in mind, I would suggest that a great way to stimulate conversation is to make time for family *play*. Sunday, the Lord's Day, is a time of leisure, a day reserved for the things that matter most—God, family, and re-creation (renewal). True leisure is not simply entertainment or relaxation but doing things that are worthwhile for their own sake, rather than for a practical end, including play. Playing games may seem like an inconsequential waste of time, but play expresses leisure, as it is done simply for its own sake. Playing games shows that we are willing to stop and enjoy time with each other. It provides a common activity, expresses shared interests, and creates space for conversations. Games are formative through cooperation, conforming to rules, finding joy, drawing out creativity, and inspiring strategic thinking. Having a weekly game time builds family culture by drawing everyone together for a common activity that requires shutting off computers, putting down phones and clearing the calendar. Families need this common time, for it is too easy for everyone to pursue their own interests apart from the family community.

Praying, talking, spending time, and building community as a family and with other families—these are the fundamental elements through which the family as the domestic church hands down the faith to children. Even if parents need the help of others in the Catholic community, they are best positioned to support the faith of their own children. Although many educators express exasperation about how parents are not engaged in this task, parents need help in understanding their role and imagining how to accomplish it. The school can provide opportunities for parents to become more comfortable praying with others, talking about what we believe, and even playing games as a group. The Catholic school truly surrounds the family with support, helping it to carry out its own primary mission. Parents send their children to school so that their children will receive a good formation. Often, they themselves continue to receive formation through this community, learning how to live as a family of faith more fully. When the parish, school, and family work together, children will experience a more fruitful education.

## A Crisis of Parenting and Childhood

Parents today need help with more than learning how to hand down the faith. Due to what Dr. Leonard Sax calls a "crisis of parenting," schools can help parents to rediscover how to exercise their God-given authority in helping their children to form virtue. Often parents take their children to Catholic schools so that teachers can impart the values they want for them. Parents need to realize how their own interactions with their children provide a much more foundational influence on their character. Our individualistic culture makes it seem like absolute freedom is a good for children that parents must respect. Parents often think they are being good parents by giving maximum freedom to their children, which, rather, leads to a crisis of emotional and spiritual health.

In articulating their hopes for their children, parents always express their desire for their children to be happy, which they often translate in their minds as being successful. Although they also want their children to learn moral and religious principles, they often, consciously or unconsciously, prioritize the things that they think will lead to material success. It is not that they do not want to hand on the faith, but they often do not make it a priority. In giving faith a back seat, they overlook the interior means by which their children can arrive at greater happiness. Leonard Sax's book, *The Collapse of Parenting*, draws upon his experience as a medical doctor and psychologist to diagnose the "a massive transfer of authority from parents to kids" that has happened in Western culture.[8] Symptoms of this transfer include disrespect toward parents, child obesity, addiction to technology and video games, declining success in education, resorting to medication to control behavior, and emotional fragility. Although parents desire happiness and success for their children, Sax points out that they have overlooked the number one factor needed for their realization: self-control. Only by teaching our children habits of discipline can they develop the emotional control and work ethic needed for personal fulfillment.

Self-control or self-discipline can be seen as synonymous with virtue, the moral habits that enable us properly to control our passions and achieve our true good. Few parents would put virtue at the top of their dream list for their children, but it is the formation they need most for both their personal happiness and their success. Sax, therefore, encourages parents to reassume control of the home by setting and enforcing clear rules to govern behavior. Establishing these boundaries and encouraging virtue provides the training necessary for becoming a rightly ordered adult. Avoiding the extremes of authoritarianism and an anything-goes mentality, "'just right'

---

8. Leonard Sax, *The Collapse of Parenting: How We Hurt Our Kids When We Treat Them Like Grown-Ups* (New York: Basic Books, 2016), 7.

parents communicate their love for their child, but they also enforce rules fairly and consistently."[9] Despite the fears of many parents, parental authority promotes stronger relationships in the family and helps children to take on greater responsibility within and out of the home.

Parents can become better parents by exercising their authority to guide their children to form habits that will help them to be happy. This does not mean acting in an authoritarian way, because parents must exercise their influence in both a loving and firm way. Sax provides more details on how parents can establish this kind of healthy relationship with their children:

> The benefits of parental authority are substantial. When parents matter more than peers, they can teach right and wrong in a meaningful way. They can prioritize attachments within the family over attachments with same-age peers. They can foster better relationships with their child and other adults. They can help their child develop a more robust and more authentic sense of self, grounded not in how many "likes" a photo gets on Instagram or Facebook but in the child's truest nature. They can *educate desire*, instilling a longing for higher and better things, in music, in the arts, and in one's own character.[10]

Parents have more influence than anyone else on the emotional and spiritual development of their children. Using this influence well helps parents to be the primary educators in assisting children to "prepare for life," be rooted in a loving relationship, and form the character needed for true success and fulfillment.[11] To be successful, children need love and affirmation, expressed in a way that leads them to responsibility.

Just as we can speak of a collapse of parenting, we could also point to a collapse of childhood. Children no longer have the free-

---

9. Sax, 141.
10. Sax, 24.
11. Sax, 189.

dom and space to remain in innocence and to play without the looming threat of ideology and perversion from entertainment, social media, and peer influence. Ironically, the collapse of parenting and childhood both have led to a prolonged period of adolescence, with children simply being left in the distraction of technology without learning to take responsibility or discover a sense of mission and adventure in life. Children need help on both ends, with parents taking more care to facilitate a protected space for youth while also giving opportunities to grow in maturity. These two points might seem paradoxical, but they reinforce one another in that parents need to be more intentional about guiding childhood and the emergence of adulthood.

Any parent could relate the unique challenges we face today in raising children. There is no manual on how to deal with the new challenges of technology or the changing dynamics of society. We can recognize, however, that our children need more than school to prepare them for life. Book learning is important, yet not sufficient for developing responsibility and finding one's place in the world. Like growing in discipline, children also need to learn how to do things, to take initiative, to solve problems, and find joy in making things. Senator Ben Sasse issued a kind of manifesto calling us to invest more attention to this aspect of education and formation in his book, *The Vanishing American Adult*. He pinpoints our failure to raise our children to become responsible and thoughtful adults: "I believe our entire nation is in the midst of a collective coming-of-age crisis without parallel in our history. We are living in an America of perpetual adolescence. Our kids simply don't know what an adult is anymore—or how to become one. Many don't see a reason even to try. Perhaps more problematic, the older generations have forgotten that we need to plan to teach them."[12] Sasse recognizes that

---

12. Ben Sasse, *The Vanishing American Adult: Our Coming-of-Age Crisis—and How to Rebuild a Culture of Self-Reliance* (New York: St. Martin's, 2017), 2, 4.

part of children's education, the part centered in the home, has been failing to form responsible adults.

If education is preparation for life, we are failing our children miserably. In order to overcome a growing "zombie-like passivity," and an "outsized sense of entitlement," Sasse recommends entrusting adolescents with more responsibility so that they can "learn how to seize the reins and do it themselves much earlier."[13] Fostering discipline should enable young people to become responsible. We need to change how we think of education to overcome this "deficit of life skills required for self-reliance," that corresponds to a "decline of agency, of initiative, of liveliness."[14] Our "kids no longer know how to produce" and so we have to teach them by "building and strengthening character" though the "intentional pursuit of gritty work experiences."[15] They are lacking in concrete experience and the ability to shape the world creatively, and so we have to create opportunities for them to grow in these areas.

Jason Craig addresses the failure to form adults from a Catholic perspective in his book *Leaving Boyhood Behind*, which examines the initiation of boys into manhood (distinct but related points could be said about girls into womanhood as well). For boys to become men, they must be taught how to work hard, to sacrifice themselves, and to live their faith. Too often boys live in a simulated reality, thinking only of themselves, and do not step up to accept the responsibilities of life. Young men do not prioritize getting married and having children, the goal of manhood, but remain unsure of their purpose, trapped in insecurity. Boys' bodies develop on their own, but they will not become men unless they also grow mentally, emotionally, and spiritually into manhood. Traditional cultures lead adolescents through elaborate rites of passage, and until recently

---

13. Sasse, 3, 123, 76.
14. Sasse, 40.
15. Sasse, 18, 139.

boys would learn how to work alongside their fathers. Today, on the other hand, many young men remain stuck in prolonged boyhood, not willing to accept a vocation of service and sacrifice for the good of others.

Education, in the most comprehensive sense, needs to include an initiation into culture, as a way of life. This is what has been breaking down in modern culture, with adolescents left to figure out their path on their own, with college as a place for continued academic formation, devoid of any real mentorship or formation in virtue or hard work. To counter this, Craig calls Catholic men to mentor boys, creating new rites of passage to initiate them into manhood.

> To mature as men, males must embrace the call to the sacrificial offering of their strength for spouse, family, and nation. Rites of passage prepare men to make this sacrifice, while providing the bulwark of a community—of brotherhood—to sustain men in living out the gift of their masculinity, and to pass that gift on to the future generations. As we have seen, there are many aspects of today's culture that make this sacrificial spirit difficult. We have to work harder than ever to create brotherhood with other men and to bring boys into manhood.[16]

Effective education today requires a greater commitment of parents working with the community.

Craig also offers specific examples of the shape this mentorship can take. "The most fundamental, practical, and first action we men should take to initiate boys into masculine maturity is this: Men must be the primary catechists and mentors for young men and for one another."[17] Fathers cannot simply allow others to educate their

---

16. Jason Craig, *Leaving Boyhood Behind: Reclaiming Catholic Brotherhood* (Huntington, Ind.: OSV Books, 2019), 124.

17. Craig, 125. You can see this principle embodied in the apostolate Fraternus (www.fraternus.net), which Craig leads.

children in the faith, but must serve as role models and teachers, as well as working with other men to make the parish a place conducive to masculine fellowship and mentorship. Secondly, fathers should teach their sons how to work, for "in his work, a man has the opportunity to give himself over to his daily burdens out of love, for the sake of his family."[18] The effort and dedication needed in work help bring boys to maturity and create a bond between men. Third, Craig recommends the experience of leisure, leading boys to disengage with technology to experience the real things of nature. "Boys need to be seeing, feeling, and touching real things in the real world—homesteading, hunting, hiking, playing, camping, swimming, carving, building, climbing, hiking."[19] Finally, Craig recognizes how mentorship extends to prayer and the spiritual life, learning how to engage in contemplative prayer, penance, fasting, the liturgical life, and fraternal community.

The insights of Sax, Sasse, and Craig all point to the important task for parents: to initiate their children into the responsibility of life. The Catholic community of the parish and school can help parents to develop their comprehensive educational role by helping them to grow in prayer and understanding, as well as living in a context of fraternal support. As parents overcome the collapse in the expression of their genuine authority, children can recover the essence of their childhood while also preparing to enter into the responsibility of adulthood.

## Fathers: Educating by Example and Affirmation

Fathers have more influence on the faith life of their children than anyone else—more than mothers, grandparents, teachers, and the parish priest. Studies have shown that if fathers do not practice the faith, children are very unlikely to do so in adulthood. If fathers do,

---

18. Craig, *Leaving Boyhood Behind*, 127.
19. Craig, 131.

children are much more likely to attend church in the future.[20] Fathers are called to lead their families in the faith and to provide a model of the Christian life for their children. Parents are the primary educators of their children, and this includes education in the faith. Simply dropping them off at a parish program will not form them in their faith. They need an apprenticeship and initiation into the Christian way of life, embracing not only faith, but also everything else. Fathers are teachers of their children primarily by providing an example for them. Fathers have to take a central role in this education, because, as we have seen, they are so crucial in the religious formation of their children. There are a number of things fathers can do to be effective teachers. First, it begins by putting God first, especially by prioritizing Sunday Mass. Everything else should be built around that central moment of the week. It speaks volumes when sports, recreation, and work fit in after worship and not before it. Making Sunday a special day also creates space just for being together as a family and having the leisure to be active outside, play games, talk together, have a bigger dinner, and enjoy each other's company.

Teaching children how to pray may be one of the most important things fathers do, but this must be followed by doing active things with them as well. James Stenson has noted that our children do not usually see fathers work, but only see them during their down time.[21] It is important for children to see fathers at their best, by drawing them into their strengths and skills when possible, but also but working on family projects together. This is not just a matter of teaching them skills, but teaching them the art of life. Fathers guide

---

20. Werner Haug and Phillipe Warner, "The Demographic Characteristics of the Linguistic and Religious Groups in Switzerland," in *The Demographic Characteristics of National Minorities in Certain European States*, vol. 2, ed. Werner Haug Paul Compton, and Youssef Courbage (Strasbourg: Council of Europe Directorate General III, Social Cohesion, 2000).

21. James Stenson, *Successful Fathers: The Subtle but Powerful Ways Fathers Mold Their Children's Characters* (Princeton, N.J.: Scepter Press, 2001).

them through challenging tasks, model how to respond to mistakes, and establish common purposes and goals for the family. Overall, children look to fathers to teach them what is really important. Concrete actions guide them in the faith and prepare them for the adventure of life.

Most significantly, fathers embody the Father's love. God does not just use fatherhood as an image of himself, because he himself is Father, even within his own triune life. Earthly fatherhood comes forth from him and should manifest his life and love. St. Paul speaks of honoring the "Father, from whom all fatherhood in heaven and on earth is named" (Eph 3:15).[22] God wants everyone to be able to see his own fatherly love and called certain men to share in his own paternal gift of bringing forth life and caring for others. Every father is called to be like Joseph, "an earthly shadow of the heavenly Father" for his own family."[23]

Our culture, however, regularly denigrates masculinity, sometimes viewing even its proper expressions as toxic. Too often, we see maleness in its fallenness—dominating and selfish—rather than showing self-sacrificial service. In fact, later in his Letter to the Ephesians, Paul speaks of the true vocation of the husband and father: "Husbands, love your wives, as Christ loved the church and gave himself up for her" (5:25). He also speaks of the role of fatherhood: "Do not provoke your children to anger, but bring them up in the discipline and instruction of the Lord" (6:4). Paul shows us the goal of fatherhood—sacrificing himself for the flourishing of the family by putting the good of his wife and children before his own desires.

No matter what the contrary voices of our culture say, we need strong men and fathers. God created man and woman in comple-

---

22. I deviate from contemporary translations that render *patria* as "family." The Douay-Rheims translates it as "paternity."

23. Pope Francis, apostolic letter *Patris corde* (December 8, 2020), 7, https://www.vatican.va/content/francesco/en/apost_letters/documents/papa-francesco-lettera-ap_20201208_patris-corde.html.

mentarity, and they need each other to thrive, helping the other in relation to their own strengths and weaknesses. And children need the strong presence of a father to discipline and teach, as Paul reminds us. Study after study has shown that fathers have the largest impact on the faith of their children. Christian Smith explains in his sociological study, *Young Catholic America*, that "the faith of Catholic fathers is powerfully determinative of the future faith of their children."[24] The same can be said for general well-being and success. When fathers are absent or refuse to exercise their role, a moral and spiritual vacuum appears. A strong majority of felons, for instance, grew up without fathers in the home.

Fathers do not lead in order to be in charge or to get their own way. They lead because God asks them to care for and protect their families. Fathers and mothers share in the great and beautiful partnership of family life, but fathers cannot simply sit back and let mothers take the lead in the spiritual life, as they are often tempted to do. Like Joseph, fathers should act firmly and lovingly to put God and the family before self, obeying God and leading the family in the right direction. They are called to model faith, work, and sacrifice to their children.

Because our children are not simply our own, but belong to God, we will have to account for our stewardship over them. God has already told us that the measure we use will be measured back to us, which is a stark warning for our parenting tactics. What is the goal by which we should measure our parenting? A father should want his child to grow to maturity as a child of God, which is to say to grow to become more like God. The goal is not simply to follow the rules that we set (and enforcing them can become a matter of pride). If the goal is not enforcing one's own will, but the will of the true Father, this gives freedom in following the path laid out by God, making parenting less about ourselves.

---

24. Smith, *Young Catholic America*, 125.

How will our children grow to become more like God? We must provide a compelling witness and example. If our parenting focuses mostly on rigidly enforcing rules and creating outward conformity, there is a risk that we will cut our children off from the real source of life in the bosom of the Father—his merciful love. We have to model his love and affection by showing our children that we care primarily about them and their good, which is why we are teaching and leading them. Conversely, children copy our behavior exactly when we do not show a good example, and they remind us often of our own mistakes.

What can we learn from the true merciful Father? Even when we rebelled against him, he sought us out. He sent his Son to reconcile us to him. He was patient, he forgave, and he accepted his prodigal sons back into his life, bestowing rich gifts upon them. The Father provides us with a perfect model of his merciful love in his Son. To love and care for others, to be a good shepherd of the flock entrusted to us, entails that we lay our life down for their good. To be a merciful father is to be a servant, who sacrifices time and energy for the good of his family.

A large part of the role of parents entails forming the identity and character of our children by giving them the support and security they need. We do this largely by loving them—willing their good, and expressing it in a way that they can understand—and affirming the goodness of their identity as children of the Father. Kent Haruf's *Benediction*, a novel set in the plains of Colorado, drives this point home. The main character, known appropriately as "Dad" Lewis, had just affirmed and blessed a young girl visiting him on his deathbed. The incident sparked a conversation with his late middle-aged daughter, Lorraine:

> "Did you touch me like that when I was little?"
> He stared at her for a long time. "I don't think so."
> "Why didn't you?"
> "I was too busy. I wasn't paying attention."

"No," she said. "You weren't." She lifted his hand to her cheek now.

"Forgive me," he whispered. "I missed a lot of things. I could of done better. I always loved you."

"You never told me that when I was her age."

"Can you forgive that too?"

"Yes, Daddy."

"I want to tell you now," he said.

She watched him, his watery eyes staring at her.

"I loved you," he whispered. "I always did. I approved of you completely. I do today."

She kissed his hand and put it back on his chest and leaned far over and kissed him on his cracked lips.

"Thank you, Daddy. I feel the same way. I hope you know that."[25]

We can take words for granted, and of course, they have to be backed up by action, but we do need to tell our children that we love them. It is crucial for their identity and coming to know the love of God the Father.

Too often children do not receive this necessary affirmation of love. The Thomistic psychologist Conard Baars spent a lifetime pointing out what happens when children do not receive love and affirmation from their parents—they themselves become incapable to giving this love and affirmation to others. Baars speaks of how a child can "not come to feel his own goodness, worth, and lovableness because those significant persons in his life were not present to him with the full attention of their whole being."[26] Our love helps our children to feel that they are "good, worthy, and lovable." Genuine affirmation reaches into the core of persons so that they know they are worthy of receiving love. This is our job as parents, and we

---

25. Kent Haruf, *Benediction* (New York: Vintage, 2014), 218.

26. Conrad Baars, *Feeling and Healing Your Emotions* (Gainesville, Fla.: Bridge-Logos, 2003), 164.

cannot wait until it is too late to let our children know our love and to feel our affirmation, which is crucial for their emotional and spiritual growth.

This love and affirmation provide an important expression of parents' essential role in education. Without communicating their own faith and love to their children, it will be hard for young people to be initiated effectively into the community of the Church. As they decide that their children will receive the sacraments of initiation, so they must follow through on initiating them into a life of faith. Through the culture of the home, children learn how to live, what matters most, and how to relate to God.

# 4 Learning to See:
## Teaching from a Catholic Worldview

What does a Catholic school teach that is distinctive from other schools? It might be tempting to answer that the Catholic faith or morality is what marks the Catholic curriculum as distinct from others. In reality, the answer should be *everything!* Nothing is the same even when it appears to be so on the surface when it is imparted through a Catholic worldview. A worldview is a way of seeing all things and fitting them within one coherent vision of reality. Even subjects such as math, science, history, and language take on a distinctive character when seen through the unity of faith and reason and in light of the eternal destiny of the human person. This chapter lays out the intellectual vision of a sacramental approach to education, explaining the integrated nature of the curriculum and how it recognizes all things as a sacramental embodiment of God's creative vision.

## What the Catholic School Teaches

The Catholic school teaches the truth of all things. Truth is the conformity or adequation of the mind to reality: correctly perceiving what *is*. Education brings us to a true understanding of things so that we can live in conformity to the truth. The Vatican document "The Catholic School" lays out this fundamental aim of Catholic education clearly, explaining how the school's "task is fundamentally a synthesis of culture and faith, and a synthesis of faith and life: the first is reached by integrating all the different aspects of human knowledge through the subjects taught, in the light of the Gospel; the second in the growth of the virtues characteristic of the Christian."[1] These two goals can be summarized as wisdom, which is the right ordering of knowledge, and virtue, the development of habits that lead to the realization of the good. In fact, this shared vision of reality constitutes the school's identity: Christ's "Revelation gives new meaning to life and helps man to direct his thought, action, and will according to the Gospel, making the beatitudes his norm of life. The fact that in their own individual ways all members of the school community share this Christian vision, makes the school 'Catholic.'"[2] School administrators and teachers, in particular, must share a Catholic vision of reality and seek to lead students in living out this truth.

We could describe this task as imparting a Catholic worldview and creating a culture in accord with this vision. The University of Mary's book *From Christendom to Apostolic Mission*, describes the power of a worldview, which it calls an "imaginative vision," in shaping how we think, feel, desire, and live:

> Every human society possesses with more or less strength a moral and spiritual imaginative vision, a set of assumptions and a way of looking at things that is largely taken for granted rather than argued for. Those fundamental assumptions provide the atmosphere the society's members breath and the soil in which the various institutions of the society take root and grow. Such a vision is holistic, a way of seeing things. It is usually secured by a religion that orders the deepest questions, but it includes more than what we usually call religion: not only a moral code, but also an accepted ideal of the good person, clear categories of success and failure, economic and political values and practices, legal codes and public policy, manners and modes of entertainment.... In a vigorous civilization this imaginative vision is more or less a

---

1. Congregation for Catholic Education, "The Catholic School" (1977), 37, https://www.vatican.va/roman_curia/congregations/ccatheduc/documents/rc_con_ccatheduc_doc_19770319_catholic-school_en.html.
2. Congregation for Catholic Education, "The Catholic School," 34.

settled matter, and the longer it is settled, the more deeply and subconsciously it is assumed. When a culture's vision is seriously contested, the society will go into a crisis until its original vision is either reconstituted or overthrown and another overarching vision takes its place.[3]

We live precisely in a time of crisis when the Christian worldview, which has survived in an ever-diminishing fashion, is now being replaced by a secular, individualist vision of life. Realizing the contested nature of a Christian worldview and addressing the hostile rise of a new anti-Christian one shapes the task of the Catholic school.

To form a Christian worldview for our students, first of all, we must ensure that all those working within the Catholic school share a conviction of its truth. Without this foundation, the school will simply transmit the prevalent anti-Christian worldview. Second, the materials and method employed by the school must consciously espouse a Christian worldview and resist the opposing vision. Third, students must receive formation in how to see the world through the eyes of faith, while also engaging parents and inviting them to share in this work. Finally, students must also understand the predominate secular worldview, why people hold to it, how it contradicts the Christian faith, and how to respond to it while living in the world. This will be no easy task, but the necessity of this kind of holistic formation justifies urgently the need for strong Catholic formation for our youth. Without a Catholic education, children will simply think and live according to a secular and individualistic view of human life.

A Catholic worldview answers fundamental questions about human life. Why do I exist? What is life's purpose? How should I live? What matters most? How do I find fulfillment and happiness? If students already espouse an anti-Christian worldview, what we

---

3. University of Mary, *From Christendom to Apostolic Mission: Pastoral Strategies for an Apostolic Age* (Bismarck, N.D.: University of Mary Press, 2020), 7.

teach will not make sense and will not impact them. It is possible for students to embrace a Christian way of thinking and living, but this will require seeing and experiencing a more compelling vision and narrative than the world offers. That will come through the witness of those in the school community, who live differently and joyfully, and the realization that the Christian vision provides more compelling answers to the deepest questions of life.

Simply imparting the content of faith without an entire worldview will not last, because faith cannot stand in isolation if the rest of one's thinking and desires oppose it. Faith will be undermined in a storm of contradictions. Catholic education provides a complete vision of life that embraces the meaning of creation and the material world, an anthropological vision of human life and love, and a sacramental imagination that sees beyond the surface of the moral life and history. This vision must navigate the vicissitudes of human culture, calling students to embrace the joys and hardships of the great adventure of life. This worldview sees life in its fullness, as a coherent whole, as opposed to a secular dualism that separates faith and reason, and nature and grace. The curriculum provides a foundation for personal formation by helping students to know what is good and noble and to form goals which transcend themselves. It provides them with a vision of what matters most in life and examples (real in the saints and imaginary in literature) of people who have served others and those who have not (examples that contrast virtue and vice). The curriculum sets students up for life, enabling them to know what to pursue in light of what they are learning.

Teaching with a robust Catholic vision embraces the entire person: body, emotions, mind, and will. The human person, as a sacramental being (body-soul unity), requires development of one's potential in all of its dimensions: strength and health of body to create personal discipline; control of the emotions in accord with the good; conformity of the mind to reality and development of the mental habits that enable one to understand and express oneself clearly; the development of the virtues of will that lead to happiness; and the encounter with the living God that enlivens our soul and enables a life of holiness. A complete formation helps students to look upward to God, but also downward to make sense of their experience of the natural world. Our students must learn to control their body and emotions and order them to the higher goods of learning and faith. They should come to love beauty, which they experience through the arts. They should learn to develop strength and discipline through physical education, which leads to self-control and team work.

Academic formation focuses on forming habits of mind ordered toward perceiving the truth of reality and articulating thoughts coherently. This occurs through proficient literacy, logical thought, and coherent and persuasive writing. Mathematics assists in the formation of logical thought in the following of ordered patterns and relations. Attentiveness to reality and the application of mathematical order occur in science. This vision draws upon the living tradition and community of the Church, which has preserved and passed down classical learning. The Catholic tradition has produced thinkers, writers, scientists, and artists of the highest caliber and these figures and their achievements should be known by our students. An integrated Catholic curriculum must also cover cultural problems, such as relativism, distorted understanding of the body and sexuality, and the saturation of technology and media which draws away from what is highest.

## A Sacramental Approach to the Curriculum

The Catholic school cannot simply offer the same instruction as a public education, with religious education and the Mass superadded onto the curriculum. Every subject must be taught in a distinctive fashion that reflects the unity of knowledge, having a common source in God—his creation and revelation—and ordered in a wisdom that communicates the ultimate purpose of all things.[4] A Catholic school approaches every subject through the two wings of faith and reason, knowing that every truth conforms our minds to the mind of God. Simone Weil captured this reality when she conveyed that every truth "is the image of something precious. Being a little fragment of particular truth, it is a pure image of the unique, eternal, and living Truth which once in a human voice declared 'I am the Truth.' Every school exercise thought of in this way, is like a sacrament."[5]

Everything is a sacrament when understood as an expression of the mind of God. Mathematics comes forth into the mind as an intellectual language that God instilled in the universe to express its order. Every material thing expresses his goodness and beauty. Human beings are made in his image and likeness to manifest him most fully within the created universe. Our faith expresses truths beyond what the eye can see, which manifest hidden realities. Catholic school students learn to look more broadly than other students, to attend to the meaning latent within creation, too often overlooked when simply seen as numerical or material, while also seeing beyond the visible. Students learn to see themselves differently as well, with their bodies as a sacrament of what lies hidden within, manifesting a divine drama, a call to the eternal.

A sacramental vision sees the deeper meaning hidden within all things. Without this vision it would be impossible to impart a Catholic worldview, because such a worldview does not flow from learning information but from learning to see, to imagine the world in a uniquely Christian way. C. S. Lewis describes the need to engage the imagination: "For me, reason is the natural organ of truth; but

---

4. For a further resource on this topic, see Brett Salkeld, *Educating for Eternity: A Teacher's Companion for Making Every Class Catholic* (Huntington, Ind.: Our Sunday Visitor Press, 2023).
5. Simone Weil, "Reflections on the Right Use of School Studies with a View to the Love of God," in *Waiting for God* (New York: Harper Perennial, 2009), 62–63.

imagination is the organ of meaning. Imagination, producing new metaphors or revivifying old, is not the cause of truth, but its condition."[6] Imagination synthesizes faith and reason by drawing them into a coherent vision of reality and the person. It is only through an imaginative vision that education will shape how we view human life, including its meaning, and purpose. We are losing the battle for the imagination by overlooking its power, allowing our students to be pulled away by competing narratives.

The entire curriculum must reflect a coherent, imaginative vision of reality. Every school subject provides an opportunity to conform the mind and the whole person to the truth of God's creation and revelation. Fundamentally, schools teach words, numbers, and things. We begin by teaching letters so that, as children learn to read, they can grasp the expression of ideas through writing. *Words* enable communication of thought, and through the development of mental habits that attend to words students learn to follow stories and information, and to be present to realities made accessible through books. Words also inspire the students' own thoughts which they learn to express through speech and writing. The mental habits and skills of words, written and oral, provide the foundation for all learning. In sacramental fashion, these words embody the thoughts and meaning that students perceive in their minds.

Students also learn logical ordering through *numbers*, by which we relate things to one another and perceive the mathematical truth of reality. Though not physical realities in themselves, numbers represent the ability of the mind to order things through counting, measuring, and creating categories. We write numbers, like words, using symbols to represent numerals and mathematical operations. Looking at the bigger picture of formation, numbers give access to the order of the universe, by which the human mind can access the

---

6. C. S. Lewis, "Bluspels and Flalansferes: A Semantic Nightmare," in *Rehabilitations and Other Essays* (Oxford: Oxford University Press, 1939), 157–58.

wisdom of the mind of God. In sacramental fashion, these numbers provide a means of accessing the hidden meaning of the created world by perceiving its order, symmetry, and relationality.

Education also teaches *things*: the physical world with its inanimate and animate beings, human persons and their deeds throughout history, artifacts of arts and culture, and the realities of faith. These things can be accessed directly by experience and observation and can be approached more indirectly with words and the logical order of numbers. Science studies the physical realities of the world, seeking to know the truth of their existence and how they fit together within the larger whole of the universe. Science is the observation of nature, conducted through experimentation, something to be *done* rather than simply studied in a secondary sense. History opens up the drama of human life and places the student within a larger narrative. Literature approaches the same drama through the use of symbols and vicarious experience to open up the psychological and spiritual depths of human choice. In sacramental fashion, students learn to see each thing as having meaning within the whole of God's creation, as something flowing from and ordered to him.

Physical education and the arts cannot be overlooked, though many modern programs downplay their significance. Formation of the body has taken on greater significance in our culture, as we must learn to respect and accept our bodies as gifts from God that need to be cared for and developed. Physical discipline lays the foundation for the discipline of emotions and mind. The arts, in turn, foster the imagination and wonder, and help guide the emotions to desire the good, true, and beautiful. The fine arts help to engage all of the senses and to inspire the imagination with the beautiful. In sacramental fashion, the body and imagination are awakened by recognizing the gift of life and its inherent beauty.

Religious education, catechesis within the school, draws students into the personal revelation of God, as the one who created the universe and, coming into this creation, speaks to those made in his image. The liberal arts help students to engage with God's revelation, understanding the words through which God makes himself known, as well as the numerical underpinning by which God has established "measure, number, and weight" (Wis 11:20) of things. Religious education should also engage with real things, the things that God uses to establish the sacraments, and the beauty of churches and ritual, along with the sacramentals which accompany them; as well as interpersonal encounter, conversation, and witness, all of which should flow naturally from the school.

The Cardinal Newman Society's "Catholic Curriculum Standards" offers an important resource for assessing curriculum from a Catholic worldview for the areas of English, math, science, and history.[7] The standards are divided between grades K–6 and 7–12 and supplement content standards with general, intellectual, and dispositional ones. The "Catholic Worldview Seminar" I helped to develop for the Archdiocese of Denver, which is required for all new teachers, draws upon these standards to give examples of how to teach from a Catholic perspective. This seminar draws upon the four pillars of the *Catechism* and connects them with the liberal arts and the four major content areas addressed by the Cardinal Newman Society standards. For instance, the first day engages the doctrines of God the Creator and the Incarnation, the unity of faith and reason, and how math expresses the order and beauty of the universe. Teachers can make concrete applications through the standards and examples are given by an experienced teacher in each area.

Teaching from a Catholic worldview does not impose theology onto other areas of the curriculum. Rather, it calls forth the contribution of each subject area within a vision of the whole. Everything that is learned in the Catholic curriculum finds its place within a

---

7. Cardinal Newman Society, "Curriculum Standards," https://newmansociety. org/catholic-curriculum-standards/.

coherent vision and can relate to the other areas. A Catholic vision deepens the subject taught by being able to ask more profound questions about its origin, purpose, connections, and applications, because of its context within the whole compass of reality, drawing upon faith and reason together.

## The Liberal Arts within the Catholic Worldview

The Church embraced the liberal arts in order to help her members, especially religious, to understand and contemplate the Word of God, as well as to speak and write effectively to share this knowledge. Out of the teaching of the seven liberal arts at the cathedral and monastery schools, medieval universities arose to teach philosophy and three terminal degrees in theology, law, and medicine. The Church's mission of salvation grew to include the complete formation of the person, uniting faith and reason in the common mission of seeking the wisdom to live well in the world and order all things to the glory of God.

Catholic schools and public schools both are rooted in the liberal arts because their curriculum is built around language, math, science, and history—the core subjects of the liberal arts. Even if we look at STEM, seen as an alternative to a liberal arts focus, two of its four core subjects are liberal arts—math and science—and the other two are practical applications of the liberal arts—technology and engineering. Today, we learn to read and count so that we can get to practical outcomes. Many employers have recently noted, however, that critical thought and creativity are more important for success than practical training, because, rather than narrowing outcomes, general dispositions make graduates more ready to do anything that a job or career may require. Catholic schools have always been liberal arts schools, but in the last fifty years we have embraced the pragmatic approach of public education more and more. The previous decades are out of step with the Catholic tradition of the last two thousand years.

The liberal arts have grown thin as American education has been dumbed down without an overarching vision of the purpose of education. John Dewey, the main philosophical influence on public education, was a pragmatist and led the public schools in moving away from a focus on the transmission of content. He shifted their aim to forming democratic citizens ready to contribute to society, and saw truth as an imposition onto the student. His thought represented one expression of a movement away from the liberal arts tradition that originally had shaped American universities and public education. For instance, following that tradition, in light of attacks on the humanities in the early nineteenth century, Yale responded that the purpose of education was to "sharpen the intellect, strengthen the faculty of reason, and to induce a general habit of mind favorable to the discovery of truth and the detection of error."[8] Traditionally understood, education seeks first to shape the person, fostering intellectual traits and personal discipline, and only secondarily to impart skills needed for practical tasks.

Returning to the Church's own liberal tradition more robustly would help us focus on the formation of the mind and soul, to teach our students how to think and live in accord with truth. Education must first be about the person, helping students to be who God is calling them to be, fostering right thinking about the truth, desiring the right goods, and then living and acting in accord with them. A stronger approach to the liberal arts, focused on being before doing, would recover rich content in the humanities and integrate it into a vision of the whole with mathematics and science. Students need better literacy (as it is decreasing across the country), they need more wonder and creativity (as technology has restricted them), and to see how math and science are more than numbers and facts

---

8. Yale University, *Reports on the Course of Instruction in Yale College* (1828), quoted in Eric Adler, *The Battle of the Classics: How a Nineteenth-Century Debate Can Save the Humanities Today* (New York: Oxford University Press, 2020), 67.

but relate to an integrated vision of life (against the dominant materialism).

In order to teach the liberal arts more effectively from a Catholic worldview, I would offer six principles. First, strive to form dispositions, habits of mind, rather than practical outcomes, enabling education to form the person rather than be used for mere utilitarian purposes. Second, offer a direct engagement with reality, rather than simply imparting abstract formulas and data, enabling students to be active and involved in the process of learning. Third, show a unified vision of life through an interdisciplinary approach that draws connections between the subjects taught. Fourth, help students to grasp the relevance of what they are learning, pointing their studies to their ultimate purpose for themselves and others. Fifth, offer content rich materials that engage the robust cultural heritage of the Christian past, implementing good and great books that ask the big questions using eloquent poetry and prose. Finally, draw upon beauty not only by teaching the fine arts but also by pointing to natural, artistic, and spiritual beauty in every subject.

First, the initial principle of the Catholic liberal arts—forming dispositions (a readiness to receive and respond to learning) and habits (which enable to students to perform actions related to learning)—recognizes that education aims primarily to form the person rather than to achieve practical outcomes. The most fundamental dispositions are to be open to, receive, and even seek the truth, fulfilling the fundamental human desire to know. Education should foster receptivity through wonder, attention, discipline, and perseverance. The active search for understanding will be furthered by developing the faculty of memory, forming ideas, logical thinking, and clear communication. Students must take an active role in understanding, while being open to the guidance of others in humility and docility. There is one key skill, language fluency, expressed traditionally by grammar, mastering the way language works, which opens up the possibility of learning most broadly. This is followed by the disciplined thought of logical thinking that seeks precision and accuracy in understanding (as embodied in mathematics), as well as the well-crafted communication of ideas and words in the speaking and writing of effective rhetoric.

Second, the Catholic liberal arts should offer a direct engagement with reality, which calls forth greater involvement from students. Rather than receiving information in a passive way, students should directly interact with the "matter" at hand in each subject, whether that is getting their hands dirty in an experiment or learning from primary sources. When conducted second hand only, education becomes dry because it focuses on the ideas and conclusions of others. Young people should have the opportunity to move through the process of discovery in the classroom so that they can see directly how things work and how to draw conclusions from their own experience. This direct method follows the natural progression of learning from experience to abstract thought, as well as the nature of the human person. As body-soul unities, we must recognize that all knowledge begins in the senses and that the way we learn must therefore engage the whole person—senses, emotions, and mind. Students should experience and learn from nature, drawing them into a tactile encounter with the realities of God's creation and salvific economy that is rooted in concrete reality.

Third, the Catholic liberal arts present a unified vision of life, guided by an interdisciplinary approach to the curriculum. Modern education has become fragmented, with discrete content taught without any seeming relation to the whole. We could call this the "synthetic impulse" of a Catholic vision. The "synthetic impulse" of faith should provide unity for the entire curriculum, showing the coherent order and relation of all things.[9] This synthetic vision should break down

---

9. Bishop Daniel Flores, "The Synthetic Impulse in Catholic Life," lecture at the University of Mary, February 24, 2017, https://www.primematters.com/perspectives/synthetic-impulse-catholic-life; see also Patrick Reilly, "Bishop Flores: What

the dualism between faith and the others subjects of the curriculum, not by sprinkling in religion where it does not belong, but by forming a worldview that enables us to see the connection and purpose of things and to live in accord with it. The example of math stands out. The answer to a math problem does not change in a Catholic school, but the entire context for learning math does. The student can ask why math works at all, and discover that it comes forth from the mind of God as an intellectual language that suffuses the universe. When a student learns math, the mind becomes attuned to the language of the cosmos, as well as becoming stronger in its own reasonings and ability to perceive objective truth. The perseverance and precisions of math should flow into one's study as a whole. A Catholic worldview can draw what is learned from every subject into a coherent whole, a unified and synthetic vision of the truth.

Fourth, the liberal arts in a Catholic approach help students to see the "why," the relevance for life of what they are learning. Although Catholic education does not focus on utilitarian goals, everything learned is relevant for life by shaping one's mind and soul, and guiding how one lives. Ultimately, study forms a response to God, the creator and redeemer who offers us the truth of his work of creation and redemption as the beginning of an eternal conversation with him. Studies in a Catholic school have an ultimate purpose and relevance. Carissa Romero pointed out the importance of seeing this relevance: "Students value school when they understand how it is related to things they care about and how school can help them reach their long-term goals. Students value their schoolwork when they believe it is relevant to their lives and/or will help them connect to a purpose that is bigger than themselves—whether it is a contribution to their family, their community, society at large, or

---

Every Catholic Kid Needs for School," *National Catholic Register*, March 4, 2017, https://www.ncregister.com/blog/bishop-flores-what-every-catholic-kid-needs-for-school.

something else."[10] When presented as part of the ongoing drama of the story of salvation history, one's own life takes shape within the great arc of God's love for us. The love of learning arises when life has meaning, when there is a role for us to take the fruits of our learning and apply them within the great vocation of our own lives in service of God and others.

Fifth, the liberal arts within a Catholic worldview offer rich materials that engage the greatest achievements of human history. It does so not for antiquarian purposes but to present the most important ideas and most inspiring stories that will help students to come alive to the story of humanity. I often describe this point to teachers as reading good books together and talking about them with your students. Anyone can do that! Rather than elaborate and prepared lesson plans, the classroom comes alive with the living voice of the greatest books, which elicit new ideas from students who want to think with the great authors, under the guidance of their teachers and fellow students. Reading rich texts develops complex thinking and a stronger vocabulary, rather than holding our students back by dumbing things down every year another level in the wrong direction.[11] The best way

---

10. Carissa Romero, "What We Know about Purpose and Relevance from Scientific Research," (September 2019), *Student Experience Research Network*, https://studentexperiencenetwork.org/research_library/what-we-know-about-purpose-relevance-from-scientific-research/.

11. American College Testing (ACT), in lamenting low literacy rates in America and their impact on workforce readiness, proposed that "the clearest differentiator in reading between students who are college ready and students who are not is the ability to comprehend *complex* texts" ("Reading Between the Lines: What the ACT Reveals About College Readiness in Reading" [2006], 2, https://www.act.org/content/dam/act/unsecured/documents/reading_summary.pdf). Although Common Core standards have sought to simplify reading materials, the ACT recommends the opposite: "In most cases, a complex text will contain multiple layers of meaning, not all of which will be immediately apparent to students upon a single superficial reading. Rather, such texts require students to work at unlocking meaning by calling upon sophisticated reading comprehension skills and strategies" (7).

to increase literacy in our children is to have them read more, not less, and to read stories that are worth reading, are beautifully written, will inspire them, and will get them thinking about the most important realities of life. Good books will draw them out of themselves and will lead naturally to great conversations.

Sixth, and finally, the Catholic liberal arts thrive upon beauty. Beauty is the splendor of truth that radiates the goodness and being of things, expressing their nature and form in a powerful and attractive way. We see this in music, the arts, and literature most powerfully, although beauty can be appreciated in every subject, including math and science, where the proportion and harmony of God's handiwork become apparent. Beauty draws forth love from our hearts, while ugliness, boredom, and banality close our minds and hearts, obscuring the deep, and often hidden, goodness of life. Beauty tills the soil of our humanity, softening our minds and hearts to receive truth and to love what is good. It leads us to wonder and awe, inspires greatness and sacrifice, and leads us to a gift of self—in our learning, relationships, and in prayer.

In response to an articulation of the Catholic liberal arts, I often hear a number of objections. Many think the liberal arts are too "Western," an objection that will receive the response of an entire chapter. The great ideas truly unite us all around contemplation of the most important and universal truths of life. Some wonder if the liberal arts are a code word for classical education. I define classical education as "an intense expression of the liberal arts drawing upon the language, history, and culture of classical civilization." Teaching the liberal arts in a Catholic context can often benefit from classical culture, even if it does not require it. Some think this approach sounds elitist and too difficult. I have seen it in action many times: every student loves learning, listening to stories, thinking, admiring, and discussing. These things often unite students of different abilities, and those who struggle with literacy, for instance, tend to respond better to stories and ideas that inspire us. They grow in literacy by being drawn into the beauty of books that may seem too hard at first. Finally, some think the liberal arts do not prepare students well enough for their careers. In fact, many corporations, including tech companies, have found that graduates of liberal arts programs are better prepared for work because they are more creative, are problem solvers, can be trained easily, and have a deeper intelligence to bring to their work.[12] The liberal arts prepare us first to be someone, and being formed at this deeper level, graduates find themselves prepared to do things as well.

---

12. See for instance: Jessica Stillman, "The Most Unexpected Workplace Trend Coming in 2020: The Return of the Liberal Arts Major," *Inc.*, November 26, 2019, https://www.inc.com/jessica-stillman/2020-workplace-trends-liberal-arts-major-hiring.html; Chad Engelland and Chris Mirus, "Businesses Looking for Perceptive Thinkers Are Looking for Philosophy Majors," *Dallas News*, June 19, 2018, https://www.dallasnews.com/opinion/commentary/2018/06/19/businesses-looking-for-perceptive-thinkers-are-looking-for-philosophy-majors/; Sydney Johnson, "As Tech Companies Hire More Liberal Arts Majors, More Students Are Choosing STEM Degrees," *EdSurge*, November 13, 2018, https://www.edsurge.com/news/2018-11-13-as-tech-companies-hire-more-liberal-arts-majors-more-students-are-choosing-stem-degrees.

# 5 Books, Beauty, and Truth:
## Inspiring Intelligence and Imagination

Recall that we are "made for the stars but rooted in the soil," as explored in the introduction. As human beings, we reach for the heights; and yet, despite our spiritual nature, we have bodies rooted in the physical stuff of this earth. Due to the sacramental nature of Catholic education, we need to take the meeting of these two sides of our nature seriously. Truth often does not "stick," because it has been divorced from its relation to goodness and beauty. Our students do not know why they should learn at all, and need to be inspired by the beauty of truth in order to desire to learn. This chapter connects the role of the intellectual life within education to the complementary awakening of the imagination, looking at how books play a role in imparting truth in a way that can capture the hearts of students.

## The Relation of Truth, Goodness, and Beauty in Education

You cannot force someone to learn. True, you can make students go through the motions of doing busy work and force them to repeat information back, but the act of understanding must proceed from within. Simone Weil said that "intelligence can be led only by desire."[1] Without delight in the truth, learning becomes drudgery, turning one's interest and affections in another direction (which is not to say that learning should not engage in difficult work, only that it should not do so apart from delight). Focusing on truth to

---

1. Weil, *Waiting for God*, 66.

the exclusion of goodness and beauty is a mistake. We tend to think of truth as something cold and hard, perceived in isolation. Perceived alongside of goodness, however, we see that the truth, as something pursued and lived with others, moves us out of ourselves. Its beauty leads us into communion with others.

Truth has become a bad word, as too many people parrot Pilate's response to Jesus, "What is truth?" (Jn 18:38). Thomas Aquinas defined it very simply, however: Truth is the conformity of the mind to reality. Truth is not creative, something that each person makes up. Truth entails grasping and understanding *what is*. It is really that simple. Something either is or it is not, and if we figure that out correctly, we have grasped the truth. Grasping truth relies on humility, as it requires subordinating ourselves to something outside of ourselves and accepting its reality. We cannot impose the truth; we must receive it.

There are parts of reality that are beyond our reach. Although reason can discern with certainty that God does exist, we cannot know God in himself on our own. God is beyond the universe, completely transcendent from his creation, and in order to know him, he has to reveal himself to us (literally, to pull back the veil that separates us from him). In faith, God elevates our minds to him, giving us grace to know him in a way that exceeds our ordinary abilities. He also gives us clarity about our own nature and God's plan of salvation for us. Faith enables us to affirm that Jesus is the Son of God made man who came into the world to save us. This supernatural knowledge opens a whole world to us, helping us to see further than we could ever imagine—into the very life of the Triune God.

Is faith imaginative in the sense that it opens our mind beyond what it can see? Perhaps this is why J. R. R. Tolkien called the Gospel a true myth.[2] The whole mythic or symbolic way of seeing reality

---

2. See, for example, Tolkien's relationship of fairy stories to the Gospel: "Of course I do not mean that the Gospels tell what is only a fairy story; but I do mean very

has been denigrated in the modern West. Symbol can often, more powerfully than fact, convey truth in an imaginative way. Returning to a broader understanding of truth that includes not only the metaphysical but also the imaginative sense would enable students to perceive the deeper meaning of things more readily. Reality is more than meets the surface through our senses, as non-believers continue to be drawn to fantasy and the occult out of a sense that life remains mysterious. Can we give an account of reality as a whole that includes these deeper senses of meaning, mystery, and purpose?

Faith affirms the truth of nature, even as it points to a higher path—the conformity of our minds to God. If truth is the conformity of the mind to reality, we can then recognize that God is Truth itself, because he is the only One who knows the reality of his own life completely and he knows the whole not only of what exists but also of what could exist. Even within himself, we see this Truth expressed in his Word, the one who comes forth from the Father to express his being and to speak forth creation. God is also Goodness itself, because in knowing the fullness of truth, he also wills it, affirming the Good in himself and bringing forth the good in his works. Within God, the Spirit proceeds according to the mode of love, expressing the love of Father and Son. God has freely chosen to manifest his own truth and goodness outside of himself, creating both spiritual beings (the angels) and the material world, resounding to his glory. God is Beauty itself because his Being radiates forth glory, expressing who God is and drawing his creation to him. The works of his creation reflect his truth, goodness, and beauty as mirrors, though rational beings consciously participate in giving him glory by knowing the truth, loving the good, and delighting in beauty.

---

strongly that they do tell a fairy story: the greatest. Man the storyteller would have to be redeemed in a manner consonant with his nature: by a moving story. But since the author of it is the supreme Artist and the Author of Reality, this one was also made . . . to be true on the Primary Plane." *The Letters of J. R. R. Tolkien*, ed. Humphrey Carpenter (New York: Houghton Mifflin Harcourt, 2013), 116.

Being made in the image and likeness of God is not a static reality but a call to become ever more like God. Education helps us to
realize this potential. The more we conform to the truth, love what
is good, and reflect his beauty, the more like God, and therefore the
happier, we will become. To be like God entails both receiving what
is true, good, and beautiful from him, including as reflected in his
creation, and also actively transmitting these to others, using them
to shape God's creation. Education, most broadly, fulfills the task of
becoming human, responding to the fundamental order within us
that propels us to know the truth and love the good. All of human
history could be seen as either a proper or distorted response to
these longings that distinguish us from all other material beings.
Our response to them does not entail a reflex or passivity, but a free
and creative response. Human beings, made into the image and likeness of God, are beings who imitate him in creative thought and
work, figuring things out and making things within the canvas of
creation. We are not merely to perceive but also conceive.

Entering into the truth entails learning how to think. This
requires an initial receptivity in coming to understand the reality of
things, but it quickly moves from there to extending and combining
ideas, laying out an entire vista for perceiving the world. Education
should emphasize forming the right dispositions for both accurate
and dynamic thinking, which comes from engaging the great ideas
that precede us, examining them, imitating them, and building upon
them. This happens most fruitfully in conversation with others, as
the great texts and ideas of the past become alive in the give and take
of discussion. Seeing rightly requires a response, not simply repeat-
ing what is learned, but giving it one's own expression in word and
writing. This prepares the student to respond to life in this fashion,
gaining wisdom by perceiving, ordering, and directing things rightly
in thought and action.

The most important response to truth is to live in accord with it.
Our free will desires things that are *known* to be good, in contrast to

our sensitive appetite, which in animalistic fashion simply desires natural good based on our bodiliness. We rise above the animals because we desire things that go beyond immediate needs and we can make free choices based on an intellectual desire. Education, as learning how to live, could be rightly described as learning how to love. An educated person knows what to desire and how to pursue it. This entails the disciplining of freedom, so that we do not simply follow our emotions, which come and go, but shape our life according to deeper truths. An educated person knows what is truly good, that which will fulfill our being, rather than meeting a fleeting desire. Education has always sought to teach a kind of discipline of life that helps students to learn how to live in an ordered way, to live a noble and worthy life. In short, education should help us to become good, as we develop the moral habits of virtue that lead to true and lasting happiness.

Why do students not desire truth and love what is most noble and worthy? Perhaps it is because they do not delight in the beauty of truth and goodness. Instead, their hearts follow immediate pleasures, and they treat learning as a burden. We have made it into a burden, in fact, with long regimented hours confined to a desk, with heads buried in a boring textbook, with the threat of an exam looming over them. If education lacks beauty, it will lack delight. For education to teach students what to love, it must help them to fall in love with truth and goodness, even being willing to give their lives for it. Beauty moves us most deeply, opening us up to truth and goodness, inspiring toil to obtain them and effort to maintain and protect them. Everything within the curriculum can lead to beauty: discovering the order, proportion, and harmony of the cosmos; the splendor of the design of each created thing; the pleasing expression of words, sounds, and stories; ideas that speak to the depth of the mind and heart; and the drama of human life and history. All this beauty points back to and instantiates the source of beauty in the Word himself, the one who made us and who can make our souls to be beautiful in him.

In imparting a rational soul to us, God wants us to think rightly about this world and delight in its beauty, even as he prepares us for what surpasses it. Divine beauty draws us beyond the logic of this world. We look for a beauty that surpasses the surface of things, thinking with "the mind of Christ," who "emptied himself and took the form of a slave" (1 Cor 2:16; Phil 2:7). God's beauty inspires us to fall in love with what lasts beyond the world's logic. The world says, "stay safe and take more for yourself." Christ says, "take up your Cross and follow me" (Mt 16:24), for this is the true path of happiness. He calls us not simply to take but to give, turning the world's logic upside down. Faith elevates reason to encompass more, inspired by a supernatural love that recognizes that we gain our lives when we give them away. We are drawn to a beauty that surpasses all understanding, that wounds our hearts and transfixes our minds by fulfilling them in a way beyond our capacities. Thus, we stand before the supernatural character of Catholic education: a mystical encounter with the One who is reality itself.

## Books, the Intellectual Life, and Community

Even if God draws us beyond the logic of this world, faith still inspires reason to contemplate earthly truth more fully. Faith and reason stand firmly together, leading the Christian to think and understand even more than the mind could do on its own: pushing it to see further and encompass the whole of reality with God's help.

The intellectual life, however, often gets a bad rap. Just the mention of it makes people think of professors writing books that no one cares about or giving lectures on obtuse ideas. The intellectual life, however, represents the heart of education, as coming to knowledge, understanding, and wisdom. It seeks truth for its own sake, recognizing it as life-giving and good in and of itself. There are four major goods we pursue, as indicated by the precepts of the natural law: (1) one's own life (self-preservation), (2) the family (preservation of species), (3) society (the common good), and (4) the truth;[3] it is the clear that there is a progression of goods, with one's self as the foundation, not the culmination. One's own life should work to advance the good of one's family, the good of society, and the one good that unites everyone most perfectly: the truth. We live for the intellectual life, particularly when we understand that life as ordered to the perfect knowledge of the beatific vision: seeing God face to face.

I have found resistance to the intellectual life to constitute the greatest challenge to the renewal of Catholic schools. Many teachers consider themselves as professionals who gravitate toward best practices over ideas. Teaching as a craft certainly requires skills and practical experience, but we also have to remember that its entire purpose is to draw students into an understanding of the truth. If teachers are not passionate about discovering the truth, how could we expect that of their students? Although schools speak freely of forming life-long learners, and teachers embody this principle, it can be difficult to have an intellectual conversation with teachers, administrators, and parents. The intellectual life may have been educated out of us through the memorization of facts and the focus on acquiring skills.

To become a great teacher, one must love learning—love the process of discovering new ideas, thinking through them, sharing them joyfully, discussing the things that matter most, and being always ready to grow. Professional educators can become comfortable with the way they have always done things and stick to a routine of imparting information and looking for measurable outcomes from their students. Fostering the intellectual life sounds like going back to school or even wasting time on content that will not be taught in the classroom, but it simply entails loving to read, think, and discuss. Someone who cares about the intellectual life is never satisfied, would never say, "I know enough about that." No! The lifelong

---

3. See Thomas Aquinas, *Summa theologiae*, I-II, q. 94, a. 2.

learner wants to continue to grow, to understand better even what
has been taught for decades, to develop new interests, to rethink
things, to be willing to approach things differently, and to explore
natural and supernatural realms.

In order to grow in the intellectual life, one must commit to
learning, making time for reading, thinking, and discussing. It is not
enough to go along unwillingly with a degree program or professional development requirement. For the intellectual life to prosper,
it must go beyond any requirement or utility. Even as teachers commit to learning what they are teaching, so they need time to read for
personal growth and to develop their interests. Out of this time, it
is important to have opportunities to share and discuss the fruits of
this learning. Learning happens through the give and take of
expressing ideas and having them refined by contradiction, affirmation, and complementary additions. This commitment will in turn
inspire students to seek the truth, joining its discovery as a quest,
rather than simply receiving information. Teachers can enter into a
shared process of discovery with their students—approaching the
truth together, standing before it in unison with them, with each
class a fresh approach to an idea, no matter how frequently repeated
over the years.

The intellectual life is more important for education and life
than any practical outcome. Josef Pieper famously reminded us that
external activity does not constitute life's goal. Rather, we find our
fulfillment in leisure, which is both the basis and height of culture.
His book, *Leisure, the Basis of Culture*, points to internal activity,
particularly contemplation, as the source of our happiness and fulfillment, especially when directed to God in worship and prayer. Leisure is not an absence of activity or mere recreation and
entertainment. It enters into the highest goods; it is drawn into them
as if receiving them as a gift. Pieper clarifies: "Leisure, it must be
remembered, is not a Sunday afternoon idyll, but the preserve of
freedom, of education and culture, and of that undiminished

humanity which views the world as a whole."[4] It withdraws from distraction so as to appreciate the goodness of the world, inspiring us to "waste" our time relating to the source of all goodness in God. Leisure fights against the boredom of constant distraction by insisting that our time is ordered and that all work and free time find meaning when directed to their ultimate purpose. Pieper recognizes boredom as a spiritual crisis: "The vacancy left by absence of worship is filled by mere killing of time and by boredom, which is directly related to inability to enjoy leisure; for one can only be bored if the spiritual power to be leisurely has been lost."[5] Noise or silence—frenetic activity or leisure—this choice will shape the state of our soul.

Leisure forms the basis of education, as the word "school" coming from the Greek *skole*, literally means leisure in its etymology. We give our children many years to immerse themselves in what is highest, not simply so that they can get a job but so that they can live. Ultimately our children need an intellectual conversion, a turning toward the truth in a way that becomes definitive for their entire life. This generally happens not by reading a book, although that does occur occasionally, but through the friendship that forms within a community devoted to learning. So many people report falling in love with learning because of a particular teacher or class where their eyes were opened, and that led to many conversations and experiences beyond the classroom. The intellectual life only grows in friendship through a shared pursuit of the truth.

The greatest educational impact occurs when the school fosters a culture dedicated to the ardent pursuit of truth. This does not arise simply from having high academic standards. It is the integration of faith, life, and friendship that makes a deep and lasting impact. My own transformative experience occurred in the Catholic Studies

---

4. Josef Pieper, *Leisure, the Basis of Culture* (San Francisco: Ignatius Press, 2009), 53.
5. Pieper, 69.

program at the University of St. Thomas in Minnesota, which not only explored the great writings and cultural achievements of the Christian tradition, but also embodied them in common prayer, lectures, meals, a study abroad program in Rome, a leadership program, and sponsorship of the arts (I watched the writing of an icon in the center). Likewise, the Integrated Humanities Program at the University of Kansas took students through two years of the great books, while also leading them through the culture behind the great books through poetry recitation, the singing of folk songs and ballads, conversational Latin, ballroom dance, trips to Europe, country fairs, and stargazing. Education loses its great power when distilled only to the transmission of ideas in schools. The search for truth needs a holistic embodiment rooted in a communal life that teaches students how to learn, what to love, and how to give their lives to beauty.

## What to Read? Choosing Literature for a Moral Imagination

I have heard educators say, "it doesn't matter what kids read as long as they are reading." This clearly is not true. Just as we recognize that "we are what we eat," so "we are what we read," what we consume with our minds and our hearts. If our children read junk, or worse, this will shape how they think and what they desire. This same principle certainly applies to what they listen to and what they watch. As we have become drowned in a sea of information, books, media, music, videos, and games, it is more important than ever to ask, "what should we read?" To be educated a hundred years ago would have entailed mastery of a clear set of authors and books. Today, the question of what to read has become a battle.

There is, of course, much censorship in today's culture. Much of it, however, remains subtle, through the controlling of how information is disseminated and what is presented as most appealing in a consumerist context. Neil Postman picked up on this, remarking that we will not be controlled by pain or overt control, but by pleasure, the constant distraction of false loves. He pondered the contrast between George Orwell's *1984* (1949), which presented the overt manipulations of a Communist society, and Aldous Huxley's *Brave New World* (1932), where people were controlled rather through pleasure:

> What Orwell feared were those who would ban books. What Huxley feared was that there would be no reason to ban a book, for there would be no one who wanted to read one. Orwell feared those who would deprive us of information. Huxley feared those who would give us so much that we would be reduced to passivity and egoism. Orwell feared that the truth would be concealed from us. Huxley feared the truth would be drowned in a sea of irrelevance. Orwell feared we would become a captive culture. Huxley feared we would become a trivial culture, preoccupied with some equivalent of the feelies, the orgy porgy, and the centrifugal bumblepuppy. As Huxley remarked in *Brave New World Revisited*, the civil libertarians and rationalists who are ever on the alert to oppose tyranny "failed to take into account man's almost infinite appetite for distractions."[6]

Even if *1984* remains a must read, we live in a *Brave New World* where too many people have abandoned the search for truth for the comforts of TV and their smartphone.

Reading itself has become a revolutionary act, if we do not use it as another distraction. Helping our children to read and to re-read the right things will mark them as truly educated, leading them to think through things more deeply and respond with creativity. This still leaves us with the question of what to read. Children will be drawn to stories more than anything else. The humanities humanize, and reading the right fiction will form their moral imagination by helping them to conceive of reality, the interior motivations of

---

6. Neil Postman, *Amusing Ourselves to Death: Public Discourse in the Age of Show Business*, 2nd ed. (New York: Penguin, 2005), xix–xx.

characters, the outcome of action, and how to overcome adversity. Vigen Guroian's *Tending the Heart of Virtue* describes how literature helps to form character:

> The great fairy tales and fantasy capture the meaning of morality through vivid depictions of the struggle between good and evil, where characters make difficult choices between right and wrong or heroes and villains contest the very fate of imaginary worlds. The great stories avoid didacticism and supply the imagination with important symbolic information about the shape of our world and appropriate responses to its inhabitants.... I am calling this way of looking at life the moral imagination.[7]

Great literature draws out the moral dimension of education, reflecting on the centrality of choice in shaping the person within and society without. In addition, good literature will teach language and expression, providing students with a model of communication.

All literature is not created equal. Both style and content matter in choosing the appropriate book to read and teach. In making a decision to use precious classroom time and to make an impact upon students' minds, questions need to be asked. Certain books should be ruled out, and priority given to others. There are certain authors who are great thinkers and masters of language, and students should come to know them and learn from them. Some books are more inspiring and formative and worth imitating.

A number of middle school teachers and administrators reached out to me in my role as associate superintendent, asking for advice about literature for middle schoolers. I also started looking at what my children were reading at their own school. I realized that while I was well read on the high school and college-level literature lists, I had skipped over many books that were classics for middle

---

7. Vigen Guroian, *Tending the Heart of Virtue: How Classic Stories Awaken a Child's Moral Imagination* (New York: Oxford University Press, 2002), 17–18.

school. I decided to go back and read the selections from four local middle schools to get up to speed.

I asked a number of questions in evaluating whether a book would be a good choice for middle school students. My evaluatory questions would also apply at other levels:

1. Does it support a Catholic worldview or provide an important contrast that can lead students to a deeper understanding of a Catholic worldview? How does it fit within the larger plan and vision of the curriculum? A book does not have to be Catholic to fit a Catholic worldview, but books that undermine it should be avoided.

2. Is it age appropriate in style, vocabulary, and complexity of thought? It could be too advanced or too basic. Is it of a high enough literary quality that would embody beautiful expression of images and ideas?

3. Does it contain inappropriate moral issues or language? Although some middle schoolers may have lost their innocence, texts should be chosen with the aim of preserving innocence. Difficult issues can be addressed in a way that is not graphic, disturbing, or inappropriate.

4. Does it raise essential questions and contain enough depth? Will the book get students to think or is it too superficial?

5. Does it treat diversity in a way compatible with a Catholic worldview and that affirms the human dignity of all people?

6. Does it avoid the occult and images that can give rise to spiritual harm?

7. Does it speak to the students' particular developmental stage? In middle school students are just beginning to think about larger issues, and there is the excitement and difficulty of adolescence. Stories should explore the larger ideas through adventure and appropriately modeled relationships, and preserve the innocence that some middle schoolers still possess. Thinking about an issue for the first time is different than being able to explore that idea in a deep and complex way. Some teachers want to teach great classics, although there are more

basic works that will prepare students for a higher level of expression later.

Based on these questions, I came up with different levels of appropriateness for use in a school: (1) highest recommendation, (2) generally recommended, (3) neutral, (4) not recommended, (5) never use.

Here are some examples of my "highest recommendation" for books in middle school.[8] Elizabeth George Speare's *The Bronze Bow* presents a young outlaw/blacksmith in ancient Israel who longs for revenge against the Romans and to expel them from the Holy Land. He cares for his reclusive sister while forming a band of young men to fight. He becomes friends with a brother and sister, children of a well-to-do rabbi, who teach him about the Bible. He also meets Jesus who helps him to understand the power of love. The story would definitely help students to enter into the biblical milieu through the eyes of adolescents. It introduces themes of suffering, loss, anger, revenge, forgiveness, caring for others, and sacrificial love. Another strong recommendation would be Lois Lowry's *The Giver*, a story of a dystopian community that has eliminated all emotion and regiments everything in people's lives. Only one person can have memories of the broader world and normal human life, including deep pain, and he must pass this on to another, the main character of the story, a twelve-year-old boy. It explores the components that make up human life—for better and worse—and how we become inhuman when we try to remove them. I see it as an important book for middle schoolers as they think through the nature of human life, learning, memory, love, and self-sacrifice. It deals with the onset of puberty and also euthanasia, both in an age-appropriate way. Some other classics would be the works of J. R. R. Tolkien, C. S. Lewis, and select works of Shakespeare.

---

8. See the appendix for a fuller list.

The next level are books that I "generally recommend" for middle school. They did not get the highest level because they did not fit the age group as well or as compellingly draw the students into deep reflection. A good example of this would be Natalie Babbitt's *Tuck Everlasting*, which narrates the story of a girl who discovers a family that does not age or die and helps conceal their secret. The story follows the purpose of a fairy tale, introducing a magical element to help us see an element of reality from a new perspective. The story stimulates thought on change and death and how living forever in this life is not really a good thing. It lacks, however, the power and depth of a more complex work. Another example would be Harper Lee's *To Kill a Mockingbird*, told through the perspective of a young girl nicknamed Scout, who with her brother is caught up in her father Atticus's defense of a black man unjustly accused of rape. The story works well in dealing with the serious issue of racial discrimination from a child's perspective without graphic intensity. The issue of an unjust trial and courageous defense provide very important moral considerations to form the imagination, although they could be supplemented from a Catholic perspective. Elizabeth Janet Gray's *Adam of the Road* tells of a boy in medieval England searching for his father and presents a good imaginative entry into the Middle Ages. It is not a masterpiece, with a simple literary style that would be good for sixth grade or even younger. It does provide a great entry point to Catholic life and traditions, such as the monastic life. Other examples of this level would Pam Muñoz Ryan's *Esperanza Rising*, Tracy Barrett's *Anna of Byzantium*, or S. D. Smith's *The Green Ember* series.

Next, some popular books struck me simply as "neutral," such as Robert Louis Stevenson's *Treasure Island*, which certainly captures the desire for adventure, Jack London's *The Call of the Wild*, with its naturalistic worldview, or Gary Paulsen's *Hatchet*, the ultimate survival story. Those books present fine stories, but they did not strike me as noteworthy in provoking deep thought or profound expression. I would not object to using them in the classroom but would not recommend them highly. Some of them could be effective simply as engaging reading to capture student interest to set up a following book.

The list of "not recommended" books will be more controversial. Although I would recommend *Frankenstein*, I butted heads with a principal over Bram Stoker's *Dracula*. He sees it as a powerful image of how someone is seduced into sin and corrupted. I agree but also found it to be too dark and intense for middle schoolers, and also too tied to the occult. Another popular book I would not recommend for a Catholic school would be Madeleine L'Engle's *A Wrinkle in Time*, because it conflates religious ideas with natural phenomena (such as angels and stars) and combines them with science fiction and fantasy in an ambiguous and misleading way. Another book, which I liked but would not recommend, is Katherine Paterson's *The Bridge to Terabithia*, a tale of friendship between a ten-year-old boy and girl who create a magical realm. The book has a strong literary quality and convincingly explores child psychology (for the most part). I appreciate its engagement of C. S. Lewis and the imagination, but I recommend avoiding it because it speaks of magic taking the place of religion in Terabithia and the children pray to spirits. The text takes the Lord's name in vain often and presents cussing as normal in middle school.

Finally, we come to the category that I would recommend to "never use." This category directly contradicts a Catholic worldview. For instance, John Steinbeck's *The Pearl* is a novella of a young Mexican couple who find suffering in the fortune of finding a valuable pearl. I think it is chosen for middle school because of its length and accessibility. Steinbeck's naturalism, however, paints a bleak and fatalistic picture of human life. There are moral lessons to be found in the story but only through brutal events, without redemption, and accompanied by a syncretistic portrayal of religion. Catholics disagree about the value of reading J. K. Rowling's *Harry Potter* series, although the serious objections by exorcists to its use of witchcraft (including genuine spells) should rule it out completely for a Catholic school. Although I have seen schools use these two works, I thankfully have not found anyone using Philip Pullman's *His Dark Materials*, a trilogy of books pushing an atheistic worldview. I include it as an example of an explicitly anti-Christian work designed for children, which should alert us to the need for caution more generally.

Catholic schools need to exercise care about the works that are chosen within their curriculum, library, and book fair. Sometimes schools do not want to offend anyone who is reading a book or likes a particular work, and so will refuse to remove a book from a library or reading list. More than simply avoiding what is evil, reading lists should be designed to lead students into the great adventure of life. In their task to form minds and imaginations, however, Catholic schools need to exercise vigilance and ensure that their books provide good nutrition for the mind and soul.

# 6 Progressive or Sacramental?
## The Need for Poetic Pedagogy

Contemporary education is marked predominately by turning away from the search for truth as the goal of education in favor of the pursuit of practical skills. We cannot live without education, which does intend to enable students to thrive within society, but what is the best way to gain it? What do we do with it after? The progressive approach argued that more traditional methods fundamentally missed education's purpose, wasting time on useless languages and books.

Education was essentially classical until the early twentieth century, meaning it was focused on reading the great works of Western civilization, in the original languages when possible. To this was certainly added the advancements made in mathematics and science in the modern period. John Dewey provided one of the most succinct modern summaries of the aims of traditional education versus that of the progressive. He characterizes the tradition of schools as passing down "bodies of information and of skills that have been worked out in the past; therefore, the chief business of the school is to transmit them to the new generation," which includes moral training within a distinct community.[1] The community of adults must impose this on the child, he claims, because "The gap is so great that the required subject matter, the methods of learning and of behaving are foreign to the existing capacities of the young. They are beyond the reach of the experience the young learners already possess. Consequently, they must be imposed."[2] This approach, he contrasts with that of the progressive:

---

1. John Dewey, *Experience and Education* (New York: Touchstone, 1938), 17.
2. Dewey, 19.

> To imposition from above is opposed expression and cultivation
> of individuality; to external discipline is opposed free activity; to
> learning from texts and teachers, learning through experience; to
> acquisition of isolated skills and techniques by drill, is opposed
> acquisition of them as means of attaining ends which make direct
> vital appeal; to preparation for a more or less remote future is
> opposed making the most of the opportunities of present life; to
> static aims and materials is opposed acquaintance with a chang-
> ing world.[3]

How could anyone oppose this change from outward imposition to
inward self-discovery? What has been lost and gained by this fundamental shift? Laying out the heart of a sacramental pedagogy, this
chapter will look at both the positive and negative aspects of the last
century's move from seeking truth to focusing on the individuality
of the student.

## The Promise and Problem of the Progressive Approach

The move to a progressive approach has been centuries in the making, birthed under the legacy of two Swiss men: Jean-Jacques Rousseau (1712–78) and Johann Heinrich Pestalozzi (1746–1827).[4]
Their views held that outside influences would corrupt the child,
while nature herself, coming forth from within—rather than
imposed by the teacher, religion, or culture—would lead to true
learning and freedom. This child-centered approach would even-
tually lead to the breakdown of the classical system, though, ironi-

---

3. Dewey, 19.
4. For Rousseau's views of education, see his influential work *Emile*, originally published in 1762 (https://www.gutenberg.org/files/5427/5427-h/5427-h.htm). Pestalozzi sees the purpose of education as to "prepare the individual to make free and
self-reliant use of all [of his] faculties." This statement comes from within his aphorisms, which I have found to provide the easiest and most direct access to his
thought. Johann Heinrich Pestalozzi, *The Education of Man: Aphorisms* (New York:
Philosophical Library, 1951), 41.

cally, it would allow the State to use education for social conditioning. It led to greatly decreasing the emphasis on knowledge and shifted the focus of education to a self-guided process of discovery. Education moved from the transmission of culture to the self-discovery of the individual, with an erosive effect on culture itself, weakened by an excessive focus on individuality.

Although Pestalozzi has been called the father of modern education, perhaps we should look to the previous centuries to St. Joseph Calasanz (1557–1648) and St. Jean Baptiste de La Salle (1651–1719).[5] It was Calasanz who founded the first public school, free and open to the public (at Rome in 1597), and de La Salle who established the first regular school for the training of teachers in 1685. It would be impossible to understand education as we know it today without these men, who founded orders dedicated to teaching the poor and established the norms of the classroom. Calasanz novelly grouped students into grades by age rather than ability, since he had hundreds of students to supervise, and de La Salle laid out the school day in a recognizable way in his *Conduite* (*The Conduct of the Christian Schools*), also outlining a positive approach to discipline.[6] They both established principles we would take for granted, namely that all children should have access to education (since they are made in the image and likeness

---

5. Calasanz likewise founded one of the Church's first religious orders specifically dedicated to teaching, the Piarists (Order of Poor Clerics Regular of the Mother of God of the Pious Schools), founded in 1617. See General Congregation of Piarist Fathers, *Spirituality and Pedagogy of Saint Joseph Calasanz* (Madrid: Publicaciones ICCE, 2005), https://edicionescalasancias.org/wp-content/uploads/2021/10/Spirituality_and_pedagogy_web.pdf. In France, there was a similar movement for the free education of children, spearheaded by Augustinian Canon Regular St. Peter Fourier and Bl. Sr. Alix Le Clerc, foundress of the Canonesses of St. Augustine of the Order of Our Lady, dedicated to teaching.

6. John Baptiste de La Salle, *The Conduct of the Christian Schools*, trans. F. de La Fontainerie and Richard Arnandez, FSC, ed. William Mann, FSC (Landover, Md: Lasalian Publications, 2007).

of God and ordered toward knowing and loving him), offered to them in the vernacular language to guide them into their future work and family life. Although the school day should be conducted in a strictly controlled and orderly way, they said, children should be respected in how they receive discipline and directed toward virtue. These two men, along with countless other religious, launched our modern conception of education.

In a way, we can see the progressive school espousing similar ideas, though unmoored from their Christian underpinning. Perhaps this is why the opposing side, especially Rousseau and Pestalozzi and not Calasanz and La Salle, receive credit for laying the groundwork for modern education. Can we, as Catholics, agree with any of its principles? We cannot avoid their influence, even as we identify problems. For instance, a child-centered approach to education has undermined the passing on of tradition. The claim that children learn incrementally only in set stages has translated into the dumbing down of the curriculum, putting off complex thoughts into the future (or not at all). That children should be active rather than passive in the classroom has itself resulted in a different form of passivity in not aspiring to knowledge. That education should relate to the child's direct experience and environment has cut students off from consideration of the transcendent. That education should provide useful preparation has sidetracked the need to enrich the human person with noble thoughts and aspirations.

Following the promptings of nature seems like a harmless principle. After all, God has established our nature and ordered it toward particular goods, the foundation of the natural law. Two problems, however, emerge from this progressive view. First, Rousseau and his followers denied original sin, finding the origin of evil within the society and culture into which education traditionally sought to initiate its young. Rousseau, rather, would have education become subversive to the status quo of society, a trend that has continued in contemporary education.[7] Second, the focus on nature took a more biological turn under the influence of Herbert Spencer (1820–1903), who thought that education should follow a Darwinist progression from a primitive to a more advanced state. Science became the model for education under Spencer's influence, asserting that learning follows an evolutionary principle of development from simpler to more complex ways of thinking. His assertions mark a turning point for pedagogical principles, beginning to claim the backing of science. Education, nonetheless, remains rooted in the human sciences, rather than biology, making it prone to pseudo-scientific claims, with the latest fads claiming scientific backing though rarely with concrete results.

Kieran Egan points out, in his book *Getting Wrong from the Beginning*, that Romantic and progressive notions of how children learn claiming to be scientific have been refuted by developments in science and psychology. For instance, the progressive views posit children developing from a more primitive to advanced state of mental capacity in linear fashion, whereas Egan points out that younger children possess greater capacity in certain regards in earlier stages of development, geared toward what children need to learn at that stage. Younger children can learn a language more easily than adults, for instance.[8] Children in the lowest grades have a stronger imaginative sense.[9] Spencer, on the other hand, contended that "children's

---

7. For a helpful overview of Rousseau's positions contrasted with Aristotle's, see Curtis L. Hancock, "Catholic Wisdom and the Recovery of the Person in Elementary Education: A Response to Rousseau's Educational Utopianism," given at the international congress on "¿Una Sociedad Despersonalizada? Propuestas Educativas," at the Abat Oliba CEU University, Barcelona, April 13–15, 2010, https://repositorioinstitucional.ceu.es/bitstream/10637/11005/3/Catholic_Hancock_2010.pdf.

8. Kieran Egan, *Getting It Wrong from the Beginning: Our Progressivist Inheritance from Herbert Spencer, John Dewey, and Jean Piaget* (New Haven, Conn.: Yale University Press, 2002), 93.

9. Egan, "If we look at children's imaginative lives, rather than their slowly accumulating logico-mathematical skills, we do not see intellectual activity dominated

understanding can expand only from things of which they direct experience."[10] Why then, Egan asks, do children love fantasy? It must be, in fact, that they love to think beyond their ordinary experience. He uses this line of thought to criticize the abandonment of history in favor of social studies, which has been consistently proven to be the least effective and interesting discipline.[11] False notions of child psychology, derived from Jean Piaget among others, asserts that the stories of history are not developmentally appropriate, even though children enjoy listening to stories of the past.[12] The presuppositions of modern progressivist educators run counter to the natural development and interests of children.

Egan demonstrates something that should be intuitive, although it may shock us somewhat, that we have been too focused on "what children cannot do: 'Generations of schoolchildren, deprived of challenging tasks because Piaget said they were incapable of them, bear evidence of this impact.' This, of course, reflects Piaget's low opinion of children's intelligence—an opinion he shared with Spencer."[13] In the name of what is "developmentally appropriate" children have been deprived of imaginative wonders and deep thinking. Egan rejects progressivism's rejection of so-called passive learning and rote memorization because he acknowledges that this effort to master content enriches the mind with knowledge. "Knowledge just doesn't seem to have the same relation with the mind that food has with the body; it constitutes the mind in a way that food doesn't constitute the body."[14]

---

by the concrete, the simple, the indefinite, the empirical, and so on. We see prodigal metaphoric invention, talking middle-class rabbits, titanic conflicts of good and evil, courage and cowardice, fear and security, and so on" (94).

10. Egan, 17.

11. Egan, 112, 130.

12. Egan, 102, 106–7.

13. Egan, 106, quoting Filipe Fernández-Armesto, *Truth: A History and a Guide for the Perplexed* (London: Bartam, 1997), 18.

14. Egan, *Getting It Wrong*, 90.

This is true because "knowledge does not exist in books or in computer files. They contain only codes that require a living mind to bring them back to life as knowledge. *Knowledge exists only as a function of living tissue.*"[15] Significantly, young children enjoy the rote memorization of songs and poems, and even facts, especially when connected to stories. Rejecting the importance of gaining knowledge, especially at a young age, has led to much greater ignorance, a reality we can affirm through experience simply by watching the educational decline in modern culture.

Modern methods claim scientific sanction and elusively promise greater educational progress. Egan also pushes back on pseudo-scientific claims that educational methods could develop through greater empirical research.[16] He sees this as a serious "error" stemming from Spencer, which has led to the "common belief that children's minds have some preferred natural kind of learning and that if we can isolate and understand it we can then make the educational process more efficient and effective."[17] Educators often hear of new methods and curricula based on science and verified by studies. Nonetheless, they never seem to lead to higher levels of learning; a magic bullet continues to evade public educators. Learning cannot be equated to an empirical or biological process; the deepest elements of education transcend empirical methodology because the human person transcends biology. The most important things cannot be measured or manipulated. In fact, if we only taught students based on their past experiences, building incrementally from there, we would never be able to arrive at God's revelation, which is offered to us by him by a free, unmerited, and unsolicited gift. Education ultimately must transcend our experience to offer us what is most needed for our nature, which transcends the material.

15. Egan, 68.
16. Egan, 151.
17. Egan, 39.

Modern methods, in fact, which claim to be adapted to the developmental stages of children, work contrary to the natural joy that children find in learning. We educate their natural dispositions out of them by making education conform to modern notions of scientific knowledge. We kill their love of learning. Even though science is held up to be the highest form of knowledge, science is now taught in a way similar to the approach criticized by progressives. We teach scientific information to be memorized rather than leading children to do science. Although younger children tend be more receptive and interested, after conforming to modern methods of education, they lose their natural interest in learning and simply conform to the regiments of school life.

Progressive education has failed according to its own criteria. If we look at this statement from John Dewey, we can see how the system of public education he helped to shape has led precisely to what he criticized in traditional education:

> What avail is it to win prescribed amounts of information about geography and history, to win ability to read and write, if in the process the individual loses his own soul: loses his appreciation of things worthwhile, of the values to which these things are relative; if he loses desire to apply what he has learned and, above all, loses the ability to extract meaning from his future experiences as they occur?[18]

We could affirm the desire of progressives to make education formative and relevant to students, while acknowledging that they failed miserably to fulfill this promise.

Unlike earlier progressive theorists, Maria Montessori observed the way young children learn and supported their strengths, allowing them to prepare themselves for more abstract learning, rather than

---

18. Dewey, *Experience and Education*, 49.

forcing it upon them.[19] She seems to fulfill Rousseau's promise of attending to nature by allowing the child complete freedom for spontaneous activity, as well as rejecting the traditional approach of pouring information into the student: "The method of observation is established upon one fundamental base—*the liberty of the pupils in their spontaneous manifestations.*"[20] She also recognizes, however, that education must attend to the spiritual dimension of the person, which has been written out of modern pedagogy: "But in all this progress of modern child education, we have not freed ourselves from the prejudice which denies children spiritual expression and spiritual needs, and makes us consider them only as amiable vegetating bodies to be cared for, kissed, and set in motion."[21] Her guiding principle centers around enabling children to learn through their own interests and activities, which provide the foundation for further learning when the child has become receptive to receiving a lesson.

The modern world has been built around freedom. Montessori saw this as central to education: "The pedagogical method of *observation* has for its base the *liberty* of the child; and *liberty is activity.*"[22] Although an emphasis on freedom may seem to contradict a Catholic approach, she recognizes this freedom as the ability to enter into

---

19. She says: "One very simple means for helping the child in his activity was suggested to me by my observation of the children themselves." Maria Montessori, *The Montessori Method*, trans. Anne E. George (New York: Frederick A. Stokes Company, 1912), 140. Contrast this with the extremely influential Piaget, whom Egan asserts showed "little interest in individual children" (Egan, *Getting It Wrong*, 104).
20. Montessori, 80. She viewed the traditional approach as hindering learning: "The teacher *hindered* the child, in this case, from educating himself, without giving him any compensating good in return" (93).
21. Montessori, 154.
22. Montessori, 86. She seems to agree with Egan's assertion that modern psychology, especially through Piaget's influence, has restricted proper child development: "We must not start, for example, from any dogmatic ideas which we may happen to have held upon the subject of child psychology. Instead, we must proceed by a method which shall tend to make possible to the child complete liberty" (29).

adulthood, overcoming a servile culture by enabling children to become adults who can care for themselves. Students who do not learn "how to live" within school cannot be free. I agree with her recognition of the physical makeup of schools (whether Catholic, traditional, or progressive) as restrictive to the free inquiry and expression of students. Montessori explains, "Today we hold the pupils in school, restricted by those instruments so degrading to body and spirit, the desk—and material prizes and punishments. Our aim in all this is to reduce them to the discipline of immobility and silence—to lead them—where? Far too often toward no definite end."[23] Students find themselves in a highly regulated environment, performing arduous or monotonous tasks, restrained from vigorous physical or tactical activity, without even knowing why they are there. We send our children to school and educate them with vague notions of its necessity but too often with "no definite end."

Catholic education also aims at freedom, but it recognizes its source as coming from outside of the students, as proposed by the greatest Teacher: "If you continue in my word, you are truly my disciples, and you will know the truth, and the truth will make you free" (Jn 8:31–32). Simply being child-centered with no outside influence makes freedom itself to be absolute without grounding it upon the truth. It runs the risk of becoming a deadly influence, the kind of freedom sought after by Eve. Progressive education sought freedom for students, hoping to find it within the purity of nature, freed from the shackles of the corruption of society. We can see the positive aspirations of drawing students into a gradual process of discovery, engaging their experience, and helping all children to prepare for their life in society. Progressivism fails, however, even fatally so, in lacking an orientation to the truth, leaving students allegedly free from outside influence with no ultimate horizon for the purpose of human life and their own ultimate direction. Rather than an impo-

---

23. Montessori, 27.

sition, the Truth is the pearl of great price, and, if our students discover it, it will be worth more than any other possession.

## John Dewey and Spiritual Culture

There is good to be found in focusing more on the nature and freedom of children, drawing forth their own initiative in moving toward the truth. This approach could be seen as a tilling of the soil through attention to the dispositions and needs of children to prepare for learning. We cannot lose sight, however, of education as an initiation into something greater than the individual. Education invites the student to become an active participant within a community, coming to understand its values and partake of its common life, which transcends the individual. We must maintain a balance between the freedom of the individual and the call to participate in a community, especially the spiritual community of the Church.

In light of this tension, we might ask if we need to react against the general education system established by Calasanz and de La Salle and inherited by modern schools, which has been harnessed by the progressives. Is it too rigid and restrictive, too focused on textbooks, too individualistic? Catholics created a universal system of education so that every child would have the chance to come to know God and be better prepared for their future. To what end has this been put?

Progressive educators have used genuine critiques of educational methods to destroy the heart of education. Dewey translated the progressive vision into the American public schools in the name of pragmatism, and, through his socialist proclivities, he grasped the social implications of education, though at the expense of truth. Progressivist educators could ask with Pilate, "What is truth?" To them, it is nothing more than a distracting illusion that leads children away from the practical aims of socialization and becoming a productive citizen. Here again, we can see how progressive educators have grasped an essential reality, one that I am trying to reinforce throughout this book, that the education of the individual necessarily has social and cultural implications. We can take note of their critiques and insights, while reestablishing contact with the lost goal of the liberal arts: to find freedom in the truth.

In his *Democracy and Education*, Dewey narrates a history of education that completely skips over any Christian contribution, focusing predominately on the tension of the individual and culture. Dewey took Plato's critique of democracy as each one pursuing his own individual interest and turned it on its head. He rejects Plato's notion that society is held together by a common conception of the "final and permanent good," which could not readily be known in an ordinary society.[24] Plato, according to Dewey, lacked a sense of "the uniqueness of every individual, his incommensurability with others," leaving man in bondage to static ideals (perhaps this is where Christianity fits for him, as a remnant of Platonism).[25] It was left to the eighteenth-century heralds of a new liberating gospel to correct Plato's subordination of the individual to such a static notion of universal truth. Although focusing on nature over society sought to liberate the individual, he notes that the State soon subsumed education into its own nationalistic and utilitarian aims. His own theory would try to strike a balance in describing how education could be ordered to a democratic society.

In describing the aim of education, Dewey asserts that "the object and reward of learning is continued capacity for growth."[26] We might accept that assertion on the surface, but we would be left ignorant regarding the end of this growth. It brings us back to the question of freedom and its purpose, because, for Dewey, there should be no "external dictation" to students that would hinder "the free growth of their own experience."[27] How could education be

---

24. John Dewey, *Democracy and Education* (New York: The Free Press, 1916), 103.
25. Dewey, 105.
26. Dewey, 117.
27. Dewey, 117.

related to a community of people, the initiation into a group with shared ideas and goals? For Dewey, democracy precisely allows individuals to focus on themselves as a culture unmoored from overarching ideals, such as found in the thought of Plato. Education does not aim for ends beyond activity in itself, only the pragmatic application gained by those engaging in those activities. In education "there are not aims, but rather suggestions to educators as to how to observe, how to look ahead, and how to choose in liberating and directing the energies of the concrete situations in which they find themselves."[28] He recognizes no "general and ultimate" ends, only those individual ones of the students themselves.[29]

Although Dewey affirms Rousseau's desire to favor nature over scholasticism (that is, traditional pedagogy), he also seeks to correct him by asserting that nature is not an end in itself but must directed somewhere. He proposes reintroducing a relationship to society, seeking to preserve the natural freedom of the individual while relating it to social efficacy, the give and take of experience. When the mind becomes socialized, Dewey sees it as more communicable in breaking down barriers between others, enjoying their experience, and sharing sympathy. Nature must be ordered toward culture, which adds to it the ideas and art of human experience. Culture, for Dewey, however, remains a means of individual fulfillment, in helping to complete education in the development of the personality in relation to others.

This view of culture remains rooted in the immediacy of the individual, cut off from any transcendent ideal. Dewey views spiritual experience as opposed to democratic culture: "What is termed spiritual culture has usually been futile, with something rotten about it, just because it has been conceived as a thing which a man might have internally—and therefore exclusively."[30] Although Thomas

---

28. Dewey, 125.
29. Dewey, 127.
30. Dewey, 143.

Aquinas saw God as the common good of all creation, because only he can be possessed fully by all without any division or rivalry, Dewey sees a culture rooted in transcendent truth and goodness as cutting people off from mutual exchange. Ironically, what has been a unifying force throughout history, uniting people together in faith and love, becomes a conflict in refusing to work for the practical good of others:

> Why then should it be thought that one must take his choice between sacrificing himself to doing useful things for others, or sacrificing them to pursuit of his own exclusive ends, whether the saving of his own soul or the building of an inner spiritual life and personality? ... There is no greater tragedy than that so much of the professedly spiritual and religious thought of the world has emphasized the two ideals of self-sacrifice and spiritual self-perfecting instead of throwing its weight against this dualism of life.[31]

Religion breaks down the relationship of personal culture and social efficiency, apparently threatening the nature of democracy itself. To summarize, according to Dewey, modern education seeks to unite individuals together in mutual self-realization, while religion creates a source of disunity by looking to something else above and more important than this immediate community of individuals.

John Dewey's most concise statement of his view of education can be found in his essay "My Pedagogic Creed." His view of the school's social role reinforces his antagonism to the spiritual and transcendent, focusing on education's relation to immediate experience:

> I believe that the school is primarily a social institution. Education being a social process, the school is simply that form of community life in which all those agencies are concentrated that will

---

31. Dewey, 143–44.

be most effective in bringing the child to share in the inherited resources of the race, and to use his own powers for social ends.

I believe that education, therefore, is a process of living and not a preparation for future living.

I believe that the school must represent present life—life as real and vital to the child as that which he carries on in the home, in the neighborhood, or on the playground.

I believe that education which does not occur through forms of life, forms that are worth living for their own sake, is always a poor substitute for the genuine reality and tends to cramp and to deaden.[32]

The relationship of the person to the community stands at the center of education. For Dewey, education enables an individual to live within an individualistic society by coordinating his own experience to that of others.

For a Catholic, however, Dewey misses the essential way in which the person (who is not an isolated individual) finds fulfillment in communion with others. The goal of life transcends immediate actions, having a true end beyond this world. Dewey saw the threat of this transcendent aim, by relativizing society and action in relation to an external standard to which both the person and society must conform for their true realization. Based on Dewey's view of the school, the curriculum should be rooted in the immediacy of human experience. A Catholic view of the curriculum and pedagogy, however, must insist upon more—that education, relationships, and learning all find their ultimate purpose in a communion of persons that reaches beyond our democratic society, stretching to the divine persons, the deceased, and all those united by faith throughout the world.

Pedagogy, therefore, must respect the fact that the human person is made for a communion that arises through a shared experi-

---

32. John Dewey, "My Pedagogic Creed," *School Journal* 54 (January 1897): 78.

ence of what is true, good, and beautiful—the transcendentals that relate present experience to ultimate reality. Because the human person is not simply material, the student cannot be manipulated technologically or through educational techniques to reach practical outcomes.[33] Even if outward conformity could be achieved, the person would remain unsatisfied by a culture of individuals that perceive nothing beyond immediate experience. True communion with others arises precisely by standing underneath greater realities together, which unite us in understanding and common aims that create peaceful cooperation rather than competition for limited material resources. Knowing that reality transcends the immediate offers true freedom from the bonds of material exigencies and coercions. Those dedicated solely to a democratic notion of education feel threatened by objective realities that stand above the State, the economy, and the individual.

While Dewey understood culture solely from an exterior perspective of conditioning students for the right behavior in society, the historian Christopher Dawson understood that it arises from an interior unity, one that is imparted by education. According to Dawson, the essential task for Catholic education today is to initiate our students into a Christian culture that encompasses all aspects of life and the formation of patterns of behavior and action to shape the way we live in the midst of a secular world. Dawson notes that the Catholic faith is no abstract idea, or simply informative, but a concrete reality into which we are initiated:

> As the Christian faith in Christ is faith in a real historical person, not an abstract ideal, so the Catholic faith in the Church is faith in a real historical society.... Hence ... it is necessary to be incorporated as a cell in the living organism of the divine society and to enter into communion with the historic reality of the sacred

---

33. Egan recognizes that "education is unlike engineering in that education is value-saturated in ways that engineering is not" (*Getting It Wrong*, 155).

tradition . . . a member of a historic society and a spiritual civilization . . . which influences his life and thought consciously and
unconsciously in a thousand different ways.[34]

Christian education, in his view, "taken in its widest sense . . . is
simply the process by which the new members of a community are
initiated into its way of life and thought from the simplest elements
of behavior up to the highest tradition of spiritual wisdom. Christian education is therefore an initiation into the Christian way of
life and thought."[35]

It is not that Dewey is wrong in his sense of education teaching
us how to relate to others through culture. The problem stems more
from cutting off that communal experience from the primacy of
truth and the transcendent. Education should teach us how to live
in the world, true, but informed by the most important and even
eternal things. Stratford Caldecott expands on the relation of teaching to lived experience in the world:

> The process of education certainly involves the communication of
> useful information and skills, but only in the context of an initia-
> tion into a community of relationships extending through time,
> the family first of all, then broadening to the lived experience of
> cultural tradition. The more human we become, the more our own
> lives and experience connect with different aspects of the culture
> into which we are progressively initiated by the school.[36]

---

34. Christopher Dawson, "The Kingdom of God in History," in *Christianity and European Culture: Selections from the Work of Christopher Dawson* (Washington, D.C.: The Catholic University of America Press, 1998), 210.

35. Christopher Dawson, *Understanding Europe* (Washington, D.C.: The Catholic University of America Press, 2008), 196.

36. Stratford Caldecott, *Beauty in the Word: Rethinking the Foundations of Education* (Brooklyn, N.Y.: Angelico Press, 2012), 34. He also says on this topic, "Ideally, Catholicism fulfills and brings to perfection the natural educational process, which is the transmission in creative freedom of a cultural tradition" (9).

Initiation into culture and thriving through its shared life are true goals of education. Culture exists for the same reason that human beings exist: to find truth and love what is good.

The spiritual dimension of culture lies at its very roots, which is why the task of cultural formation lies at the heart of the Catholic school. Only faith can integrate all the diverse subjects and pursuits of the school and order them to the ultimate goal of life and education in God. As Jacques Maritain points out, "culture is essentially the inner forming of man."[37] St. John Paul II states the case even more clearly by showing why culture and the faith are connected so strongly:

> Culture and holiness! We must not be afraid, when saying these two words, of pairing them unduly. On the contrary, these two dimensions, if well understood, meet at the roots, they unite with naturalness on their journey, they join together in the final goal. *They meet at the roots!* . . . Therefore, cultural commitment and spiritual commitment, far from excluding one another or from being in tension with each other, mutually sustain one other.[38]

Culture and faith are not unrelated realities as both spring from the same root—the reality of God and his creation of man. They have the same goal as well—to order all things to their final end, though faith does this more directly than culture. There is a reciprocal relation between holiness and culture, as holiness lies underneath genuine culture and culture embodies and expresses this holiness. Faith and culture need each other, as culture is the soil on which a life of faith depends and faith provides culture the meaning that it lacks

---

37. Jacques Maritain, *The Education of Man*, ed. Donald and Idella Gallagher (Garden City, N.Y.: Doubleday & Company, Inc., 1962), 154.
38. John Paul II, Address to the Catholic University of the Sacred Heart, November 9, 2000, 3, 4, https://www.vatican.va/content/john-paul-ii/en/speeches/2000/oct-dec/documents/hf_jp-ii_spe_20001109_gemelli.html.

without its ultimate vision of reality. John Paul explains that "a faith that does not become culture is not fully accepted, not entirely thought out, not faithfully lived."[39] The Catholic school, therefore, must foster the cultural soil for faith to grow into a way of life. Our individuality will only be fulfilled by overcoming it so that we do not stand apart as isolated and autonomous beings. We are not meant to be consumed by society, made into a cog by a mass society or subsumed into a communal whole that loses sight of individual good. The individual finds meaning precisely in communion with others. Education is ordered toward culture in arriving at this kind of spiritual communion, opposed to any material communitarianism, such as Communism, which destroys our spiritual longings. Education should open up the true spiritual horizon of life; and, rather than leading to solipsism like Dewey alleged, it provides the deepest source of communion with others, even to the point of being willing to die for them, knowing that a greater good unites one another in friendship. Dewey introduced a false dichotomy between society and the spiritual life, and the answer to his assertion can be found in a sacramental vision of culture that approaches the highest goods through their exterior expression.

### Experience: The Foundation of a Sacramental Pedagogy

Progressive pedagogy has also sought to engage the whole person, moving away from a focus on content that marked the so-called traditional approach. It is true that we largely tend to overlook the

---

39. John Paul II, Address to the Italian National Congress of the Ecclesial Movement for Cultural Commitment, January 16, 1982. Although the original address was delivered in Italian and has not been translated, John Paul quoted the line in other documents, which have been translated, such as his address to Plenary Assembly of the Pontifical Council for Culture on March 18, 1994, https://www.vatican.va/content/john-paul-ii/en/speeches/1994/march/documents/hf_jp-ii_spe_18031994_address-to-pc-culture.html.

importance of the body, emotions, and senses in how we teach. These physical and emotional elements, along with our relation to nature, provide the natural foundation for placing oneself in relation to one's culture by discerning meaning (in an intellectual sense of grasping how things fit together within a particular cultural pattern) and purpose (in a practical sense of how to live within this culture).

We need a sacramental pedagogy that engages the human person as a sacramental being—a body-soul unity—that unites the interior and exterior, the highest and lowest, and draws together the human capacity for wonder, emotions, thinking, and affections. It is common to find the liberal arts and practical skills put at odds, although it is possible and even desirable to draw them into a synthesis. A sacramental vision recognizes the exterior as ordered toward the spiritual reality, and the Catholic view of the body, relationship, work, and play are ordered toward communion with God. We should not pit these against the search for truth and our transcendent desires but help students to draw them together in a coherent way of life that teaches them how to find the highest good through the concrete choices of their life. Teachers can lead students into what is true, good, and beautiful in a way that will shape their future life by providing a storehouse of good experiences that refine their thinking and desires.

Engaging the whole person by relating intellectual and practical education brings us back to progressive attempts to engage experience, a hallmark of Dewey's theories. For instance, he writes, "The desirability of starting from and with the experience and capacity of the learners . . . has led to the introduction of forms of activity, in play and work."[40] Dewey rightly notes that these activities bring joy into edu-

---

40. Dewey, *Democracy and Education*, 194. In "My Pedagogic Creed," he also states: "I believe, therefore, that the true center of correlation of the school subjects is not science, nor literature, nor history, nor geography, but the child's own social activities" (79).

cation, even as he misses the way in which they differ from and support learning. They are not learning in themselves. Play, as Romano Guardini pointed out in relation to the liturgy, is an activity done for its own sake, as an expression of leisure.[41] It is not a backdoor to learning, as if the student's experience of play or work could substitute for the classroom. In discussing gardening, Dewey praises what students pragmatically could derive out of the activity, such as "the place of farming and horticulture have had in the history of the race and which they occupy in present social organization," missing the point that gardening is a worthwhile activity in itself for the development of the student as a person—establishing contact with nature, taking responsibility for living things, attending to details, and awakening the senses.[42] These aims are not pragmatic, leading to a future practical application, but formative of the person. They will bear fruit in the classroom in indirect ways, and without these sorts of activities, which could have been taken for granted in the past, students become one-sided in their development. Students should take joy in play and work, while also learning to derive joy at the proper time from higher expressions of leisure that foster the deeper refinement of the person.

Like the mind, the body and senses need to be formed, as Maria Montessori points out, in a way that exceeds vague notions that Dewey proposed of what could be learned from an activity of work or play. With her attention to children, she recognized that "the development of the senses indeed precedes that of superior intellec-

---

41. See Romano Guardini, *Spirit of the Liturgy* (New York: Crossroads Publishing Co., 1998), 42–50.

42. Dewey, *Democracy and Education*, 200. For a much more profound account of the potential of gardening for education, see Ravi Scott Jain, Robbie Andreasen, and Chris Hall, *A New Natural Philosophy: Recovering a Natural Science and Christian Pedagogy* (Camp Hill, Penn.: Classical Academic Press, 2021), 200–204. Sr. Janet Stuart, RSCJ, remarked that "little gardens of their own are perhaps the best gifts which can be given to children. To work in them stores up not only health but joy." *The Education of Catholic Girls* (Charlotte, N.C.: TAN Books, 2011), 140.

tual activity."[43] This may seem obvious, but it receives little direct attention, with many early childhood programs focusing primarily on moving children to more abstract learning as quickly as possible. Montessori contends that "The education of the senses has, as its aim, the refinement of the differential perception of stimuli by means of repeated exercises."[44] The engagement of the senses, the movements of the child, the stimulus of materials and activities lead children to conform to something outside of themselves, animating growth in perception and control. "The didactic material *controls every error*. The child proceeds to correct himself, doing this in various ways."[45] Although these actions may refine the senses, they also bring about a refinement of the person that prepares for intellectual learning. To see Montessori's insights on the education of the senses in action, we could turn back to the example of gardening:

> But if for the physical life it is necessary to have the child exposed to the vivifying forces of nature, it is also necessary for his psychical life to place the soul of the child in contact with creation, in order that he may lay up for himself treasure from the directly educating forces of living nature. The method for arriving at this end is to set the child at agricultural labor, guiding him to the cultivation of plants and animals, and so to the intelligent contemplation of nature.[46]

Exterior experience should not be denigrated in Christian education, even though it is directed toward higher experiences of intel-

---

43. Montessori, *The Montessori Method*, 215. She relates in more detail: "This is, therefore, the time when we should methodically direct the sense stimuli, in such a way that the sensations which he [the three- to six-year-old child] receives shall develop in a rational way. This sense training will prepare the ordered foundation upon which he may build up a clear and strong mentality" (216).

44. Montessori, 173.

45. Montessori, 171.

46. Montessori, 155.

lectual and spiritual contemplation. A sacramental approach recognizes the necessity of exterior signs and life in the world, because they provide a necessary and enduring ground for higher experiences. Without a sensory foundation of experience, in fact, students struggle to grasp higher level concepts, which remain remote and abstract.

Perhaps we have misconstrued the connection between sensory experience and higher levels of intellectual knowledge, which relate more than we often realize. Students need rich experiences that refine their senses, spark their imagination, lead to wonder, and, as a result, inspire them to think. They need a sensory spark to inflame their intellect. Egan points out that we cannot overlook the relationship of perception, feeling, and knowing, because "the mind is an organ that perceives and feels as well as knows, and the three, along with other features of our mental lives, are combined in ways we haven't the vaguest understanding of. What we know forms a resource for our imaginations."[47] It is just as false to lock students in direct experiences without any attempt to teach them truth, a fault of progressive educators, as it is to teach truth without any foundation in perception and feeling. Students need to do and to think in order to live well.

Matthew Crawford pointed out in his *Shop Class as Soulcraft* that we have denigrated the intelligence of practical knowledge to our own diminishment. He claims, for instance, "A decline in tool use would seem to betoken a shift in our relationship to our own stuff: more passive and more dependent. And indeed, there are fewer occasions for the kind of spiritedness that is called forth when we take things in hand for ourselves, whether to fix them or to make them."[48] This builds up a practical knowledge, a "knowing

---

47. Egan, *Getting It Wrong*, 137.
48. Matthew B. Crawford, *Shop Class as Soulcraft: An Inquiry into the Value of Work* (New York: Penguin Books, 2009), 2.

how" that complements the more abstract knowledge of the classroom.[49] Although it is easy to denigrate this kind of learning, it does create a dignity of action, overcoming our modern passivity, that enables us to imitate the creative action of God. As St. Benedict taught his monks, the contemplation of highest truths by no means abrogates the dignity of manual work, because the higher can shape the lower and the physical undergirds and supports the spiritual sacramentally.

## Poetic Knowledge: The Move from Senses to Contemplation

Knowledge begins in the senses! Therefore, we need to use the senses to begin the process of learning. We often want children simply to accept what others have learned, appropriating their results without learning the reality of what is taught through their own sense experience and reasoning. Have we attended enough to the foundational reality of the senses in Catholic education? Even though progressive educators have called for the engagement of students' experience, do not even they teach their primary subject of science in an abstract way without letting the students themselves engage in the scientific process of discovery? We lack a poetic engagement with nature and beauty to ground the experience of students' process of learning.

The philosopher Alfred North Whitehead (no traditionalist) criticized education for working against the natural development of children. He argued for a rhythm that begins with romance, then moves to precision, and ends in generalization. By romance, he meant the "stage of first apprehension" when the "subject-matter has the vividness of novelty," which inspires a kind of mystery in coming

---

49. Crawford, 161. Bob Schultz outlines the discipline and interior dispositions that arise from work in his *Created for Work: Practical Insights for Young Men* (Eugene, Ore.: Great Expectations Book Co., 2006).

to know the material.[50] He speaks of "romantic emotion," which we could also call "wonder" in the realization of previously undiscovered insights, whether concrete or literary. The mind must be stirred, he asserts, setting it on a process of fermentation and eventual ordering. Here we can say that Whitehead perceived a general problem of seeking precision, generalization, and order in education without the initial spark of romance within the mind. Perhaps students' minds fail to ferment and come to order because they lack this initial spark. Although he does not use this term, romance comes close to what I will call poetic knowledge.

What is poetic knowledge? The word "poetic" immediately conjures thoughts of poetry and the arts. Though these have an important place in poetic knowledge, the poetic as a way of knowing embraces a broader meaning, reflecting the most fundamental way of encountering something through direct contact with it. Poetic knowledge could be defined as "not strictly speaking a knowledge of poems, but a spontaneous act of the external and internal senses with the intellect, integrated and whole, rather than an act associated with the powers of analytic reasoning."[51] Joseph Ratzinger, commenting on the thought of the Orthodox theologian Cabasilas, makes a similar distinction between "two kinds of knowledge." He outlines these distinct forms as "knowledge through instruction which remains, so to speak, 'second hand' and does not imply any

---

50. Alfred North Whitehead, *The Aims of Education and Other Essays* (New York: The Free Press, 1929).

51. James Taylor, *Poetic Knowledge: The Recovery of Education* (New York: State University of New York Press, 1998), 6. Even in attempting to define Catholic poetry, Angela Alaimo O'Donnell speaks in broad terms: "What defines a Catholic poet and Catholic poetry cannot be readily summed up in terms of content or technique; instead, Catholic poetry reflects and embodies a particular disposition towards the world. It is corporeal, perhaps even bloody minded, in its insistence upon an embodied, incarnate faith." "Seeing Catholicly: Poetry and the Catholic Imagination," in *The Catholic Studies Reader*, ed. James T. Fisher and Margaret M. McGuinness (New York: Fordham University Press, 2011), 337.

direct contact with reality itself. The second type of knowledge, on the other hand, is knowledge through personal experience, through a direct relationship with the reality."[52] The ultimate meaning of the poetic consists in knowing directly from experience rather than from secondhand mediation.

Hylomorphism, the principle establishing that human nature exists in a body-soul unity, provides the ultimate foundation for poetic knowledge. All knowledge begins in the senses, and from this foundation we ascend to higher forms of understanding. According to John Senior, "the ancients distinguished four degrees of knowledge," building upon the primary encounter of reality by the senses. This first degree, "the poetic," occurs when "truths are grasped intuitively." The second, "rhetoric," follows when "we are persuaded by evidence . . ; next the dialectical mode in which we conclude to one of two opposing arguments beyond a reasonable doubt . . ; and finally, in the scientific mode . . . we reach to absolute certitude."[53] Aristotle points toward this progression of knowledge in Book I of the *Metaphysics*, as he moves from experience, which is rooted in the "delight we take in the senses"; to art, "when from many notions gained by experience one universal judgment about a class of objects

---

52. Joseph Cardinal Ratzinger, *On the Way to Jesus Christ* (San Francisco: Ignatius Press, 2005), 35–36. The chapter, "Wounded by the Arrow of Beauty: The Cross and the New 'Aesthetics' of Faith," in which this quote is found, derives from a lecture Ratzinger delivered to Communion and Liberation in 2002, titled "The Feeling of Things, the Contemplation of Beauty," https://www.vatican.va/roman_curia/congregations/cfaith/documents/rc_con_cfaith_doc_20020824_ratzinger-cl-rimini_en.html.

53. Senior, *Restoration of Christian Culture*, 115. In this division, it seems that Senior may be drawing upon Plato's distinction of four faculties: "Let there be four faculties in the soul—reason answering to the highest, understanding to the second, faith (or conviction) to the third, and perception of shadows to the last—and let there be a scale of them" (quoting Plato, *Republic*, VI, 511d–e). For a succinct overview of poetic knowledge and its importance, see Caldecott, *Beauty for Truth's Sake*, chap. 2, "Educating the Poetic Imagination," 37–52.

is produced"; and finally science, through which we have "knowledge about certain principles and causes."[54] According to this theory, the natural way of knowing comes first by encountering what is known through the senses, having direct contact with it. The poetic is foundational, as Aristotle states, for art and science must build upon experience: "really science and art come to men through experience; for 'experience made art,' as Polus says."[55] Learning has a natural progression, beginning with sense experience.

Thomas Gilby, OP, in an early twentieth-century work on poetic knowledge, *Poetic Experience*, describes this form of knowledge as a "direct way ... real things can be immediately and nobly experienced in themselves, without the go-between of abstraction, representation, and argument."[56] Aquinas describes knowledge as the conformity of the mind with the thing known.[57] Direct contact with the reality under study protects against abstraction and superficiality. Jacques Maritain, in *Creative Intuition in Art and Poetry*, explains how poetic knowledge fundamentally brings the soul into conformity with the truth of things: "By Poetry I mean, not the particular art which consists in writing verses, but a process both more general and more primary: that intercommunication between the inner being of things and the inner being of the human Self which is a kind of divination. . . . Poetry, in this sense, is the secret life of each and all of the arts."[58] The poetic draws upon intuition: "When it comes to poetry,

54. Aristotle, *The Metaphysics*, trans. W. D. Ross, bk. 1, part 1, http://classics.mit.edu/Aristotle/metaphysics.html.
55. Ibid.
56. Thomas Gilby, *Poetic Experience: An Introduction to Thomist Aesthetic* (New York: Sheed & Ward, 1934), 1–2.
57. Aquinas, *Summa theologiae*, I, q. 16, a. 2, c.: "For this reason truth is defined by the conformity of intellect and thing; and hence to know this conformity is to know truth. But in no way can sense know this."
58. Jacques Maritain, *Creative Intuition in Art and Poetry* (New York: Pantheon Books, 1953), 3. Maritain cites Samuel Taylor Coleridge in support of the second sentence of the quotation: "Coleridge used the word 'poesy' with the same

the part of intuitive reason becomes absolutely predominant . . . an intuition of emotive origin."[59] Maritain describes this, drawing from Aquinas, as a "knowledge through connaturality," by which something is "embodied in ourselves, and thus . . . in accordance with it or connatured with it in our very being."[60] This "knowledge through union or inclination" provides a foundation for all other knowledge by placing the knower in intimate union with the reality of things.[61]

James Taylor's *Poetic Knowledge: The Recovery of Education* presents a more contemporary articulation of the importance of the poetic. Taylor critiques the predominance of abstract ideas in education flowing from Descartes's insistence on "clear and distinct ideas" and his distrust of the senses: "The Cartesian view is one of the great disintegrating philosophies of all time with its tendency to set the mind against the sensory and intuitive powers of the body-soul harmony."[62] In response to this modern epistemological turn, Taylor articulates a vision of the poetic as one that "reverberates . . . throughout the body and mind as a kind of real *experience* of the concept."[63] It "sees in delight," "gets us *inside* the thing experienced," and "derives from the *love* of a thing."[64] This may sound overly sentimental, yet Taylor quotes Socrates's vision of education in Plato's *Republic* for support: "But to love rightly is to love what is orderly and beautiful in an educated and disciplined way . . . for the object of education is to teach us to love what is beautiful."[65]

---

universal meaning: 'poesy in general, as the proper generic term inclusive of all the fine arts as its species.'" Maritain quotes Coleridge, *Lectures and Notes on Shakespeare and Other Dramatists* (New York: Harper, 1853), 181–82.

59. Maritain, *Creative Intuition*, 76.
60. Maritain, 117.
61. Maritain, 117.
62. Taylor, *Poetic Knowledge*, 93.
63. Taylor, 21.
64. Taylor, 6, 7.
65. Taylor, 17.

Taylor's account provides an important example of the difference the poetic can make by describing its embodiment within a collegiate program of studies, the Integrated Humanities Program (IHP) at the University of Kansas, co-founded by John Senior. The IHP has been described as a Great Books program, but "it was never the plan of the IHP to simply teach the books of Western culture, but rather to discover the roots of that culture and give, to the extent possible, the actual experience of that civilization."[66] The IHP did not simply teach the ideas of the great books, but rather it sought to engage the whole person and to bring wonder and enthusiasm to study, in a way that transformed many lives. Taylor uncovers the program's resounding success within the philosophy of the program: "There can be no real advancement in knowledge unless it first begins in leisure and wonder, where the controlling motive throughout remains to be delight and love."[67] The poetic encounter with a reality in itself, rather than simply an idea of reality, brings about greater wonder and joy, initiating the learner into the subject rather than approaching it abstractly from a distance.

As the most foundational way of knowing, the poetic itself does not provide the culmination of learning, but the necessary foundation for it. Learning must follow the natural patterns of human development and take the body and emotions seriously. Taylor describes the way in which the IHP achieved this: "Literally and figuratively, in this way the IHP was a musical education, observing in poetry, dance, song, star gazing, and calligraphy, an understanding of what Socrates, Aristotle, [and] Aquinas . . . all called for as preliminary and prerequisite music and gymnastic for humanizing the student prior to any advanced study."[68] Thus, poetic knowledge serves as a means of awakening the student to the wonder of reality

---

66. Taylor, 153.
67. Taylor, 153.
68. Taylor, 150.

so that a transformational encounter with the truth may occur as a gateway for further learning.

We need poetic knowledge because an abstract approach to knowledge has not captured the imaginations of our students. Vigen Guroian makes this case in relation to morality in a way that could be extended to education as a whole:

> Mere instruction in morality is not sufficient to nurture the virtues. It might even backfire, especially when the presentation is heavily exhortative and the pupil's will is coerced. Instead, a compelling vision of the goodness of goodness itself needs to be presented in a way that is attractive and stirs the imagination. A good moral education addresses both the cognitive and affective dimensions of human nature. Stories are an irreplaceable medium for this kind of moral education—that is, the education of character.[69]

Likewise, in their study of Catholic higher education, Melanie Morey and John Piderit, SJ, note that "knowledge of Catholic culture is not gained most effectively through purely intellectual means. . . . The relationship between the imaginative and conceptual components of the faith is circular. . . . It is through . . . living theological experience that the content of Catholic culture is integrated, experienced, and lived."[70] The integrated, experienced, and lived contact with the reality of Catholicism as a culture, or a way of life, only strengthens the central role of the poetic for Catholic education. Daniel McInerny points out that the poetic translates the Catholic vision concretely, helping students to recognize its living dimensions: "When it comes to a loving appreciation of how the essentials of happiness might plausibly be lived out, then poetry is the more

---

69. Guroian, *Tending the Heart of Virtue*, 20.
70. Melanie M. Morey and John J. Piderit, *Catholic Higher Education: A Culture in Crisis* (New York: Oxford University Press, 2006), 151.

adequate mode of expression."[71] The poetic translates the reality of faith to life in a tangible way, assisting students in applying the content of instruction to their lives. It can lead Catholic schools to a sacramental pedagogy that truly engages the whole person.

## Words Made Flesh: A Truly Holistic Approach

Liberal education focuses predominately on the formation of the mind in truth. As St. John Henry Newman tells us, it focuses on the cultivation of the intellect for its own sake: "This process of training, by which the intellect, instead of being formed or sacrificed to some particular or accidental purpose, some specific trade or profession, or study or science, is disciplined for its own sake, for the perception of its own proper object, and for its own highest culture, is called Liberal Education."[72] The intellect is the highest part of our nature, and it deserves robust formation, drawing us into the contemplation of the truth and the proper ordering of human life toward it. We must return to this lofty goal, while also making it more realistic by supporting it from the bottom up.

Currently, we face a challenge from above and below. First of all, education does not cultivate the intellect in any serious fashion. Standards of excellence have fallen precipitously over the last fifty to a hundred years, and currently are in free fall. Most schools do not even aspire to the truth and scorn the pursuit of wisdom that marked education in the past. And secondly, despite contemporary aspirations, education also does not provide adequate practical preparation. Students do not really know how to do anything when they graduate. We are failing according to what is loftiest in us and at the same time according to what is most immediate. The Church

---

71. Daniel McInerny, "Poetic Knowledge and Cultural Renewal," *Logos* 15, no. 4 (2012): 29.

72. John Henry Newman, *Idea of a University* (New York: Longmans, Green, and Co., 1907), 152.

has always prioritized liberal education, because a well-trained mind becomes capable of entering into any task with discipline, order, and wisdom. Practical training is useful, but it pertains only to whatever practical end that was the focus of the training. A liberal arts graduate can be trained to program computers or conduct business, but a computer programmer may struggle to change careers without the foundation of logical thought and effective communication. One approach is broad and the other narrow, but both are necessary, for we are spiritual beings who must find a practical way through this world.

A sacramental approach draws the two together, teaching ideas and helping students to embody them. Embracing poetic knowledge, for instance, could serve as a wake-up call for students, forcing them to engage directly with what they are learning and to break out of passivity. By starting with the concrete, rather than the abstract, students will encounter the "real," directly standing before reality, rather than an abstracted account of it. School is not about memorizing the right answer. It must be received as a process of discovery that calls the student forth out of self and into the great adventure of life. Can schools facilitate this in an organic way? Can they tell stories that convey the great romance of the journey of life? Reading them out loud or memorizing and reciting poems makes words come to life off of the page. Can we invite students to become scientists in their own right by observing nature and learning from it directly? Can students make things, beginning in imitation and then calling forth their own contributions in the arts and crafts? Can we get them out of the classroom and into the world to observe for themselves and to do, applying what they are learning?

The words they receive must become flesh in their lives, incarnating into a reality that they can experience. There is no curriculum that can simply solve the current problems of education. Rather, the teacher must simply find ways, no matter what is being taught, to engage students in experiencing reality, thinking about it, and acting upon it. This is the heart of any effective education. Good books will help by providing content worthy of reflection and that more readily stimulate action in response to them. A sacramental approach to education does not require teaching an exact set of principles in one precise way. It rather emphasizes the things that make us human, as they come forth from the curriculum, and facilitates a more human response to them—emotionally, intellectually, and volitionally.

This approach forms a call to action to go back even to the very beginning of our primary vocation, given to us by God, and how we can respond to it today. God made man in his image to participate in his work of creation. Even though he made us to be able to perceive the truth of his work, he also gave us the task to continue the work of creation through our own creativity. John Paul spoke of this in his "Letter to Artists":

> God therefore called man into existence, committing to him the craftsman's task. Through his "artistic creativity" man appears more than ever "in the image of God," and he accomplishes this task above all in shaping the wondrous "material" of his own humanity and then exercising creative dominion over the universe which surrounds him. With loving regard, the divine Artist passes on to the human artist a spark of his own surpassing wisdom, calling him to share in his creative power.[73]

What St. John Paul II perceived of the vocation of the artist could be said for all of us. God calls us to know him and to share in his work of creation, exercising dominion over the earth in his name. Catholic education draws out the divine spark within in both of these dimensions as a sacramental and cultural mission that flows from the image of God in us.

---

73. John Paul II, "Letter to Artists" (April 4, 1999), 1, https://www.vatican.va/content/john-paul-ii/en/letters/1999/documents/hf_jp-ii_let_23041999_artists.html.

What about the progressive approach? Does it have anything to offer the modern Catholic educator? A sacramental approach can fulfill the genuine desires of modern educators to serve students by drawing forth their potential. For a Catholic educator, the goal does not stop at the child, but reaches to God, as the teacher leads the child into truth out of charity as a servant. The goal also should not stop in the student's experience in and of itself, because there is a goal outside the student, but truth must be encountered in an incarnational and sacramental way that engages experience. Freedom also cannot be the goal, for it is too open-ended, but by receiving training in virtue the student will be able to direct his freedom toward the good. Catholic education should produce good citizens, who are ready to serve the common good, because they focus on a vocation and mission that transcends loyalty to country and provides the ground for true patriotism.

A sacramental approach emphasizes the intellect and body, avoiding the false dichotomy of the search for wisdom and practical training. Words must become flesh in the classroom and beyond it. Every teacher can find ways to make reality more accessible to students, engaging more of themselves in a complete and holistic formation. To devote more attention to the emotions and body should not distract from the goal of liberal education to form the mind. In fact, it will do so more effectively, flowing from a sacramental vision of reality, engaging the whole person and inspiring the imagination in wonder and delight. Engaging reality will awaken the mind and help students to experience the truth within the life of the Catholic community.

# 7 A Great Inheritance:
## Cultural Literacy and the Role of History

Most people have some level of distaste for history. Having taught the subject for more than a decade, I can attest to how many students have shared this sentiment. I love to see them experience a conversion, coming to recognize how both interesting and relevant history can be. It helps to rely on primary sources, tell it as a story (that is what history means after all), and reveal how the events of history have shaped our world. Unfortunately, schools have turned away from emphasizing history directly, subordinating it to the new and abstract discipline of social studies. Recovering history can strengthen the curriculum and culture of our schools and can invite our students to enter into the great drama of the human story.

The sacramental mission of education recognizes the school as participating in the historical mission of the Church, receiving a mandate from Christ to spread his kingdom through the world. Two thousand years into this effort, we can look back upon a great legacy of saints and cultural achievements. Too often Catholics remain ignorant of this tradition and, therefore, living without its enriching influence. Catholic schools must teach the great story of the Church so that Catholics can find their place within it, receiving and handing on their spiritual and cultural inheritance.

## Catholic Cultural Literacy

Cultures survive through education. We are born into a particular group of people with a shared inheritance of ideas, beliefs, and practices. In the past, formal education was reserved for leaders, who consciously appropriated and handed on to others the constituent elements of the culture. Cultures die when either an external threat overwhelms it from the outside or, as often happens, it becomes weak from within, no longer imparting conviction about its own beliefs or translating them into a coherent way of life. A breakdown in education quickly brings a crisis of civilization.

Within our own educational crisis, E. D. Hirsch contemplated why some students excel and others do not, coming to the conclusion that there is a certain level of literacy concerning the specific content needed to function within a culture. "To be culturally literate," he explains, "is to possess all the requisite knowledge needed to thrive in the modern world."[1] Disadvantaged students often lack this requisite literacy and, therefore, struggle to keep up and gain additional knowledge in school. He proposed that American schools teach this specific content as a social equalizer, and his proposal was taken up by the Core Knowledge movement and curriculum used in some charter and private schools.

Hirsch held that reading literacy and knowledge are connected:

> The decline in our literacy and the decline in the commonly shared knowledge that we acquire in school are causally related facts. . . . No one is surprised by a correlation between a rich vocabulary and a high level of literacy. A rich vocabulary is not a purely technical or rote-learnable skill. Knowledge of words is an adjunct to *knowledge of cultural realities signified by words*, and to whole domains of experience to which words refer. Specific words go with specific knowledge. And when we begin to contemplate how to teach specific knowledge, we are led back inexorably to the contents of the school curriculum.[2]

---

1. E. D. Hirsch Jr., *Cultural Literacy: What Every American Needs to Know* (New York: Vintage Books, 1988), xiii.
2. E. D. Hirsch Jr., "Cultural Literacy," *The American Scholar* 52, no. 2 (Spring 1983): 160, emphasis added. A 2020 study from the Thomas B. Fordham Institute, "Social Studies Instruction and Reading Comprehension" by Adam Tyner and Sarah Kabourek, also found a correlation between between strong literacy and "rich

Abstract ideas do not stick effectively in students' minds. Ideas need to be embedded within a cultural framework to anchor them within a broader vision. Students require content to access a culture, and yet the culture itself provides a matrix for situating that knowledge in a way that gives purpose to it within a community. American schools, however, have moved away from a content-focused curriculum, driven more by an emphasis on skills, socialization, and career preparation. Hirsch points out that "our elementary schools are … dominated by the content-neutral ideas of Rousseau and Dewey," who saw more traditional approaches as imposing upon the freedom of students." To thrive," Hirsch contends, "a child needs to learn the traditions of the particular human society and culture it is born into," however "the fragmentation of the American school curriculum" has led to a "gradual disintegration of cultural memory, causing a gradual decline in our ability to communicate."[3] It is common knowledge that most young Americans lack basic knowledge of American history and government, undermining the country's tradition and culture.

If a lack of cultural literacy marks American education, this is equally true of American Catholics. Catholics, including Catholic school graduates, lack literacy of the biblical, theological, historical, and cultural traditions of the Church. One serious alarm went off when a 2019 Pew survey revealed that only 50 percent of Catholics know that the Church teaches that Jesus is truly present in the Eucharist, while only 30 percent believe it.[4] Too many Catholics do not know the basics of their faith, let alone the Church's rich historical and cultural legacy. Catholics need literacy of more than

---

content about history, geography, and civics" (https://fordhaminstitute.org/national/resources/social-studies-instruction-and-reading-comprehension).

3. Hirsch, *Cultural Literacy*, 31, 110, 113.

4. Gregory A. Smith, "Just one-third of U.S. Catholics agree with their church that Eucharist is body, blood of Christ," *Pew Research Center*, August 5, 2019, https://www.pewresearch.org/fact-tank/2019/08/05/transubstantiation-eucharist-u-s-catholics/.

doctrine—including prayers, such as the Rosary, practices such as Eucharistic adoration and processions, and cultural artifacts of her literature, music, and art. Without an overall knowledge of Catholic teaching, history, and life, they will lack the requisite experience of Catholic life to be able to access its riches.

Many Catholics do not even realize the depths of their own tradition. Bishop Robert Barron articulates the great fullness of the Catholic life that requires a more deliberate immersion. In speaking of how Catholics come to understand the meaning of the Incarnation, God's enfleshment in the world, it is necessary to know the whole trajectory of the Church's life in the world, the great thinking, figures, and cultural achievements that have manifested her truth over time:

> The Incarnation is one of the richest and most complex ideas ever proposed to the mind, and hence it demands the space and time of the Church in order fully to disclose itself. This is why, in order to grasp it fully, we have to read the Gospels, the Epistles of Paul, the *Confessions* of Saint Augustine, the *Summa theologiae* of Thomas Aquinas, *The Divine Comedy* of Dante, Saint John of the Cross's *Ascent of Mount Carmel*, *The Story of a Soul* of Thérèse of Lisieux, among many other master texts. But we also have to *look and listen*. We must consult the Cathedral of Chartres, the Sainte-Chapelle, the Arena Chapel, the Sistine Chapel ceiling, Bernini's *Ecstasy of Saint Teresa*, the Church of the Holy Sepulchre, Grünewald's Crucifixion in the *Isenheim Altarpiece*, the soaring melodies of Gregorian chant, the Masses of Mozart, and the motets of Palestrina. Catholicism is a matter of the body and the senses as much as it is a matter of the mind and the soul, precisely because the Word became *flesh*.[5]

Simply attending Sunday or even Catholic school, with our current approach in place, would not be enough to receive these great treas-

---

5. Robert Barron, *Catholicism: A Journey to the Heart of the Faith* (New York: Image Books, 2011), 3–4.

ures. We are missing out on the full picture, without a Catholic worldview and sensibility. The Catholic tradition encompasses more than doctrine, and grasping this cultural fullness could guide Catholics more deeply into their own faith.

We can take the concept of cultural literacy even further, however, through the importance of tradition. Through tradition, the Church hands down her entire life from one generation to the next. She imparts her spiritual inheritance through the sacraments, proclaims God's revelation, celebrates Mass, engages in popular piety, tells stories of her saints, celebrates cultural traditions, and imparts the Christian life. All of this entails a living memory, which is received interiorly through grace, conforming the soul to Christ, alongside of an immersion into the living community of the Church in the world.

Catholic education may entail academic formation, but it situates this task within a supernatural mission of immersion into the spiritual community of Christ's Body. The Church's culture, her way of life, extends beyond this world, making contact with the entire communion of saints. One image stands out to me as capturing the supernatural character of education as a spiritual initiation; it depicts the fourteenth-century Russian St. Sergius of Radonezh as a boy (then known as Bartholomew). The young Sergius, who would go on to become the great monastic father of Russia (akin to St. Benedict's role in the West), struggled to learn how to read. As seen in Mikhail Nesterov's nineteenth-century painting, an older monk appeared to him and offered him a piece of bread, telling him, "Take and eat it, this is given to you as a sign of God's grace and for understanding of the Scriptures," which miraculously stimulated his studies.[6] The monk himself stands as if a wizened tree, representing the deep roots of the tradition rising up to bring forth new fruit in another generation. His literacy served as an entry point into the great tradition, granting access to the words of Scripture and the

---

6. "Life of St. Sergius," *st-sergius.org*, http://www.st-sergius.org/life1.html.

Figure 1. Mikhail Nesterov, *Vision of the Young Bartholomew*, 1890, Tretyakov Gallery, Moscow, Russia.

text of the liturgy. The monk represents the task of the Catholic educator, to receive gifts handed on by the mystical communion of the Church and to pass them on.

Tradition may point us to a deeper understanding of the cultural initiation offered by Catholic education, but we can also ask if this seemingly unbroken chain has broken today. Mass attendance, baptisms, and weddings have all plummeted in the last decade. The problem is not so much a lack of knowledge as a lack of attachment to a community. People no longer find their identity in the Church and have become disconnected from the living reality of Christian community. In a consumerist culture, the Church constitutes one choice among many, and young people do not see anything compelling about the ideas and rules of the Catholic tradition, remaining ignorant of the riches of holiness, art, and genuine community. Young Catholics are simply overwhelmed by choice and the infinite possibilities made present in technology, drowning out their own tradition.

Pope Francis spoke to young people about the disorientation of the many choices before them, comparing it to entering into a bookstore:

> In this regard, I often think of the experience a young person can have today entering a bookshop in his or her city, or visiting an Internet site, to look for the section on religious books. In most cases, this section, when it exists, is not only marginal but also poorly stocked with works of substance. Looking at those bookshelves or web pages, it is difficult for a young person to understand how the quest of religious truth can be a passionate adventure that unites heart and mind; how the thirst for God has inflamed great minds throughout the centuries up to the present time; how growth in the spiritual life has influenced theologians and philosophers, artists and poets, historians and scientists. One of the problems we face today, not only in religion, is illiteracy: the hermeneutic skills that make us credible interpreters and translators of our own cultural tradition are in short supply. I would like to pose a challenge to young people in particular: begin exploring your heritage. Christianity makes you heirs of an unsurpassed cultural patrimony of which you must take ownership. Be passionate about this history which is yours.[7]

How can young people become passionate about their history when our own culture as Catholics has become foreign to us? This deficit requires an urgent response in a deliberate program of education and immersion.

Much of what has been forgotten will need to resurface. Learning the faith itself will always remain preeminent, but it will

---

7. Pope Francis, apostolic letter *Scripturae sacrae affectus* (September 30, 2020), https://www.vatican.va/content/francesco/en/apost_letters/documents/papa-francesco-lettera-ap_20200930_scripturae-sacrae-affectus.html.

take root more effectively with greater cultural context, coming alive in the life of great figures and the accomplishments that embody it through the ages. To us today, much of Catholic history will seem obscure at first, but over time greater consciousness of our Catholic heritage will emerge and become a storehouse of inspiration for the future. To assist in this growth, see the appendix, which offers "A Guide to Building Catholic Literacy," offering suggestions for the key doctrinal, liturgical, historical, and artistic landmarks of Catholic life.

## History as Immersion: Christopher Dawson on the Study of Christian Culture

Christians in the early Church made the decision to appropriate and preserve classical culture. The oldest Christian school, the Catechetical School of Alexandria, taught the liberal arts as a way of helping Christians to read and think so that they could access the truth of the *Logos* (the Word) in both Scripture and creation. It was only in the fifth century AD that Martianus Capella articulated the division of the seven liberal arts in a way that would be definitive for Western education. Not long afterwards the great Christian figures, St. Boethius and his friend Cassiodorus, began gathering texts, producing translations of the Greek philosophers into Latin, and writing a collection of textbooks on the liberal arts that would prove definitive for the Middle Ages. Other saints, such as Isidore of Seville, sought to gather all the learning of the classical period together in encyclopedic form, for example, Isidore's *Etymologies*; and even the great missionary, St. Boniface, began his work by first writing a treatise on Latin grammar. The Church clearly discerned a mission to preserve the learning of the classical period and transmit it to her new barbarian converts.[8]

---

8. For a thorough history of Catholic education, including the development of education in the Middle Ages, see Augusta Theodosia Drane, *Christian Schools and*

In recent time, it has been fashionable to frown upon the Hellenization of the faith, alleging a corruption of the biblical vision through Greek philosophy and learning. Pope Benedict XVI, responding to this accusation in his famous Regensburg Lecture, argued for a providential and even necessary inculturation of the faith in Greco-Roman culture, drawing together the unity of faith and reason.[9] Christians studied classical culture not simply because they wanted to preserve its fruits after the Roman Empire collapsed; they also wanted to use its learning to enrich their own understanding of the Christian faith itself. The monastic tradition of theology offers a prime example, dedicated to contemplation of the Word of God while also treasuring classical authors, such as Virgil, meticulously copying them, and transmitting them from monastery to monastery. As Jean Leclercq, OSB, famously described in his *The Love of Learning and the Desire for God*, their attention to the Word demanded a deep penetration of the way words work, which they learned at the feet of classical authors.[10] Western education preserved this dedication to the classics all the way until the beginning of the twentieth century. This continuous tradition provided an entry point into an ongoing exploration of truth, goodness, and beauty through common texts and ideas surrounding human nature, the clear expression of ideas, the purpose of politics, and the ideals of virtue.

Christopher Dawson, looking back on this two and a half thousand-year tradition of classical learning, pointed out that we now need a similar approach focused on Christian culture. When

*Scholars or Sketches of Education from the Christian Era to the Council of Trent* (New York: E.G. Stechert & Co., 1907).

9. Benedict XVI, "Faith, Reason and the University: Memories and Reflections," lecture delivered at the University of Regensburg, September 12, 2006, https://www.vatican.va/content/benedict-xvi/en/speeches/2006/september/documents/hf_ben-xvi_spe_20060912_university-regensburg.html.

10. Jean Leclercq, *The Love of Learning and the Desire for God: A Study of Monastic Culture* (New York: Fordham University Press, 1982).

living within the great civilization of Christendom, this study may not have been necessary, but in a post-Christian society it is vital to preserve and transmit a Christian worldview and way of life. Dawson's proposal would not excise classical culture. Rather, it would make Christian culture—its ideas, artifacts, and ways of living—central to education. He rightly posits that without explicit attention and a committed effort to passing on these things, our young people will simply overlook or discard them. Dawson, more than any other Catholic thinker, recognized the centrality of religion in culture and education's role in forming culture, and produced a vast synthesis of history, the human sciences, and theology stretching from prehistoric times to the crisis of Western civilization today. The thread that united all of his works was the thesis that religion is the heart of culture. Tracing that thesis throughout history, he noted that our own culture has a void in place of this heart, which it attempts to fill with secular ideologies. Without a religious renewal, Dawson thought the material advances of technology would prove self-destructive for our culture, a prediction which partially came true in the world wars.

Dawson laid out an agenda for reversing this problem by rediscovering the vital power of Christianity to reinvigorate Western society by immersing ourselves in both its spiritual power and the more material, cultural fruits of its living tradition. In *The Crisis of Western Education*, he reacts against the practical and utilitarian nature of modern education, and attempts to resituate the work of Catholic education within the realm of building culture:

> The essential function of education is "enculturation," or the transmission of the tradition of culture, and therefore it seems clear that the Christian college must be the cornerstone of any attempt to rebuild the order of Western civilization. In order to free the mind from its dependence on the conformist patterns of modern secular society, it is necessary to view the cultural situation as a whole and to see the Christian way of life not as a

number of isolated precepts imposed by ecclesiastical authority but as a cosmos of spiritual relations embracing heaven and earth and uniting the order of social and moral life with the order of divine grace. Christian culture is the Christian way of life. As the Church is the extension of the Incarnation, so Christian culture is the embodiment of Christianity in social situations and patterns of life and behavior. It is the nature of Christianity to act as a leaven in the world and to transform human nature by a new principle of divine life.[11]

Dawson provides a bold goal for Catholic education: change the entire life of our students.

For him, cultural literacy concerns not so much knowledge about the Catholic tradition as understanding it from within. He sees Catholic cultural literacy, which he calls the study of Christian culture, as an immersion into the Catholic way of life. This is not simply a Christian great books program, but more interdisciplinary and connected to life. Dawson calls for the "study of the culture-process itself from its spiritual and theological roots, through its organic historical growth to its cultural fruits. It is this organic relationship between theology, history and culture which provides the integrative principle in Catholic higher education, and the only one that is capable of taking the place of the old classical humanism which is disappearing or has already disappeared."[12] A new Christian humanism would exceed the old humanism because it is supernatural and involves the whole person in a complete way and initiates one into a community that goes beyond this world. "Thus Christian education was not only an initiation into the Christian community, it was initiation into another world; the unveiling of spiritual realities of which the natural man was unaware and which changed the meaning of existence. And I think it is here that our

---

11. Dawson, *Crisis of Western Education*, 115.
12. *Crisis of Western Education*, 106.

modern education—including our religious education—has proved defective."[13] Because of this, "From the beginning Christian education was conceived not so much as learning a lesson but as introduction into a new life, or still more as an initiation into a mystery. . . . Christian education was something that could not be conveyed by words alone, but which involved a discipline of the whole man."[14] The focus on the study of Christian culture would be more than theological thought and artistic artifacts, even if it includes these elements, because it encompasses the "whole tradition of Christian life and thought through the course of history."[15]

Taking the example of monasticism, we could say that without knowing about this essential facet of Christian life, students would not be able to grasp the reality of the Church in the world. They need to learn what a monastery is, who St. Benedict is, and about monastic contributions to culture, such as forming early hospitals, copying books, and perfecting Gregorian chant. This knowledge would be edifying, but there should be more to it than that. Understanding monasticism should begin to shape students' imaginations, as they conceive of models for how to live as a Christian in the world and adapt them to their own lives. Catholic students should learn why people flocked to monasteries in the ancient world, how monks live according to the Sermon on the Mount, how poverty, chastity, and obedience perfect human life, rather than denigrating it, what the life of the monks is like, how they balance work and prayer, and how they model the centrality of prayer in the Christian life. This deeper knowledge is not abstract, looking in academically from the outside, but begins to step into this social institution of the Christian life in a way that could inspire its continuity in the lives of the

---

13. Christopher Dawson, *Understanding Europe* (Washington, D.C.: The Catholic University of America Press, 2008), 197.
14. *Understanding Europe*, 197.
15. Dawson, *Crisis of Western Education*, 119.

students. This literacy is handing on a legacy to them to be continued. The same could be said about the formation of universities, confraternities, the mendicant orders, guilds, and pilgrimage as social and cultural expressions of Christian culture.

Because public schools have provided the model for Catholic school curriculum, Catholic students have remained largely unaware of key aspects of their own story. I have heard many educators react to teaching medieval history as if it were theology. The events of medieval Christendom are no less historical than any other period and are more relevant than other periods for Catholic students! The Middle Ages are truly the deliberately forgotten age of history, that stuff in the "middle" that does not really matter. History books remain replete with prejudicial inaccuracies about the alleged barbarism, backwardness, and bigotry of medieval Christendom, even though it laid the foundations for modern democracy and science (whereas most people would think the Middle Ages were an obstacle to their development). Absolute monarchy, for instance, arose out of the early modern period, and the same is true for "medieval" instruments of torture, which were invented mostly in the sixteenth and seventeenth centuries. We could also cite the persistent falsehood that people in the Middle Ages thought the earth was flat. Even a prominent conservative charter school network said that it rejected "medievalism" in favor of Americanism, seemingly to turn away from a direct focus on religion and metaphysics. Like the European Union Constitution, which falsely asserted that Europe was a combination of classical and modern influences, so has American education simply skipped over these rich and important years as too religious.

Dawson, however, would point Catholic schools more to their own great legacy as a focal point for the curriculum. He saw the study of Christian culture as providing the unity needed to overcome the fragmentation of subjects that leaves students overloaded with disconnected information and skills. Christian culture provides an integrated vision of reality, giving education a spiritual purpose and depth that secular culture lacks: "It is vital to the survival of the West that we should recover some sense of our moral values and some knowledge of the spiritual tradition of Western Christian culture. The way to do this is by education, and specifically by making the study of Christian culture an integral part of our educational system."[16] He spells out this program as using Christian thought and life as the lens through which to see and approach the whole. "What is needed," he contents, "is a study of Christian culture as a social reality—its origins, development, and achievements—for this would provide a background or framework that would integrate the liberal studies which at present are apt to disintegrate into unrelated specialisms."[17] This would situate Catholic education within a particular community, inviting students to enter into a concrete tradition that makes sense of their lives within the unfolding of God's work of creation and salvation. The ultimate goal, however, is to reinvigorate Christian culture itself, inspiring students to continue this tradition and make it come alive again within our secular world.

## Teaching History

The most controversial decision of which I have been a part in education was the reversion from teaching social studies back to history. This entailed moving from a new discipline, part of the social sciences, back to a liberal arts approach of the past that emphasizes narrative over information. Teachers literally quit over this move, claiming that emphasizing history was racist, too hard for children to follow, and too theological. They also claimed that, even though most of the old curriculum was retained, now placed within a new historical framework, essential social studies skills would be lacking, such as placing a stamp on an envelope, learning about fire stations, and knowing in which state they live (to give some examples we heard from teachers).

---

16. *Crisis of Western Education*, 117.
17. *Crisis of Western Education*, 105.

Americans truly believe in "the religion of progress," a reality described by Dawson and addressed by Pope Benedict XVI in his encyclical *Spe salvi*. Even though society suffers from abandoning faith in God, with the family deteriorating and attacks on life ever increasing, most people still think things are getting better and life in the past was worse. It would break the mold of this mentality to consider that things might have been better in the past, even without the technology and conveniences with which we are accustomed. To value the past is to realize that the ideas, accomplishments, arts, and faith of past ages still have something to teach us, perhaps providing something we lack even with material advancement. If the life of the spirit is more important than that of the body, perhaps we should learn from the life of Catholics in past generations.

The move from history to social studies is related to the religion of progress. Although many claim it to be interdisciplinary in its approach, social studies lacks an integrating principle. It draws information from history, placing this alongside of additional information from geography, anthropology, and political science, for instance, without any overarching purpose. Students do not know why they are studying the past, other than vague notions of learning about influential people and events that are disconnected from their present experience. Its original advocates, such as John Dewey, put it forward to advance skills for citizenship rather than passing on an inheritance of ideas and culture. Dewey held that the curriculum should focus on "present social concerns" even though "children show a marked preference for narrative history, dealing with personalities, conquests, heroism, the exotic, drama."[18] Social studies, a pseudoscientific approach to the study of society, has proven to be uninteresting and ineffective in American education.[19] In contrast, I witnessed students enthusiastically embracing the change to history,

---

18. Egan, *Getting It Wrong*, 130.
19. Egan, 130.

showing stronger interest and even fascination in the stories of ancient heroes and saints. Somehow defenders of social studies see it as more developmentally appropriate than telling stories, despite the opposite reaction of children.[20]

The religion of progress, by definition, urges us to forget about the past. In fact, it seems that many educators express hatred for history and the values of past cultures. Yet, this position remains naïve, for there is no reason to believe the future will be better than the past if we lose the wisdom, example, and warnings of previous generations. Cicero affirmed the importance of history within ancient Rome: "To be ignorant of what occurred before you were born is to remain always a child. For what is the worth of human life, unless it is woven into the life of our ancestors by the records of history?"[21] Just as literature forms the moral imagination through a fictional exploration of human psychology and spirituality, so history forms prudence and wisdom by exploring the consequences not only of individual action but also the progress and decline of entire civilizations.

Even with a larger focus on the narrative of the human story, history is driven by human decisions. It communicates the drama of human action that can only be understood as a story of the human Fall in action and God's response to save humanity from within. Ultimately, it is not politics that drives history, but the interaction of human freedom and divine providence, a drama that can be seen playing out in politics, warfare, economics, art, and religion. The Vatican's Congregation for Catholic Education provided just such as a vision for teaching history in the Catholic school, in its

---

20. Egan, 107.
21. Cicero, *Orator (ad M. Brutum)*, chap. 36. Vitruvius, in his *Ten Books on Architecture*, also relates the importance of studying history in the ancient world: "Let [the architect] be educated, skillful with the pencil, instructed in geometry, know much history, have followed the philosophers with attention, understand music, have some knowledge of medicine, know the opinions of the jurists, and be acquainted with astronomy and the theory of the heavens" (bk. I, chap. 1).

document "The Religious Dimension of Education in a Catholic School" in 1988:

> The teacher should help students to see history as a whole. Looking at the grand picture, they will see the development of civilizations, and learn about progress in such things as economic development, human freedom, and international cooperation. Realizing this can help to offset the disgust that comes from learning about the darker side of human history. But even this is not the whole story. When they are ready to appreciate it, students can be invited to reflect on the fact that this human struggle takes place within the divine history universal salvation. At this moment, the religious dimension of history begins to shine forth in all its luminous grandeur.[22]

History remains unintelligible on the surface, requiring the cooperation of faith and reason to approach its true driving forces, both within the soul and beyond the universe.

Approaching history in this way reinforces a Catholic worldview by helping the students to learn how to see and process the events of history and the contemporary world. Although some people do not acknowledge history as part of the liberal arts, because of the approach of the modern social sciences, the study of great figures, events, and sources of the past certainly finds a place within the Catholic liberal arts.[23] Like literature, it explores human action,

---

22. Congregation for Catholic Education, "The Religious Dimension of Education in a Catholic School" (April 7, 1988), 59, https://www.vatican.va/roman_curia/congregations/ccatheduc/documents/rc_con_ccatheduc_doc_19880407_catholic-school_en.html.

23. St. John Henry Newman describes Augustine's organization of the liberal arts, including history: "Augustine, in his enumeration of them, begins with arithmetic and grammar, including under the latter history; then he speaks of logic and rhetoric; then of music, under which comes poetry, as equally addressing the ear; lastly of geometry and astronomy, which address the eye." "The Benedictine Schools," in *Historical Sketches*, vol. 2 (New York: Longmans, Green, and Co., 1906), 461–62.

although it has a broader narrative by focusing on the chief characters and action of the drama of the entire human race. This study provides models of action and societies for students, teaching them the consequences of action on a grand scale, while also providing them with both positive examples and warnings. Students will learn why things are the way that they are in the world, the root of different forms of government, the impact a great figure can make, the consequences of evil and betrayal, and the fragility of civilization. It expands the imagination of what is truly possible within the scope of human action, like St. Ignatius laying in his recovery bed reading the lives of Sts. Francis and Dominic. Like Ignatius, our students can ask, "Why can't I imitate these past figures?"

Teaching stories of the most important events and people of the past enriches the minds and lives of our students. Teaching primary sources enables them to hear voices from the past, which broadens how they think about life, pulling them out of the ever-narrowing confines of modern thought. This is true for all students, but Catholic students have the opportunity to learn their own story and heritage more deeply, recovering what is too often overlooked in history. Why should students, even public school students, learn about Caesar but not Charlemagne, Buddha and not St. Francis? There are also many dark legends to overcome, such as gross exaggerations and falsehoods about the crusades and inquisition, or claiming the Church was an obstacle to science when in reality she helped to birth it. This is not to say that Catholic educators should whitewash history. Rather, they need to present it accurately, with primary sources instead of false popular narratives, and help students to analyze it and acknowledge when Catholics have acted contrary to the faith. This also helps them to understand the inner workings of grace and sin in the soul, and in history when writ large.

A Catholic approach to history reincorporates the lost history of the Middle Ages within the narrative of ancient civilization and the modern world, making the lost "middle" to be the true center when we see the Christian faith shaping and forming human society to the fullest. Teaching events of Catholic history is not the same as theology. Throughout human history, religion has always been a part of culture, until the last few centuries, and so we cannot approach history from a purely secular perspective. Because of an anti-Catholic prejudice, history in the English-speaking world tends to downplay, discard, or distort events in history related to the Catholic Church. This leaves Catholics even more illiterate of their own story. We could say the same about the Bible. Although modern scholars dismiss it as unhistorical, there is no reason to accept other narratives from the ancient world as historical and dismiss the Bible as religiously biased. All ancient narratives bore the influence of religion. Furthermore, contemporary archaeology often confirms events and figures of the Bible that scholars quickly dismissed as fiction. Why teach ancient Sumer and not ancient Israel? Why teach Egypt and not the Exodus? In terms of historical influence, no ancient figure has impacted the lives of more people than Abraham, father of faith to Jews, Christians, and Muslims, although he would be dismissed in historical accounts as a myth. Likewise, from a purely historical point of view, Jesus has changed the world more than anyone else.

Catechesis and theology treat the events of the Bible as God's revelation, the way in which he made himself known to his people Israel and the Church. History should treat the events of the Bible for their influence in shaping our world, as the rise of Israel and the Christian Church are truly of great consequence to civilization. How could the average American hope to understand even the cultural foundation of the United States with no knowledge of the Bible, the ancient Romans and Greeks, and the history of Great Britain, which shaped the founding of the country? To understand one's country, a certain knowledge of history is required. The same is true for the Church. Just as Jerome said "Ignorance of Scripture is ignorance of Christ," I would say that ignorance of history is ignorance of the Church. It is only in history that we see how God has been working out salvation for his people through all of the ups and downs, raising up great saints, and overcoming many crises. God teaches us about how to be holy in the world by looking back at the witness of the Church. It is an exciting endeavor to open up the world of the past to students, and, in the Catholic school, to recover a whole world of Catholic thought, life, and beauty.

We can help our students to come to know the key figures, events, and works of their heritage. This is not simply a study of the past but the entrance into a living tradition that continues to unfold in our lives. The events of salvation history and the lives of the saints are not simply things that we remember. We participate in them through our faith, and they continue to shape the present through our reception of them. St. Athanasius, St. Francis, and St. Ignatius of Loyola are not dead. They are more alive than we are, and we live in communion with them. Learning about them and our connection to them helps us to understand our shared identity with the Body of Christ. Having received such a rich legacy from the Church, her saints, art, and learning, we are privileged to enter into this tradition, to appropriate it in our lives, and to share it with others. By studying history from a Catholic perspective, we also gain perspective on the many trials Christians must face before Christ fully inaugurates his Kingdom. The Church continues the Incarnation in time, as Jesus continues to take flesh in the Eucharist and the life of the Christian community. This includes embracing the suffering of the Church, as her members continue to sin and cause scandal. In history, we see how the Church faced extreme trials, even to the point of near extinction, and how God raised saints to help her overcome these challenges. We grow in hope as we see how God guides his Church even through the darkest trials and never abandons her.

Despite moments of darkness, we also find great light in the Christian story. First of all, we encounter the great witness of the holiness of the saints, who show us how God can alter the course of history through the faithfulness of those who give their lives to him.

From the illiterate St. Anthony of the desert, to St. Catherine of
Siena admonishing popes, reaching down to St. John Paul II's role
in helping to bring down Soviet Communism, God has not stopped
raising up saints who change the world. We also find inspiration in
the sublimity of the Church's unparalleled tradition of art. Christianity is a sacramental religion that uses the beauty of architecture,
music, painting, sculpture, and words to express her transcendent
faith in ways that appeal to the senses and soul. Dawson expresses
this beautifully:

> It is the very nature of the Christian faith and the Christian life
> to penetrate and change the social environment in which they
> exist, and there is no aspect of human life which is closed to this
> leavening and transforming process. Thus Christian culture is the
> periphery of the circle which has its center in the Incarnation and
> the faith of the Church and the lives of the saints. All this is to
> be seen in history. Christianity did actually come into the histori-
> cal world and did actually transform the societies with which it
> came into contact.[24]

History unveils this dynamic, making the need for the Church to
undertake this work of transformation once again.

Catholic school students will see their place as a link within a
great chain, inheriting a great story and legacy, which they in turn
will need to pass on to the next generation. Without a knowledge
of history, they will continue to see themselves as isolated individuals, grasping to find and figure out their place in the world, thinking
they need to reinvent what has already been given to them. History,
therefore, plays a crucial role in shaping the identity and sense of
purpose for our students, situating them as characters within a great
drama, in which they are called to cooperate with the great protagonist: Jesus Christ.

---

24. Dawson, *Crisis of Western Education*, 106–7.

# 8 Truly Universal:
## Unity and Diversity in the Catholic Tradition

The most common criticism of teaching history from a Catholic perspective, and indeed of teaching the entire liberal arts from this approach, is that it is too Western focused. Today this criticism comes with a latent accusation of racism. Isn't Catholic history just about a bunch of dead white guys, like the whole Western intellectual tradition? Due to the frequency and gravity of this accusation, it is worth an extended response.

The word "catholic" means universal, coming from the Lord's call to bring his message to all nations. God established the Church as a communion that is meant to extend to all people, giving them the fullness, the "whole" (another translation for the word "catholic"), of what he desires us to know in faith and to live in charity. As the Gospel reaches various nations, it does not take away or diminish what is good in each culture, but elevates, purifies, and enriches it through an encounter with revelation and grace (a principle called inculturation). The Catholic story truly touches every continent and involves a rich encounter with every major culture in the world. This does not mean that the encounter of Catholics with indigenous people did not involve injustices, which must be addressed. Nonetheless, there is no other story in human history as diverse and far-reaching as the Catholic story, making it ideal for addressing the important topic of diversity.

A sacramental approach to education takes the particularity of cultures seriously but refuses to fall into the fragmentation of cultural relativism. Christ is the one who enables us to understand and redeem the fallenness of our history. He draws forth fruit from every culture and elevates this fruit within the universal community of the Church, his body on earth. To be Catholic is to inherit a rich cultural tradition that stretches across every continent, offering a source of unity and integration for people across the globe.

## Salvation History as a Unifying Thread

"Why not Japan?" This was a question from a Catholic school principal, asking why our new history curriculum would focus on Greece and Rome but not the cultures of the Far East. In fact, Japan did enter the curriculum, but through a missionary presence and the many Catholic martyrs. My response was that we could, of course, choose many cultures to address in our curriculum, but we chose salvation history as an anchor that addresses the civilizations surrounding the story of the Bible: the Ancient Near East, Egypt, Greece, Rome, and then following the story of the Church from there. Following the Church does lead to the corners of the earth, including the Far East. If you choose Japan, on the other hand, the viewpoint would be much more insular (and the same could be said for China and India, despite not being islands). Every approach to history must draw from some overarching viewpoint or narrative that is used to organize what content is worth studying and how to approach it. There is no such thing as a solely objective or neutral history because human beings must choose what is worth studying, in how much detail, which sources to use, and what lessons to take away from it.

Salvation history provides the perfect backdrop for teaching history because it offers the deepest *ratio* for the human story. It situates history within the universal story of humanity rather than one particular people. To teach it, we must rely on faith, rooting the school's perspective on history in a Catholic worldview. Through faith we know that all human beings were created by God, made in his image and likeness. This is the beginning of the story of history. The first human beings were given the task of dominion over creation, but our first parents fell from God's grace, causing disunity and strife, evident in the story of Cain and Abel. The disunifying effects of sin can also be seen in the story of Babel, where human pride became a catalyst for isolation within distinct languages and groups, in a kind of tribalism. God works to reestablish the unity of humanity, beginning with the formation of his chosen people.

A Catholic view of history recognizes that God intervened in a real way in history, calling one particular people to be his own, the nation of Israel. Through this nation, however, God himself would enter into the story, taking a role within it on behalf of all of humanity. This all important historical event becomes the very center of the story, which gives the whole its ultimate purpose and meaning. The story of salvation history continues to unfold within the Church, which, as Catholic, reaches beyond the confines of any single ethnicity or culture to all peoples universally. The mission of the Church to draw all people into the unity of communion with God forms the great arc that leads to the final act: the second coming of Christ, which will give history its completion in the moment when all things will be made manifest and all injustices set right.

No matter one's ethnicity, through faith the story of salvation history becomes one's own history, with Abraham as the father of faith for all. This approach to history does not teach the events of salvation history as theology, but situates the *historical* events of salvation history in relation to the surrounding civilizations. For instance, in the Archdiocese of Denver we started the history curriculum with the civilizations of the Ancient Near East in kindergarten, relating them to Abraham's call and the movement of God's people to Egypt. The next year focuses on the Greeks in relation to the story of the Maccabees, with the Romans following in second grade, leading into the coming of Christ. Third grade explores the culture of Christendom in the Middle Ages. Fourth grade focuses on Colorado history, drawing out connections to native cultures, Mexico, and Spanish missionaries in the Southwest. The following year provides an overview of American history, drawing in over-looked elements from the Catholic settlers. Middle school offers an overview of the whole cycle again, with ancient, medieval, and modern years.

The Church's own teaching points to this approach to history, saying it should be seen as a "mystery," in that "human history unfolds within a divine history of salvation: from creation, through the first sin, the covenant with the ancient people of God, the long period of waiting until finally Jesus our Savior came, so that now we are the new People of God, pilgrims on earth journeying toward our eternal home."[1] Another Church document, "The Catholic School," laid out a vision of history as "part of that salvation history which has Christ, the Savior of the world, as its goal."[2] History is not just a bunch of names, dates, and places, because it has an intelligible beginning and end, with a unifying center in Christ. The chief protagonist not only gives us our own supporting role, but also provides a common source of unity for all people.

Jesus said that he would both divide and unite, making us choose a primary affiliation to him even over spouse, parents, and children. On the other hand, in becoming a disciple one becomes part of the people of God, a spiritual society that stretches over the whole course of history and knows no boundaries of nation or ethnicity. Even for those separated by hostility, such as Jew and Gentile, Jesus has become a source of unity and peace: "But now in Christ Jesus you who once were far off have been brought near in the blood of Christ. For he is our peace, who has made us both one, and has broken down the dividing wall of hostility" (Eph 2:13–14). The rebirth of baptism, an adoption into the life of the Triune God,

---

1. Congregation for Catholic Education, "Religious Dimension of Education," 76.
2. Congregation for Catholic Education, "The Catholic School," 46.

transcends the particularities of this life: "For as many of you as were baptized into Christ have put on Christ. There is neither Jew nor Greek, there is neither slave nor free, there is neither male nor female; for you are all one in Christ Jesus. And if you are Christ's, then you are Abraham's offspring, heirs according to promise" (Gal 3:27–29). This does not mean that distinctions disappear; rather, they are integrated in Christ, so that we can understand and appreciate the role of femininity, cultures, and freedom even more deeply. God loves variety, as we see in creation, but he keeps this variety in harmony through the order of the cosmos. In the spiritual life, he works to draw all things into communion in him. The Church is the greatest single organization for manifesting the diversity of the human race in an integrated way. We have had popes who were Jews, North Africans, Greeks, Syrians, Germans, Italians, and, so far, one Slav and one Latin American. We celebrate the feast days of Egyptians, such as Anthony of the desert; Korean and Japanese martyrs; sub-Saharan Africans, such as St. Charles Lwanga; slaves such as St. Josephine Bakhita; Native Americans, such as Juan Diego and St. Kateri Tekakwitha; and South Americans, such as St. Martin de Porres. The Church overcomes the sinful divisions of Babel through Pentecost, manifesting how God's grace draws the whole world into God's oneness, while respecting the distinctions of persons and cultures, even as he himself is triune.

History provides a unifying principle in the Catholic curriculum, situating all subjects within the great human story of the search for truth and the drama of salvation. It leads students to recognize that they are part of God's people, a story that reaches back to the beginning and continues to unfold in their lives. They will come to see Abraham, the prophets, St. Peter, and St. Francis, among many others, as familiar figures, helping them to grasp their place within this broader narrative and community. By learning a common story, history imparts a shared identity, as well as a common frame of reference, heritage, and aspirations. Using salvation history as a thread is at once the most universal approach as well as the greatest integrating factor for drawing in the many cultures of the world. Through Catholic education, we learn that we are part of one people no matter our ethnicity or geographical location. Catholics are at home in any country, so long as they can worship in common at the Mass. God is the greatest source of unity, and he helps us to overcome all division, appreciating distinctions within a greater unity.

## Should We Cancel or Defend the West?

Every community has its own way of remembering. Throughout history, communities have found ways of keeping track of time based on the sun, moon, and stars. Nations remember times of want and plenty, and keep track of the important figures and events that have shaped their life. The buffalo count is a great example of this from Native American culture. Egyptians tracked time through the reigns of pharaohs, Romans by their consuls, and the Chinese through their dynasties. This memory is not yet what we would call history. It was among the Greeks that people began to be interested in preserving more than their own story. Herodotus, often called the father of history, explored the life of the Greeks' archenemy and the Persians, along with a culture the Greeks honored, the Egyptians. He claims to have traveled throughout the ancient world, learning from the similarities and differences of peoples, and sharing stories from other cultures from which the Greeks could learn. We call him the father of history for showing this universal interest in human history, no matter the nation. We could simply dismiss him as a dead white male, but his inquiries spanned three continents, from Europe into Asia and Africa.

Dawson explains, "Today, no less than in the past, the uneducated man accepts the culture in which he lives as culture in the absolute sense. It requires a considerable amount of study and imagination to understand the difference of cultures and the existence and value of other ways of life which diverge from the dominant pattern."[3] Ironic as it may seem, the Western tradition offers the best vantage point for this consideration. The book *The Heart of Culture: A Brief History of Education in the West* uses what may seem like a paradoxical term "the universal West."[4] The word "West" would seemingly negate universal as only one particular strand or tradition. That may be true to a point, but the expression leads us to consider how the Greeks were the first ones to look beyond the confines of their own culture and to ask universal questions. Not what it means to be a good Greek, a citizen of Athens, a Persian, or Egyptian, but what it means to be a good human being based on the nature of humanity itself. Thinking of human excellence based upon human nature, rather than a particular tribe or city, lent itself to universal questions. The myths of various cultures certainly posed important questions in symbolic form, but the Greeks paved the way for a philosophy that would be accessible to the mind of people from any culture.

Europe did not form around one ethnicity. The barbarians who settled along the Atlantic Ocean did not have linguistic or ethnic ties to the Greeks and Romans. They chose to accept the cultural heritage of the Mediterranean region because of the religious, philosophical, and legal value it imparted to their illiterate culture, learning from the ancients how to think about reality (just as most nations accept Western science today). From this chosen inheritance, the converted barbarians of the West created universities and laid the foundation for science. It was precisely from the universal approach to the study of things, including the investigation of nature, that the scientific method arose in Oxford and Paris in the thirteenth century. The nations of the world have accepted the fruit of Western tradition in modern science and medicine because of its

---

3. Dawson, *Crisis of Western Education*, 112.
4. Habiger Institute for Catholic Leadership, *The Heart of Culture: A Brief History of Education in the West* (Providence, R.I.: Cluny Media, 2020).

universal nature that can be understood and applied by anyone throughout the world. To defend the West is to defend the universality of truth, which reveals itself through universal questions on the nature of things and general methods of inquiry, the articulation of which began in Greece and was perfected in Western Europe.

The West is under attack, however, by those who see its tradition as imperialist and oppressive, evidenced, many claim, even by the traditional assertion of universal truth. Postmodernism would root us, rather, in our individual perception of reality, expressed in our own narratives which cannot be universal. Modern ideology, such as Marxism, which has influenced our public educational system and teacher training programs, advocates for the destruction of the Western tradition as a way to achieve true equality. A similar sentiment has found its way into the mainstream thinking through a radical understanding of freedom. Our cultural inheritance has been likened to perceived restrictions of traditional morality, which restrict the absolute freedom of the person to define what is good and what constitutes one's own happiness. Carl Trueman traces the influence of what he calls "expressive individualism" into education, which has led people to think that the "traditional notion of education must be abandoned. History for example, becomes a tale of oppression, not a source for contemporary wisdom. It is something that must be overcome, not something to be embraced and upon which we can build."[5] Many forces are converging today, leading to a cultural restlessness, a kind of revolution centered on individual freedom. We are attempting to recreate human nature and society around limitless freedom, leaving the Western tradition in the dustbin of history.

Beyond a doubt, we are witnessing an internal upheaval within Western culture. The American founding, despite its secular aspirations, relied upon an undergirding of Christian culture for its

---

5. Trueman, *Strange New World*, 162.

success. One of the chief characteristics of a Christian culture stems from its integration of faith and reason: recognizing that human nature and reason arose from the same God who has revealed himself in the Bible. The Bible itself led the way for early Christians by referring to Jesus as the *Logos*, the word or reason of God made flesh. The Church helped build Western civilization by preserving and synthesizing the philosophical, literary, political, and artistic legacy of the ancient world and drawing these contributions into a Christian way of life. That civilization, however, has been tottering under unrelenting attacks, as modern thinkers and politicians have driven a wedge between faith and reason and sought to replace it with utopian dreams of continual, material progress. The split has undermined the integrity of both faith and reason, as everything seems up for grabs in a world shaped by individualism and the will to power.

Defending the West entails overcoming this modern split. Samuel Gregg, in *Reason, Faith, and the Struggle for Western Civilization*, explains the philosophical fragility of the West, built upon a synthesis of the natural and supernatural, now tottering as its underpinning gives way:

> The West's integration of creation, freedom, justice, and faith is always fragile, and undermining any one of them undercuts the others. Without creation, the intelligibility of the universe is hard to sustain. Without intelligibility, freedom is only a mirage, justice a sophism, and faith nothing more than emotivism or ideology.... Again and again, we see that belief in the *Logos*—or at least an acknowledgement that it is a more plausible position than assertions that all is flux or that everything begins in nothingness—is crucial for preserving the West's civilization achievements from the rule and consequences of irrationality.[6]

---

6. Samuel Gregg, *Reason, Faith, and the Struggle for Western Civilization* (Washington, D.C.: Regnery Gateway, 2019), 147.

Gregg points out that the preservation of the liberty and justice sought by our culture will succeed only by upholding the great tradition, allowing reason and faith to speak harmoniously to us about the order of the universe and integrity of human life. We could even point to this reality of the harmony of faith in a quest for universal truth as the essence of the West. This great quest, which has derailed in many ways, must continue. To do this, we must defend the fruits of the Western tradition and hand them on to the next generation in our schools.

Rather than pitting one group against another, the Western tradition, as a universal search for truth, can promote unity. Rather than remaining trapped in our individual narratives or desires, truth is the common good that unites us in a shared understanding. The Western tradition can engage many diverse voices in its exploration, because, as St. Thomas Aquinas put it, truth is truth no matter the source: "In fact, every known truth from any source is totally due to this 'light which shines in the darkness,' since every truth, no matter who utters it, comes from the Holy Spirit."[7] This is a Western approach to truth. The Western tradition may privilege certain texts that ask the most important questions, but it does not hold to them as dogmatic positions that must simply be accepted without thought. The whole point of the Western tradition is to investigate and consider truth from any source, angle, or aspect. This is why it unites students from various cultures.

Critics of a more traditional liberal arts program often allege that this approach constitutes elitism, and is not meant for minority students. In fact, the dumbed-down, contentless approach of modern education does nothing to inspire literacy for minority students. Inviting them into the great conversation of the Western tradition

---

7. Thomas Aquinas, *Commentary on John's Gospel*, vol. 1, *Chapters 1–5*, trans. Fabian Larcher, OP, and James A. Weisheipl, OP (Albany, N.Y.: Magi Books, 1998), lect. 3, no. 103.

opens up a world of ideas for all students. The emphasis on reading great works inspires students to grow in vocabulary, and the inspiration of the works draws forth greater interior motivation. I have seen this in minority schools which have embraced a "classical" approach. In one such parochial school, predominantly Hispanic, though encompassing a diverse immigrant population, students were not making it through one book a year in eighth grade and were showing up to high school unprepared. In the first year of reading works in the Western tradition, students were devouring six books a year and even writing their own epic poetry in imitation of Homer. Another parochial school with a large Hispanic culture saw students in first and second grade rushing to the public library to check out additional books on Greece and Rome. Great ideas, a shared inquiry with the greatest minds, and an immersion into beautiful language—these things inspire learning by breaking out of the mold of dry textbooks and stale information.

Contrary to those who accuse a traditional approach to education of being racist, I have found the opposite to be true. Why would minority students not deserve the greatest works and ideas? I have heard Catholic educators tell me that "those students" are not capable of accessing these resources. I have found these accusations to be completely false, containing their own latent racism. The Western tradition believes that all human beings, because they share the same nature and rational faculty, together can understand the truth. Educators are contradicting their vocation by holding back the truth from students and keeping the greatest educational riches from them. St. Thomas Aquinas wrote that "whoever teaches the truth enlightens the mind, for truth is the light of the mind," even if the teacher only guides the students as an instrument of the true teacher, the Word, who takes root through the work of the Holy Spirit.[8] The student, however, does

---

8. Thomas Aquinas, *De Veritate*, vol. 2, *Questions 10–20*, trans. James V. McGlynn, SJ (Chicago: Henry Regnery Company, 1953), q. 11.

not receive this light passively, Aquinas says, but, with their teacher as guide, should actively seek to realize their potential to know. This is what we aim to elicit from every student, without exception.

Students from an underprivileged background need the Western tradition more than other students, because it focuses on the key aspects of learning, the basics of how to read, how to think, how to speak. These three skills are often referred to as "the three ways," the *trivium* of grammar, logic, and rhetoric. The Western tradition focuses on inspiring students to read more, think about what they read, and communicate effectively about it. As we saw in the last chapter, rich content is the best way to draw forth greater literacy from students. This approach does not focus primarily on practical outcomes as the goal, but the formation of the mind. Ironically the approach has proven that it also prepares students well for their future. No matter what students will do for their careers, this approach to education gives general preparation through deep thinking, problem solving, and creative expression, which will help them to excel in any career. As the workforce becomes more automated and computer driven, classical training will be more in need and will not be replaced by machines like other practical skill sets are.

Finally, in defending the ongoing relevance of the Western educational tradition, we must remember that the concept of human dignity arose in the West. Many Islamic or Communist nations, for instance, reject the Western notion of human rights. How could we possibly ground human rights in a rational and objective way within our own individualist and relativist culture? Without God and a strong sense of reason's ability to perceive universal truth, our sense of human dignity quickly erodes. Although we tend to equate civilization with an increase in wealth and comfort, its real health stems from genuine human flourishing, which arises much more from the interior life. The twentieth century was a time of great material progress, yet it also witnessed a terrible interior collapse. Perhaps it was precisely this material progress that led to such a large-scale and systematic destruction of human life: the Armenian genocide, the Holocaust, Communist mass starvations and purges, and the Rwandan genocide. The universal West recognizes the dignity of any human being, made in the image of God. Trained to think with the two wings of faith and reason, Catholics will be more ready to act in charity, confronting any injustice against human dignity. Imitating the Good Samaritan, who did not help a fellow countryman or believer but was moved to compassion for an unknown fellow human being, Christians are called to care for everyone—no matter their age, race, or religion, whether they are born or unborn. Allowing the exploitation of innocent human beings fundamentally undermines the common good of a nation, questioning even the basic adherence to the principles of justice. Our students need to be formed in an educational approach that can perceive the universality of human nature, the way reason is ordered toward truth, and the human dignity that flows from these objective realities.

## The American Catholic Experience

Just as we skim over Middle Ages in most school curricula, the same happens to the Catholic presence in the history of the United States. Students are taught that the nation began at Jamestown and Plymouth Rock, ignoring St. Augustine, Florida, and Santa Fe, New Mexico. The United States came to be as a confluence of Spanish, English, and French colonization, interacting in various ways (mostly bad) with the Native Americans. When viewed from a Catholic perspective, however, we discover a stronger presence and contribution from Native Americans in the history of North America: St. Juan Diego, St. Kateri Tekakwitha, Servant of God Nicholas Black Elk, and martyrs, such as in Florida.

Catholic history provides an opportunity to broaden the narrative of history and to recover lost voices. In this regard, we can appreciate a good motive behind the 1619 Project in wanting to recover the important and overlooked element of African-American history in the United States (but we should also acknowledge 1565 as the arrival of the first African slave to St. Augustine, Florida).[9] The 1619 Project may fail for ideological reasons, but we are free to accept the importance of its aim in seeking to recover the history of minorities. Apart from the Catholic tradition, could we find another place where white people venerate and beseech Native Americans and African-Americans? This point was brought home to me with the cause of Servant of God Julia Greeley in the Archdiocese of Denver, watching students of different ethnicities crowding around the tomb of a former slave in the cathedral, kneeling down and reaching out their hands to her. It offers a powerful image of the unity God brings through his Church.

Recovering the diversity of the Catholic story does not mean whitewashing problematic elements of the story. Looking at how the Church, and in particular the saints, have worked for racial equality and justice can be balanced by also looking at the sins of Catholics in violent conquest, forced enslavement, and creating racially discriminatory laws. We have contradictory statements from popes, some sanctioning enslavement and others condemning it; religious orders owning slaves even while serving those who are enslaved; and religious orders accepting applicants of color but sending them to Europe for education and ordination. We own a complicated history but one that opens up important and illuminating discussions of race and faith.

Many missionaries heroically gave themselves to serve Native Americans, even to the point of death, although it is hard to discuss this contribution without a broader evaluation of colonization. Even if some natives, such as the Aztecs, engaged in brutally horrific actions, Spaniards, such as Bishop Bartolomé de las Casas or Francisco de Vitoria, held that this did not justify the seizure of their land

---

9. The first free Black settlement in the continental United States was also established there at Fort Gracia Real de Santa Teresa de Mose in 1738.

or their enslavement. Even de las Casas, in trying to stem off enslavement of natives, recommended importing African slaves instead, a terrible suggestion, for which he later repented. One may not appreciate the mission system in general, but it was used by friars, such as St. Junipero Serra, for creating a protective sphere for natives within the colonial system. Through this somewhat murky lens, the saints bear witness to the true fruit of the faith's presence in the New World. St. Kateri was born in the village where the North American martyrs died. St. Juan Diego showed that even the Aztecs could continue to shape the course of civilization, being chosen by Our Lady of Guadalupe as her special son. No one could fault the heroic witness of St. Peter Claver in becoming a slave of the slaves, or the profound humility of the mulatto brother, St. Martin de Porres.

Catholic students, as a part of their increased cultural literacy, need to recover many forgotten stories. When critics accused the Archdiocese of Denver's history curriculum of being too Western focused or even racist, we had to point out that the curriculum was much more diverse both in world and American history than the previous social studies curriculum—by far.[10] We highlighted the role of Syriac Christians taking the faith to India, Central Asia, and China (and Matteo Rici's later role there), the forgotten Christian Kingdom of Kongo, the missionary friars of the American Southwest, American educators of minorities such as St. Katharine Drexel, St. Francis Xavier Cabrini, and St. Rose Philippine Duchesne, and the African-American candidates for sainthood in the United States: Ven. Pierre Toussaint (a layman and hairdresser in New York City), Servant of

---

10. Kathy Mears of the NCEA, for instance, expressed her concerns about an overly Western focus: "The biggest concern is that, because it's the Roman tradition, it's very European-centered. . . . There's a concern that children whose ancestors don't come from Europe, that their [ancestors'] stories aren't being told or heard." Angela Denker, "Is Classical Education the Future of Catholic Schools?" *U.S. Catholic*, August 18, 2021, https://uscatholic.org/articles/202108/is-classical-education-the-future-of-catholic-schools/.

God Mother Mary Elizabeth Lange (who founded the first African-American religious order, the Oblate Sisters of Providence, in 1829), Ven. Henriette DeLille, Ven. Augustus Tolton (the first visibly African-American priest, who had to study in Europe), Servant of God Julia Greeley, and Servant of God Sister Thea Bowman. Despite many injustices, we highlighted how the Catholic faith brought together European, Amerindian, and African cultures into a beautiful synthesis in Latin America. We can say proudly, while also acknowledging shortcomings, that no other organization or group has done more to educate minorities and protect their culture in North American than the Catholic Church, with the first school for Black and Indian students opening in New Orleans in 1727.

Servant of God Thea Bowman, FSPA, spoke passionately about the need to honor the history of African Americans in the United States and their contribution to the nation's culture, despite their suffering:

> They cleaned houses, they built churches, railroad bridges, and national monuments. They defended the country as soldiers and sailors. They taught and molded and raised the children, and I'm not just talking about the Black children. They produced a music that speaks America and that has influenced the music of the world. And during the movement for Civil Rights, they challenged America to live out her freedom creed. The history must be told. In spite of oppression, exploitation, disenfranchisement, and poverty, my people helped to build and form this nation. Surviving our history, physically, mentally, emotionally, morally, and spiritually, faithfully and joyfully, our people developed a culture that was African and American, that was formed and enriched by all our various experiences.[11]

---

11. Thea Bowman, "Black History and Culture," in *Black Catholic Studies Reader: History and Theology*, ed. David J. Endres (Washington, D.C.: The Catholic University of America Press, 2021), 21.

In Denver, we were gifted with a beautiful way of entering into the contribution of African Americans in the Church through the life of Servant of God Julia Greeley (d. 1918). Julia has a compelling and deeply moving story. Born a slave in Missouri, she lost her vision in one eye when her mother was being whipped for caring for young Julia while she was sick, rather than working in the fields. After gaining her freedom, she worked as a cook and nanny before coming to Denver about 1878. Shortly after her arrival and through the witness of her employer, Julia Gilpin, she became a Catholic. And not only that, she entered the Third Order Franciscans, became a key parishioner of Sacred Heart parish and the main proponent of its devotion to Jesus' heart, especially by bringing badges and pamphlets to every firehouse in Denver each first Friday of the month, and a key fixture of the newly established Catholic community (this was the time of Bishop Joseph Machebeuf, Mother Frances Xavier Cabrini's work, and the martyrdom of Fr. Leo Heinrichs). Most importantly, she became known as an "angel of charity," and truly beloved to the city of Denver by Catholics and non-Catholics alike.

Julia certainly experienced discrimination, especially since she lived at a time when the KKK was rising to ascendancy in Denver politics. Even in the Church, she occasionally experienced derogatory comments and some complaints about her prominent pew in the front row of Sacred Heart Church. Because of that, she provides an even more powerful image of God's grace: a former slave, with face disfigured and almost no money of her own, traveled the streets of Denver at night and served needy white people! She did not leave us any written treatises on the spiritual life, but her life itself serves as an icon of holiness. She shows us the meaning of peace and her actions teach us what charity and true forgiveness look like. She could not evaporate racial discrimination, but she surely transcended it. Clergy, police, firefighters, and ordinary people all gave her money and goods to disperse among Denver's poorest.

Julia has much to teach us about living as a Catholic in the modern city, with love and respect for everyone in need. Her biographer, Fr. Blaine Burkey, OFM Cap., is clear on how Julia can guide us now: "Whatever was thrown at her, Julia kept her good eye on her lover nailed to a cross and chose to follow his lead in not fighting back, while sharing his love to all. Thus in a world, where so much racial vitriol still abounds, Julia gives all a sterling example of respecting the dignity of all our brothers and sisters."[12] Julia shows that charity, more than anything else, can change hearts and transform the world through personal encounter. She had an infectious sense of humor and loved children, giving them presents, taking them on trips through the city, and organizing wholesome dances for girls (including providing dresses when they needed them). Her saintliness can be seen in her extreme generosity, wearing rags and fasting while giving all that she had to others: "Poor, old, alone, far from her native home, Julia Greeley did not ask charity or sympathy; she gave both in unstinted measure, and according to her giving she received the good will of those whose lives touched hers."[13] Pulling her red wagon around at night, "she had even been seen going through the streets at night with a mattress on her back. Many and many a times when was seen carrying coal and groceries."[14] Her death on the feast of the Sacred Heart summarized her life: "This surely was one of the secrets of her own spirituality: to place all of her day's activities into the secret service of the Sacred Heart."[15] Students of Annunciation School in Denver have a special devotion to her, as they can even

---

12. Blaine Burkey, OFM Cap., *An Hour with Julia Greeley* (Liguori, Mo.: Liguorian Publications, 2020). See his longer work, *In Secret Service of the Sacred Heart: The Life and Virtues of Julia Greeley* (Denver: Julia Greeley Guild, 2012). For more information on Julia's life and cause for canonization, please visit the Julia Greeley Guild's website http://juliagreeley.org/.

13. Burkey, *In Secret Service*, 6, quoting a contemporary obituary.

14. Burkey, 11.

15. Burkey, 21.

see a house where she worked out a school window. They wrote and illustrated a book about her, *Julia Greeley: Denver's Angel of Charity*, which helped to spread the word about Julia to their fellow students throughout the archdiocese.

Attending to the African-American contribution to the Catholic experience brings us back to the question of the West more generally. Does an emphasis on the Western tradition mean the exclusion of minority voices? Dr. Anika Prather said she encountered that reaction in her doctoral studies: "Why are you researching classical education in the black community? Don't you realize that those books are not for your people?"[16] And yet, she said, "I stuck to my convictions and discovered that the classics not only influenced the black intellectual tradition; they were central to it. Before black Americans found freedom from slavery, through classical texts they conceived of and engaged with ideas of virtue, liberty, and the public good."[17] She gives the examples of Frederick Douglas, Phillis Wheatley, W. E. B. Dubois, Anna Julia Cooper, and Martin Luther King Jr., and speaks forcefully of the need to continue reading the classics: "We must be clear: The classics do *not* oppress us. Taking the classics away from us *did*—and we should be upset about that. The great conversation helps put our own struggle and achievement into sharp relief so we can fully engage with our history, the good and the bad."[18] Just like the Christian faith, the classics unite us, by drawing all people into the great conversation of the ideas that matter most. Everyone is invited.

---

16. Anika Prather, "The Classics Are an Instrument of Freedom for Black People," *National Review*, February 20, 2022, https://www.nationalreview.com/2022/02/the-classics-are-an-instrument-of-freedom-for-black-people/. See also the powerful book she co-authored with Angel Adams Parham, *The Black Intellectual Tradition: Reading Freedom in Classical Literature* (Camp Hill, Penn.: Classical Academic Press, 2022).

17. Prather, "The Classics Are an Instrument."

18· Prather, "The Classics Are an Instrument."

Prather, however, leads us to another key point. Why were the classics taken away, not just from African Americans, but from everyone? In response to removing the classics program from Howard University, Cornel West and Jeremy Tate wrote of this as a spiritual tragedy that touches on the nature of education itself:

> The removal of the classics is a sign that we, as a culture, have embraced from the youngest age utilitarian schooling at the expense of soul-forming education. To end this spiritual catastrophe, we must restore true education, mobilizing all of the intellectual and moral resources we can to create human beings of courage, vision, and civic virtue.
>
> Students must be challenged: Can they face texts from the greatest thinkers that force them to radically call into question their presuppositions? Can they come to terms with the antecedent conditions and circumstances they live in but didn't create? Can they confront the fact that human existence is not easily divided into good and evil, but filled with complexity, nuance, and ambiguity?
>
> This classical approach is united to the Black experience. It recognizes that the end and aim of education is really the anthem of Black people, which is to lift every voice. That means to find *your* voice, not an echo or an imitation of others. But you can't find your voice without being grounded in tradition, grounded in legacies, grounded in heritages.[19]

The spiritual catastrophe extends beyond the cancellation of classics at Howard. We should all ask ourselves why we have deprived our children of the greatest ideas in their greatest expression. The desire to include more voices does not denigrate the Western tradition, because it follows the whole thrust of Western education to pursue all truth in whatever source and to do so in union with all seekers.

---

19. Cornel West and Jeremy Tate, "Howard University's Removal of Classics Is a Spiritual Catastrophe," *Washington Post*, April 21, 2021, https://www.washingtonpost.com/opinions/2021/04/19/cornel-west-howard-classics/.

The Catholic story continues, and its future looks more global than ever. This does not mean that the Catholic tradition, with its historical connections to Greco-Roman and medieval European Christendom should disappear, rather it should continue to grow, to enrich new cultures and to be enriched by them. This will ensure that the living tradition of the Church will continue, passing on the values she preserved for centuries, as they continue to be shaped for new generations. In the United States, we face the important task of integrating and serving a new generation of immigrants. Hosff-man Ospino points out that "about 45 percent of all Catholics self-identify as Hispanic, but likely less than 4 percent of Hispanic Catholic children are currently attending Catholic schools."[20] This statistic should awaken us to urgent action. We need to ensure that Catholic education remains truly universal: drawing upon the truth destined for all, uniting people of all cultures in these truths and the Church's own heritage and offering these gifts to all those in need.

The West's future cannot remain fixated on the past, of course. In receiving its heritage, we have the responsibility to appropriate its legacy as a living thing, drawing together the old and new in a synthesis for today. Just as the West spread from Greece and Roman to northwest Europe and from there to the Americas, so it can continue to draw us together in a shared pursuit of the truth, guided by faith and reason, our common humanity, and the call of all people to work together in pursuit of the good.

---

20. Quoted in Denker, "Is Classical Education the Future."

# 9 English through Latin:
## Rediscovering the Sacred Power of Language

The word "classical" refers back to the culture of the ancient Greeks and Romans. Many parents, educated at Catholic liberal arts colleges, see the classical movement as a way of infusing new life into parochial schools by reading better works, emphasizing beauty, and returning to the study of classical languages, especially Latin. Those educated in mainstream education programs see this movement as a threat to the status quo, implicitly or explicitly challenging their own approach. Many teachers, when approached with a classical education, express fear or confusion because it speaks in ways that are unfamiliar to them.

In my experience, most people who desire classical education simply want Catholic schools to be more "Catholic" and to use better books, especially more primary sources, in the curriculum. True classical education teaches the classics, and at the center of this approach we find the study of classical languages. The Catholic liberal arts do not require the study of classical languages or texts. My own undergraduate and masters programs in Catholic Studies focused on the masterpieces of Christian culture, rather than the "classics." You cannot really avoid classical authors in Catholic education, however, considering the effort of the monks to copy and pass them down through the centuries and that all the great Catholic authors and artists found inspiration in them, including our great spiritual writers.[1]

---

1. We could also point to moments when the saints were called beyond their classical studies, such as the dream of St. Jerome accusing him of being a Ciceronian rather than a Christian or the call of St. Gertrude the Great to leave her focus on study behind for a more mystical vocation.

The study of Latin may lead into classical culture, but I would argue for its importance based on its role in the Christian tradition. Latin has been the language of the Catholic Church in the West for the predominance of its history, shaping its culture, prayer, and thought in fundamental ways. It behooves us, then, to take the study of Latin seriously so that it can open up the accomplishments of the past and continue to shape the ordering of our own thinking and expression in continuity with the great tradition. Latin provides a stimulant for Christian education and the renewal of culture. Catholic education should have some "classical" element, therefore, at least through the preservation and teaching of this great language, which provided the foundation for the Church's own linguistic and educational tradition.

## Faith and Literacy

We need language not only to communicate with another, but also with God. The first alphabet, known as Proto-Sinaitic, arose among the Semitic people who were living in Egyptian territory and borrowed hieroglyphic symbols to create the first letters (even before the Phoenicians, the Semitic people to whom the invention is generally, though falsely, attributed).[2] The Greek and Latin alphabets ultimately derive from this first creation. Viewing history from a Christian perspective, we can see how this alphabet providentially arose to enable the recording of Israelite history and revelation in this early script that predated Hebrew. As their own Semitic dialect developed, the Hebrews preserved the memory of God's saving action through literacy. Not only do we find Moses writing records in the Torah, we also see that he enjoins Israelite parents to instruct their children and inscribe the words of the Shema:

---

2. See Douglas Petrovich, *The World's Oldest Alphabet: Hebrew as the Language of the Proto-Consonantal Script* (Peabody, Mass.: Hendrickson Academic, 2017).

And these words which I command you this day shall be upon
your heart; and you shall teach them diligently to your children,
and shall talk of them when you sit in your house, and when you
walk by the way, and when you lie down, and when you rise. And
you shall bind them as a sign upon your hand, and they shall be
as frontlets between your eyes. And you shall write them on the
doorposts of your house and on your gates. (Dt 6:6–9)

The words of Scripture require diligent study and instruction, and
must be adhered to so faithfully as to bind them upon oneself. The
Jews began establishing schools in the first century BC to teach boys
Hebrew, and it is likely that the apostles attended them. By this time,
the Jews were native Aramaic speakers, preserving Hebrew literacy
in order to read God's revelation.

The Church, seeing herself as the new Israel, also sought to preserve literacy to receive and pass on the revealed Word. Priests need
to be literate, and so the Church accepted the mission of teaching
the liberal arts, which would also enable monks and lay faithful to
engage in their own study of Scripture. The two main languages of
the Church initially were Greek, the language of the New Testament, and Syriac, a dialect related to Aramaic. It was in North Africa
that Western Christians began praying liturgically and writing theological works in Latin; from there it spread to Rome, partially under
the influence of the African Pope Victor I. Knowledge of Greek
brought the Church into connection with the great philosophers,
while Latin connected the Church to the legacy of the Roman
Empire, with its own distinct literature and enormously influential
legal tradition.

When the Church brought literacy to the barbarians of Europe,
she did not do so through their own language. The Germanic, Celtic,
and some of the Slavic tribes learned to read and write in Latin, and
only afterwards began to write in their own language and to record
the stories they had passed down orally (such as *Beowulf* or *The
Táin*). The language of the Romans became their language, shaping

their own thinking about law, medicine, and prayer. Britain had
formed a province of the Roman Empire, and the Anglo-Saxons
were drawn back into this cultural orbit with the arrival of St.
Augustine of Canterbury as a missionary out of Rome. The North-
umbrian monk, Venerable Bede, remarked on the unifying force of
Latin in the British Isles: "There are in the island at present, following the number of the books in which the Divine Law was written,
five languages of different nations employed in the study and confession of the one self-same knowledge, which is of highest truth
and true sublimity, to wit, English, British, Scottish, Pictish, and
Latin, the last having become common to all by the study of the
Scriptures."[3] The converted Anglo-Saxons were drawn into the intellectual and spiritual community of Christendom through Latin,
enabling Boniface, himself a teacher of Latin, to serve among the
Franks and German missions, and Alcuin to advise Charlemagne.

Latin shaped the life and culture of the people of the West,
including England. Although we often hear that the common people
were oblivious to Latin, this simply was not the case. Although they
could not read or write in Latin, they were immersed in the prayer
and rituals of the Roman rite and could recognize the meaning of
significant words and phrases that saturated their lives. The English
language itself bears the abundant mark of this influence. The
Angles, Saxons, and Jutes who arrived in Britain spoke diverse German dialects, but the English language has absorbed a significant
portion of its vocabulary directly from Latin and also from the
Latin-derived French language. One study of the *Oxford Dictionary*
in the 1970s put the origin of its vocabulary at 28.3 percent French,
28.24 percent Latin, 25 percent Germanic (including Norse), and
5 percent Greek.[4] Other studies vary slightly, and Germanic-derived

---

3. Venerable Bede, *Ecclesiastical History of the English People*, bk. 1.
4. Thomas Finkenstaedt and Dieter Wolff, *Ordered Profusion: Studies in Dictionaries and the English Lexicon* (Heidelberg: C. Winter, 1973).

words, despite remaining a minority of the total, continue in most common usage. Although some mistakenly attribute the Latin vocabulary to Roman soldiers (which would have been lost when the Britons were displaced), the influence remained steady through the development of the English language.

In our new age of barbarism, language is deteriorating. Think of its reduction in simple text messages, symbols, and abbreviations. Our vocabulary continues to diminish, and our ability to communicate is further stunted. We are even losing our ability to read in any real sense, as Nicholas Carr points out in his book *The Shallows: What the Internet Is Doing to Our Brains*: "And what the Net seems to be doing is chipping away my capacity for concentration and contemplation," because "calm, focused, undistracted, the linear mind is being pushed aside by a new kind of mind that wants and needs to take in and dole out information in short, disjointed, often overlapping bursts—the faster, the better."[5] In this cultural environment, perhaps it is not enough only to teach English to gain literacy in a language that has always existed alongside of Latin. From its genesis as a distinct language, English drew upon Latin as essential to the Catholic culture from which it was born. Why did the Anglo-Saxons learn Latin? Primarily, as Bede tells us, to read Scripture, and to access all the texts surrounding the Catholic faith. Like the Hebrews, we need literacy, bound up, as it is, with words and their proper grammatical arrangement. Barbarians are illiterate, those who cannot express themselves clearly, logically, or elegantly. Clearly, we have reverted to barbarism.

Grammar has become a bad word to many, conjuring images of hopelessly depressing textbooks and irrelevant classes. From my own experience in English class, I would have to agree. It is hard to learn grammar in English because it does not maintain consistent rules;

---

5. Nicholas Carr, *The Shallows: What the Internet Is Doing to Our Brains* (New York: W. W Norton & Co., 2010), 10.

it simply does not make sense. It was only when I studied Latin that grammar made sense to me, as Latin has a more complex structure and greater consistency, which enables its students to glimpse more clearly how language works. Without Latin to bolster it, English speakers seem to be losing literacy of their own language, out of touch with a wellspring not simply of the language's vocabulary but also of grammar and the whole cultural memory surrounding its development. In my opinion, English needs Latin to survive in its fullness. We could say the same for the religious literacy of Catholic school students.

## English Theological Vocabulary

Beyond general literacy, Latin also reinforces religious literacy. It is harder for English speakers to access theological words and concepts. English, as we have seen, is a very odd, though interesting, language. It has its roots in the Germanic family of languages, with minor influences from Celtic and Norse languages; and it experienced a major overhaul through the influence of French after the Norman conquest. After that, during the Renaissance, a major word borrowing from Latin occurred. This melting pot means that our theological vocabulary in the English language has two major sources: the Germanic and Latin families. There are other words that have also come down from the Greek usage of the early Church. The Catholic faith necessarily entails contact with the Hebrew, Greek, and Latin languages.

In other languages, theological words mean something on the surface, whereas in English our theological words are mostly technical jargon that has to be memorized in its special meaning. Theological words are taught in religious instruction or sometimes even used regularly as a title but without the clear underpinning they once possessed. In a secular culture, these words are simply obscured and have lost their meaning. Catholics speak their own internal language, and many of us do not know exactly what it means. To provide our children with greater literacy of their faith, they need contact with the languages that have fed into English vocabulary. This forms part of the general Catholic literacy in which they are deficient. The liturgical seasons are a good example of this: *Lent* and *Easter* are both Germanic words related to spring. Lent refers to the longer days coming with "spring" and Easter refers to "dawn" (coming in the East), related to the spring equinox. Neither, of course, have a Christian connotation and originated, rather, from the rites of paganism. Compare these terms to their Latin equivalent. *Quadragesima* and *Pacha*, which mean "forty" and "Passover" and in Latin have clear meaning on the surface, pointing to the forty days of Lent and the new Passover of Christ's Paschal mystery. Lent and Easter have no apparent meaning in modern English other than the names for the liturgical seasons. In contrast, we still use the original Greek for *Pentecost*, meaning "fifty," and *Christmas* is an English contraction that still bears its original meaning: Christ's Mass. The feast of the *Annunciation* stems from the Latin *annuntiationem*, perhaps through the Anglo-French *anunciacioun*, meaning an "announcement." *Advent* is another example from Latin, meaning "arrival." Old English, Greek, more recognizable English, Latin, and Anglo-French—this variety represents the complexity of naming ecclesial things in the English language!

Names also provide important context for faith, which we also lose in English. We see this especially with our Lord's name: *Jesus Christ*. We tend to view "Christ" as a last name, but Jesus' actual last name is "of Nazareth," indicating his hometown. "Christ" is Greek for "Messiah," the anointed one, and is a title, of course. The name "Jesus," "Joshua" in English, means "God saves," and adding Christ to it indicates that Jesus, the Savior, is the true King. The *devil* and *Satan* both mean "accuser," from the Greek (*diablos*) and Hebrew (*Satan*). Both point to an action, the role of accusing, but in English have become more of a personal name, whereas the devil's personal name is Lucifer (see Is 14:12). We can also look at the names of roles in the

Church—*pope* meaning "father" (*papa*), *bishop* is "overseer" from the Greek *episkopos*, *priest* is "elder" from the Greek *presbyteros* (there is also the influence of the Greek *hieros*, meaning "priest," in how we understand the priesthood), and *deacon* meaning "helper" or "attendant," from the Greek *diakanos*. *Monk* is from the Greek *monachos*, meaning "solitary." The meaning of the names helps unlock the purpose of the role, which unfortunately is obscured in the English titles.

There are other theological words with an English/Germanic origin, such as *heaven* and *hell*, meaning "sky" and a "concealed place" respectively. Neither word points directly to their theological meaning. *Sin* comes from a Germanic root referring to a transgression, though literally deriving from an affirmation of guilt in the sense of "this is the one who is truly guilty." This differs from the Greek and Hebrew meaning for *sin*, which is "to miss the mark," derived from archery. We still use archaic words such as *hail* and *hallowed* in our daily prayers, but they are now somewhat antiquated. *Hail* is a greeting, indicating something like "to be whole," but we could translate it simply as "hello," while *hallow* means "to make holy."

In contrast, here are other examples of words with a Greek origin. *Cathedral* stems from *kathedra*, the bishop's chair, symbolizing his teaching authority. The word *Bible* stems from *biblos*, meaning "book" or "scroll," derived originally from a Phoenician port city which imported Egyptian papyrus. *Church* also has a Greek origin, *Kyriache*, meaning "belonging to the Lord," which points to the church building, versus the word for the Church as a whole in Greek and Latin: *ecclesia*, meaning a "gathering" or "assembly." English does not have a distinction between the church building and the entire Church. *Catechesis* means "echo" in Greek, referring to an oral instruction that could be repeated back. *Evangelization*, although we received it in a Latinized form, comes from the Greek for a proclamation of the Good News.

And there are many theological terms with Latin origins, which should not surprise us since England lies within the territory of the Latin Church. *Grace* stems from the Latin *gratia*, indicating "favor," related to the New Testament Greek word *charis*. *Testament* refers to a "will," from the Latin *testamentum*, but this obscures its meaning of *covenant*, stemming from the Latin *convenire*, a "coming together" or "uniting." Old and New Testament would probably be better translated as Old and New Covenant. *Sacrament* means a "holy thing," but its equivalent in Greek, "mysterion," refers to a hidden and mysterious thing. The word *Mass* comes from the Latin conclusion of the rite, "ite missa est," which is hard to translate, but as a dismissal indicates roughly: "Go, the [holy] things are sent." *Transubstantiation* in English would be something like: "thing-changing-ness," referring to the substance of bread and wine becoming the substance of Christ's body and blood. *Concupiscence*, although it has a technical meaning of our fallen desire, refers simply to a strong desire or lust in Latin. *Conscience* is literally "with knowledge" in Latin, implying a mutual knowing, which I think is crucial as it refers to knowledge based on the moral principles that God has instilled within us.

This list could go on indefinitely, but even this short survey should provide a sense of the complexity and difficulty of theological vocabulary in English. Beyond any etymological interest, it should reinforce the amount of work we have to do in catechesis so that these unfamiliar words become more familiar and laden with meaning. Otherwise, comprehension will remain on the surface and will not take root in our consciousness and life. English has a hard time standing on its own, because it is a mutt of a language. Unlike Spanish and French, with much more obvious connections to Latin, English speakers have to discover the language's dependence on classical languages, which opens up a greater depth to the English language itself. For Catholics, the need goes beyond a general literacy to the recovery of the vocabulary and concepts that undergird how we learn about and communicate our faith.

## Why Latin?

With student proficiency in their native language declining, and with
so many outside influences on the English language, why would we
prioritize Latin? There are many parallels between English and
French, making it easier to master. Spanish would be more practical.
We could certainly make a case for Greek, especially as the language
of the New Testament. On the other hand, Britain was part of the
Roman Empire, and the English language is much more significantly
influenced by Latin, and we already use the Latin alphabet, not the
Greek. Furthermore, Catholics in the United States are predominantly members of the Latin Church, which prays with the Roman
rite, and our theology flows primarily from Latin authors, such as
St. Augustine and St. Thomas Aquinas. Just as Dante looked to Virgil as guide, as he set out not only to explore the next life but also to
create a vernacular poem that spoke to the spiritual and cultural
landscape of his day, so we can be guided by the great educational
tradition of the West, centered on the study of the Latin language.

Not only has Latin served as the language of the Church since
the third century, it also has provided the key language of education
and learning. The great Cicero translated many concepts of Greek
philosophy into the language of the Romans and himself became the
chief model of polished writing. After the fall of the empire, Roman
Christians, particularly Boethius and Cassiodorus, sought to continue
the study of the Latin language, writing textbooks on grammar and
forming libraries to pass on ancient literature. The monasteries
became centers of Latin grammar, using the writings of Virgil to provide a literary standard to study the Bible and for the Church's liturgy,
teaching, and legal tradition. Latin became the *lingua franca* of the
Middle Ages and the language of the universities. Even modern
writers have found within the ancient tongue their training ground
for elegant expression and a literary tradition to guide their own work.

Our reliance on Latin suddenly ceased, not only with the introduction of the vernacular in the Church's liturgy but also with the

eclipse of liberal education. Recognizing this decline, even in the very year the Second Vatican Council commenced, Pope St. John XXIII pointed to the sacred place of Latin in the Church and its important role in preserving her tradition and promoting unity throughout the world. In his apostolic constitution, *Veterum sapientia*, "On the Promotion of the Study of Latin," he proclaimed Latin's crucial role in education:

> There can be no doubt as to the formative and educational value either of the language of the Romans or of great literature generally. It is a most effective training for the pliant minds of youth. It exercises, matures, and perfects the principal faculties of mind and spirit. It sharpens the wits and gives keenness of judgment. It helps the young mind to grasp things accurately and develop a true sense of values. It is also a means for teaching highly intelligent thought and speech.[6]

Pope St. John's reasoning points to why the Church preserved ancient, pagan literature through the centuries. The great, subsequent literature of the West built directly upon this continuous tradition of reading the Latin classics. He also sees its value not only in its venerable and even sacred status in the Church's tradition, but also for linguistic reasons, quoting Pope Pius XI: "Its 'concise, varied and harmonious style, full of majesty and dignity' makes for singular clarity and impressiveness of expression."[7] For these reasons, writing in 1962 at the very verge of Latin's collapse, John speaks of his determination "to restore this language to its position of honor, and to do all We can to promote its study and use."[8] We should embrace his determination, bringing it to effect.

---

6. John XXIII, apostolic constitution *Veterum sapientia* (1962), 9, https://www.papalencyclicals.net/john23/j23veterum.htm.

7. *Veterum sapientia*, 3.

8. *Veterum sapientia*, 10.

Latin is not a dead language, although we are working hard to make it so.[9] We need defenders of this ancient and venerable tongue, such as Tracy Lee Simmons, who has given us one of the best apologetics for both Latin and Greek in his work *Climbing Parnassus*. Simmons rightly notes the deep influence of classical learning on the nation's founders and its guiding presence within our oldest universities and even one room schoolhouses. After expressing the foundational and all-important role of words in education, he notes that flowing from "the inseparable link between words and thinking" we find that "good language makes for good thinking."[10] This is true for any language, but especially through the study of Greek and Latin, which "helped, through their rigor and beauty, to form intellects, to develop minds."[11] Engaging in the rigors of ancient grammar teaches language itself, in a much more complete way than found in modern languages. Its complexity and precision leads to discipline within the mind itself, learning the craft of words and the logical thinking needed to form them clearly and cogently.

Latin provides us greater access to English grammar and vocabulary, as I argued in the first section of this chapter. More deeply, however, with ancient language one enters into the beauty and power of the masterpieces of the past, not simply reading them quickly in translation, but sitting at their feet and laboring to learn directly from the words of the masters. Simmons argues that "Greek and Latin carry in their long wakes an entire world of thought and feeling."[12] Looking at the great deeds of the past, within our own country and the entirety of our civilization, it is necessary to reconnect

---

9. The language continues to develop in its use as the official language of the Holy See, with new vocabulary developed within Church documents. Even more so, it remains alive with the prayer of the Church as her sacred language.

10. Tracy Lee Simmons, *Climbing Parnassus: A New Apologia for Greek and Latin* (Wilmington, Del.: ISI Books, 2002), 160.

11. Simmons, 160.

12. Simmons, 164.

to the sources of life that inspired and animated their achievements. In looking to the greats, Simmons advocates, "Don't merely read about them; read what they read—as they read it."[13] The extra effort pays off, opening up a greater horizon of thinking with the ancients in their own words, not simply reading a modern translation of their thought, which can never catch the intricacies of their expression. Even during the Renaissance, which embraced vernacular literature, following the example of Dante, the study of Latin remained the core of education, learning the nature of language and artful expression. One of the best explanations for the study of Latin came from the Renaissance figure, Leonardo d'Arezzo in a letter on education to Baptista Malatesta:

> This leads me to press home this truth—though in your case it is unnecessary—that the foundations of all true learning must be laid in the sound and thorough knowledge of Latin: which implies study marked by a broad spirit, accurate scholarship, and careful attention to details. Unless this solid basis be secured, it is useless to attempt to rear an enduring edifice. Without it the great monuments of literature are unintelligible, and the art of composition impossible. To attain this essential knowledge we must never relax our careful attention to the grammar of the language, but perpetually confirm and extend our acquaintance with it until it is thoroughly our own. We may gain much from Servius, Donatus and Priscian, but more by careful observation in our own reading, in which we must note attentively vocabulary and inflexions, figures of speech and metaphors, and all the devices of style, such as rhythm, or antithesis, by which fine taste is exhibited.[14]

---

13. Simmons, 210.
14. Leonardo d'Arezzo, "Concerning the Study of Literature: A Letter Addressed to the Illustrious Lady, Baptista Malatesta," in *Vittorino da Feltre and Other Humanist Educators*, ed. W. H. Woodward (Cambridge: Cambridge University Press, 1912), 124, https://history.hanover.edu/texts/bruni.html.

D'Arezzo emphasizes broadness of thinking, accuracy, attention, access to the great monuments of the past, and attending to models of elegant writing that flow from a careful study of Latin, "observing the sense of each passage, the structure of the sentence, the force of every word down to the least important particle." Learning how language works from this kind of careful study enables the flowering of writing in the vernacular, as occurred in the Renaissance. Following the ancients in these matters of grammar and style will surely advance education!

Many of our Catholic schools offer Latin, and many more should return to it, for its study opens up to students a breadth of tradition, thought, and beauty. The language of saints and scholars can inspire our students to read deeply, think rightly, communicate clearly, and to enter more profoundly into the mystery of our faith. And the benefits will extend to other subjects through the attention to words that the study of ancient language entails. Simone Weil offers the example of St. John Vianney, "The useless efforts made by the Cure d'Ars, for long and painful years, in his attempt to learn Latin bore fruit in the marvelous discernment that enabled him to see the very soul of his penitents behind their words and even their silences."[15] The many Catholic school students who have slaved over their grammar books could sympathize with the saint, while little realizing the hidden benefits that their study may have provided in their souls through their effort, diligence, and attention to language.

## The Need for a Sacred Language

*Ave Maria, Gloria in excelsis, Agnus Dei, Dominus vobiscum, Sanctus, Tantum ergo.* These are just some of the Latin phrases that Catholics may recognize. Although we commonly speak of Latin as a "dead" language, it remains alive within the Church as her sacred language

---

15. Weil, *Waiting for God*, 108.

of prayer, study, and unity. When introducing the *Compendium of the Catechism of the Catholic Church*, Pope Benedict XVI asked Catholics to learn the basic prayers of the Mass and the Rosary to be able to pray together throughout the world: "Precisely in the multiplicity of languages and cultures, Latin, for so many centuries the vehicle and instrument of Christian culture, not only guarantees continuity with our roots but also continues to be as relevant as ever for strengthening the bonds of unity of the faith in the communion of the Church."[16] This common language roots the Latin rite of the Church in a shared identity and heritage. A sacred language also points to the transcendent mystery and reverence of the Mass, moving beyond the ordinary language of one's daily routine.

The challenge of learning a sacred language comes with its own benefits. In memorizing and translating, we must think through the meaning of the prayer rather than take it for granted. A distinct language provides a sign that the words of prayer are more important than those of everyday life. For this reason, sacred languages have played an important role throughout history. Jesus' everyday language was Aramaic, but as a Jewish boy he would have learned to read and pray in Hebrew. Even as the Jews adopted the more widespread Aramaic, a language related to Hebrew, they preserved the Scriptures in the language in which God had revealed himself. It is not that they were completely against translations—for example, Jewish scholars produced the Greek Septuagint in Egypt—but they realized no translation could perfectly capture the meaning of revelation, because it was bound to the vocabulary and culture of the Hebrews. As the Italians say: *traduttore, traditore*—"to translate is to betray." Preserving an ancient language also preserves the ideas,

---

16. Benedict XVI, "Presentation of the *Compendium of the Catechism of the Catholic Church*," June 28, 2005, 8, https://www.vatican.va/content/benedict-xvi/en/speeches/2005/june/documents/hf_ben-xvi_spe_20050628_compendium.html.

memories, and customs encapsulated by that language, elements that are essential to preserving a cultural and religious identity.

In Western Europe, the preservation of Latin as a sacred language depended more upon the Carolingians, particularly Pepin the Short and Charlemagne, than on any pope. St. John XXIII reminds us that Latin "proved to be a bond of unity for the Christian peoples of Europe. Of its very nature Latin is most suitable for promoting every form of culture among peoples. It gives rise to no jealousies. It does not favor any one nation, but presents itself with equal impartiality to all and is equally acceptable to all."[17] This is why the Roman rite of the Mass, with its accompanying Gregorian chant, served as a unifying force throughout the empire of Charlemagne in the early ninth century, with a sacred language providing a common center for people of diverse cultures and traditions throughout Europe. The common thread of Latin assured that Catholics throughout the West shared a common theological vocabulary and ritual.

It is due to the conversion of the barbarians to the Catholic faith in the Middle Ages that Latin became the common sacred language for all Latin rite Catholics. The preservation of Latin, transmitting with it the legacy of classical and ecclesial culture through the ages, is more than an historical accident, however. Even the inculturation of the faith to the Slavic tribes in Eastern Europe, a bold and controversial move at the time, led to the sacred language of Church Slavonic, still used by Eastern Catholic and Orthodox faithful today as distinct from their modern, national languages. Even the Greek used in Byzantine liturgies remains somewhat distinct from the modern Greek dialect. Christians in Egypt pray in three languages, preserving Coptic (the ancient Egyptian language), alongside some remnants of Greek and the now dominant Arabic. Most strikingly, Maronite Catholics continue to use Aramaic, the language of Jesus, for the consecration.

---

17. John XXIII, *Veterum sapientia*, 3.

Christians, like their Jewish forebears, preserve sacred languages because there is something deeply human about using a distinct language for prayer. Even though it is essential to be able to read the Bible and pray in our native tongue, the use of a distinct language for the most solemn moments manifests their transcendent importance. It also gives us precision for things such as the form of the sacraments, as evidenced by recent tweaks to overcome imprecise translations. For instance, Pope Benedict XVI adjusted the words of consecration to "shed for you and for many" rather than for "all," to match the words of Jesus. There has also been an uproar over changes to the translation of the Our Father in French and Italian, changing the prayer's meaning. In English, we saw a return to the Latin-based word "consubstantial" from "one being," to convey a clearer philosophical and theological meaning.[18] The use of Latin for our most common prayers and theological terms provides stability through the constant developments of language.

The Second Vatican Council seemed to foresee some use of the vernacular alongside of Latin in the liturgy. *Sacrosanctum concilium*, the Constitution on the Liturgy, stipulates that "the use of the Latin language is to be preserved in the Latin rites," though ecclesial authorities would "decide whether, and to what extent, the vernacular language is to be used."[19] Pope St. Paul VI, who approved the use of the vernacular within the liturgy, also spoke of the loss that would incur:

> The introduction of the vernacular will certainly be a great sacrifice for those who know the beauty, the power, and the expressive sacrality of Latin. We are parting with the speech of the

---

18. United States Conference of Catholic Bishops, "Consubstantial with the Father," https://www.usccb.org/prayer-and-worship/the-mass/order-of-mass/liturgy-of-the-word/consubstantial-with-the-father.

19. Second Vatican Council, *Sacrosanctum concilium*, Constitution on the Liturgy, 36, https://www.vatican.va/archive/hist_councils/ii_vatican_council/documents/vat-ii_const_19631204_sacrosanctum-concilium_en.html.

Christian centuries; we are becoming like profane intruders in
the literary preserve of sacred utterance. We will lose a great part
of that stupendous and incomparable artistic and spiritual thing,
the Gregorian chant.[20]

Paul clearly wanted someone in the Church to maintain this tradition, and he made a strong appeal, mostly to monastics to preserve
it within the Divine Office. Speaking to monks, he explained,

> For this language is, within the Latin Church, an abundant well-
> spring of Christian civilization and a very rich treasure trove of
> devotion. . . . Your founders and teachers, the holy ones who are
> as it were so many lights within your religious families, have
> transmitted this to you. The traditions of the elders, your glory
> throughout long ages, must not be belittled. . . . In present con-
> ditions, what words or melodies could replace the forms of Cath-
> olic devotion which you have used until now? You should reflect
> and carefully consider whether things would not be worse, should
> this fine inheritance be discarded. . . . One can also wonder
> whether men would come in such numbers to your churches in
> quest of the sacred prayer, if its ancient and native tongue, joined
> to a chant full of grave beauty, resounded no more within your
> walls. We therefore ask all those to whom it pertains, to ponder
> what they wish to give up, and not to let that spring run dry from
> which, until the present, they have themselves drunk deep.[21]

While Paul was appealing to monks, could we not see schools also
as places that could take up his call to preserve Latin as the great
inheritance of the Church's prayer, culture, and music?

---

20. Paul VI, "Changes in Mass for Greater Apostolate," November 26, 1969,
https://www.ewtn.com/catholicism/library/changes-in-mass-for-greater-apostolate-
8969.

21. Paul VI, apostolic letter *Sacrificium Laudis*, August 15, 1966, https://www.
ccwatershed.org/2014/12/22/sacrificium-laudis-english-translation/.

The very height of language comes from glorifying God. What words we use and the way we express them shape how we learn to relate and communicate with God. Within a sacramental approach, the outward expression of our prayers matter, as they surround the inward approach to God within a cultural context. Learning Latin opens up the words expressed by the Church and the saints throughout the centuries in praising God, allowing them to become our own and to shape our thoughts and sentiments. Even just the basic vocabulary can enrich our understanding of doctrine and the Church's liturgical tradition. Returning even to a limited use of Latin unites us to the past and serves as a unifying factor for the Church. The long tradition of praying in a sacred language has not lost its relevance, in our need to recover a sense of the sacred in a secularized world. Perhaps our students will discover a love for the tradition of liturgical prayer and the beauty of language by returning to the study of Latin.

# 10 Thirst for Beauty:
## The Essential Role of the Arts

What do we really need to live? Not just survive, but to live a genuinely human life? Fyodor Dostoevsky, in his novel *Demons*, answers, even if he slightly exaggerates: "Man can live without science, he can live without bread, but without beauty he could no longer live, because there would no longer be anything to do to the world. The whole secret is here, the whole of history is here."[1] We might limp along, but could we really live without beauty? Without beauty, there would be no inspiration, joy, or motivation to sacrifice—no real love.

We could say the same about Catholic education. Without beauty, it will wither and die. Hans Urs von Balthasar famously asserted that if we lose sight of the centrality of beauty, we will also lose her sisters, to whom she is inextricably bound: truth and goodness.[2] Because of this, we cannot approach the arts, both the visual arts and music, as simply "specials" or extra classes that can be dispensed with if there is not sufficient budget or interest. These areas of education are essential for the formation of youth, leading them to love what is truly good, helping them to fall in love with the highest truths of human life and the divine. Human beings thirst for beauty and if this desire is not quenched on what is worthy, we gorge ourselves on what is not, futilely seeking our happiness in the wrong

---

1. Quoted in Benedict XVI, "Meeting with Artists," Nov. 21, 2009, https://www.vatican.va/content/benedict-xvi/en/speeches/2009/november/documents/hf_ben-xvi_spe_20091121_artisti.html.
2. Hans Urs von Balthasar, *Seeing the Form*, vol. 1 of *The Glory of the Lord: A Theological Aesthetics*, trans. Erasmo Leiva-Merikakis (San Francisco: Ignatius Press, 1982), 18.

way. We need to commit to the arts for the sake of the souls of our students.

## Discovering True Beauty

Jesus offers the perfect icon of God (Col 1:15), manifesting the inner life of the Trinity to us in the flesh. As the perfect man, we understand the meaning of our lives only in light of his illumination of what human life should be. We can read about Jesus, of course, but do we need images of Christ to appreciate how he reveals God to us? Is not walking by faith enough, as Paul says, "we walk by faith and not by sight" (2 Cor 5:7)? Human beings, however, learn through their senses, and so God emptied himself, becoming one of us to speak with human words and manifest the Father's love through his own human face and action. Continuing the Incarnation, the Church uses words, images, and the sacramental life to manifest God's ongoing presence in the world. Because the Word has been made flesh, we can encounter God through images and by meditating upon them come to discover our own story in relation to Christ, the true icon. The beauty of this divine image restores us to be the image of God we were created to be.

We long for beauty, yet we are not always sure how to recognize it. There are things that immediately attract us: a stunning landscape, a Renaissance masterpiece, or a beautiful figure. Why do they grab our attention? The beauty of nature awes and offers peace. Great art transfixes us and inspires our imagination. The beauty of another person moves our heart and leads us to desire communion. That is what beauty should do, but a merely surface attraction can lead us back to ugliness—using the person for immediate gratification and pleasure. Exterior attraction might capture our eyes, yet it should lead us to more.

Our culture, however, is full of ugliness and vanity. We experience a never-ending bombardment of images and sounds that leave us in confusion and distraction. Media tempts us to a constant consumption, even of the beauty of the human body itself. In the midst of this con-fusion, we do not receive enough genuine beauty, something to inspire us to make a commitment to another and ultimately to God. Ugliness presents a spiritual roadblock. If beauty manifests the perfection and splendor of a thing, ugliness distorts it, corrupting what it is meant to be and blinding us to its true reality. A tree struck by lightning or blighted with disease is ugly. A building sculpted with cement, with little light or elegance, depresses us. The ugliness of modern art disturbs us and does not uplift our sensibilities. And the greatest ugliness of all—sin—corrupts and distorts the beauty of our soul by grasping after pleasurable scraps, trying to force happiness even though this pleasure, cut off from higher goods, only makes us more miserable.

Maybe that is what is wrong with the world, after all? It is not that we lack physical beauty. People take plenty of nature walks and remain quite aware of the power of physical attraction. Too often, however, the experience of beauty stops there. It does not lead us anywhere; it does not inspire us to make a commitment. In the end, a mere surface beauty remains vanity—an allurement that creates desire without leading to love. Beauty should do more than provide a "delight to the eyes," like the fruit that tempted Eve; it should push us outside of ourselves to lead us to what is true and good.

Beauty calls us to commitment, not just to enjoy another but to give our lives in love. When we are taken by someone's beauty it generates a spark, a desire for something more than ourselves. Falling in love is the best example of this. We are attracted to the good of the other—their looks, personality, and companionship—but the initial draw is meant for *commitment*, leading us to dedicate our lives to the good of the other. Beauty leads to love, moving us to sacrifice for the good of the other, to cultivate and protect their beauty. This love helps us to see beauty more deeply than we did before. After fifty years of marriage, a couple should be able to appreciate the other's beauty beyond the initial attraction, even if the beauty of youth has passed, because they know what is within.

True beauty is deeper than any outward attractiveness. It radiates the splendor of a soul rightly ordered that communicates what is good and true about life in the deepest sense. Beauty is spiritual in nature. The awe that we find in nature and even the depth of human love both provide a sign of divine love—of the one who is Beauty itself. Beauty truly resides more than skin deep: in its deepest expression it shines forth the essential goodness, purity, and loveliness of God and his creation. When we recognize the deepest aspect of beauty, we are drawn into this good and want to commit our lives to it. In fact, falling in love with God makes us beautiful, as he cultivates and protects our beauty in our divine communion with him.

Beauty's greatest power cannot be found in a beautiful object but in a beautiful life. One life, in particular, shows us this power to its fullest extent. The Cross expresses the power of beauty by showing us the supreme goodness of human life. The one who is Beauty itself emptied himself and took on all the ugliness of the world, even to the point of disfigurement. And yet this love and sacrifice manifests the greatest beauty—the beauty of Christ's love and also his desire to see our lives become beautiful through that love. The beauty of the Cross cuts through all the noise, vanity, and lust by unmasking their transience.

## Perceiving Beauty's Objective Nature

Our culture usually emphasizes the subjective side of beauty: "Beauty is in the eye of the beholder." This is true to a point, because beauty requires recognition, and we can be formed to recognize deeper and more intellectual elements of beauty, beyond what immediately catches the eye. Beauty, however, also contains objective elements. People generally agree that certain places, buildings, and even people are beautiful. The reason for this is that beauty is a communication of "form," the essence of what something is, presenting the nature of a thing in a compelling and attractive way. Beauty speaks to us and, when it catches our heart, it compels us.

St. Thomas Aquinas described three essential elements of beauty: integrity, symmetry, and clarity. "Integrity" speaks to the grasp of the wholeness of something, that it truly presents to us what the thing is. "Symmetry" refers to a proportionality and balance that appeals to our sense of order and our desire for the proper arrangement of things. "Clarity" entails a splendor or radiance that clearly communicates the essence of what a thing is, speaking to us of its identity in a compelling way. We could return to the example of a tree. Being struck by lighting and losing its branches, it would no longer have integrity. Or, if someone cut down all the branches on one side of a tree, it would lack symmetry. If it were covered over by vines and bushes, so that it could not be seen and appreciated, it would lack clarity in relation to us. In none of these cases would we consider the tree to be beautiful. Imagine walking through a field and finding a well-placed tree, fully grown, with lush leaves, its branches proportionately extending in all directions, and drawing our attention to it so that it moves us. We would describe this tree as beautiful.

Aquinas also spoke of beauty as a "transcendental," a quality of being that all of creation possesses. Insofar as something exists, it expresses the goodness and beauty of the Creator. Nonetheless, we recognize that the expression of the reality of beauty can be more or less. All trees may be beautiful insofar as they are trees, even though some catch our attention and direct us more to the contemplation of the essence of "treeness." We can also speak of a hierarchy and varying degrees of beauty. Creation compels us with its natural beauty, instilled by God. Human art attempts to draw out this beauty further as a kind of contemplation of nature and human life. Humanity, because we are made in the image and likeness of God, contains the deepest beauty, because our life is infused with spiritual significance. There is nothing more beautiful than love and relationship. We cannot live without beauty, as we would be lacking in the necessary joy and splendor of life. The role of beauty is life-giving and necessary for humanity to be fully human and alive. Beauty, as a sign, points us to God, who is himself the fullness of Truth, Goodness, and Beauty.

The objective nature of beauty points us also to ugliness. When something is incomplete, deformed, or turns us away from the contemplation of truth, we would speak of its ugliness. Because we see the deepest beauty in human life, it is also there that we find the greatest ugliness. Sin, violence, and hatred lead us away from the true meaning and purpose of our lives and cut us off from communion. Beauty is meant to lead us to love, into communion, peace, and harmony. Jesus, however, has redeemed even the ugly elements of life by embracing them on the Cross. He helps us to recognize beauty even in the midst of suffering, which he transforms into an opportunity for love. Beauty and ugliness themselves form a kind of harmony, because we all must experience the trial of ugliness, even as God pulls us to his beauty in and through these difficulties. Forming a Christian aesthetic in our students helps them to recognize the relation of true beauty and ugliness, which can sometimes present itself as a surface beauty of vanity that pulls us away from truth and goodness.

Faith also regenerates art, moving it beyond a mere expression of human creativity and into a manifestation of the divine. Although the Old Testament prohibited any depiction of God, so as to avoid idolatry, in the Incarnation the Son of God has taken on human flesh and made himself an icon of the living God. Christian art continues this manifestation of the divine, enlivening the imagination of the artist to cooperate with God in expressing his revelation. It helps us to relate to God by engaging our senses, which in turn helps us to meditate in prayer. The great art of our churches, icons, statuary, music, and holy vessels surrounds Christ's presence at the Mass, leading us through their beauty into an encounter with the transcendent source of all beauty.

In our relativistic age, it can be hard to engage people in conversations about truth or morality. And yet, beauty and art can cut through these barriers, catching people's attention and drawing them toward the sacred. A beautiful church, such as the great Gothic cathedrals of France, draws people inside like magnets. When they step inside, tourists are greeted by a silence and peace that speaks more powerfully than anything on social media. The candles burning before the saints create a sacred atmosphere, as they flicker on the gold leaf along the seams of their garments. The stained glass radiates with brilliant color, calling the visitor to awaken his interior senses. The arches themselves lead the mind upward to wonder, "Is there anything more than this life?" In the center of it all, treasured in a tabernacle of gold, the Lord himself awaits them and invites them quietly to meet him in their hearts.

This is why beauty is so important for education. When we discover true spiritual beauty, it makes us stop, it even wounds us, and challenges us to become more fully human. Beauty tells us there is something more than what we see on the surface—there is something and someone worth knowing and loving. Christ ultimately reveals the beauty of human life to us, especially on the Cross. Life is beautiful—it is a gift that we have received and one that is meant to be given to others. The world needs to learn how to see again, to recover its ability to recognize the surpassing beauty of knowing Jesus and living in communion with him.

Art provides an initial sign of the Christian vision, and Christian witness confirms its living reality in the world. Pope Benedict XVI spoke of this opportunity and need: "I have often affirmed my conviction that the true apology of Christian faith, the most convincing demonstration of its truth against every denial, are the saints, and the beauty that the faith has generated. Today, for faith to grow, we must lead ourselves and the persons we meet to encounter the saints and to enter into contact with the Beautiful."[3] Art, following this sacramental identity, expresses our faith, draws us into prayer,

---

3. Ratzinger, "Feeling of Things."

and mediates divine realities.[4] Within a sacramental pedagogy, it becomes a means of contemplating truth and goodness.

## Teaching and Making Art

God, the supreme artist, spoke, "Let there be light," and there was light (Gn 1:3). This primal creation on the first day manifested the order God brought into the chaos. We are blessed with eyes to receive this light that illuminates the beauty of God's handiwork. We can go further, however, and see how we too are called to share in God's work, to "subdue" the earth, contributing our own work to bring forth additional order and beauty. Everyone is called to become a co-creator with God in some sense, but the artist shares the special vocation of shining light onto human life. We may not all be great artists but we can enjoy their works which look more deeply into creation, human aspirations, suffering, and even the divine. To enjoy their masterpieces, we need to learn how to look, how to contemplate their message transmitted through the physical signs of medium and artisanship.

"Let there be light!" God not only illuminated his creation at the beginning of time. He continues to shed light into our hearts and minds, helping us to see into his divine life. The light of faith also shines into the darkness of the world, illuminating a path to order all things to the goal of heaven. Christian art casts this light on the human experience, illuminating the world through faith and a sacramental imagination. This imagination comes from God's own taking on of flesh in the Incarnation, making our humanity a way of manifesting eternal light in the world: "In him was life, and the

---

4. Elizabeth Lev details one example, the crucial role of art at a time of crisis in the Church in her book, *How Catholic Art Saved the Faith: The Triumph of Beauty and Truth in Counter-Reformation Art* (Manchester, N.H.: Sophia Institute Press, 2018). As core Catholic doctrines faced opposition from Protestants, the Council of Trent called for the creation of art to assist in renewal.

life was the light of men. The light shines in the darkness, and the darkness has not overcome it" (Jn 1:4–5).

Through the study of art, students become immersed in beauty. Beauty is an objective reality experienced subjectively in time and space that transcends time and place. Beauty arrests the heart, sparks wonder and awe, and leads to the Divine. Beauty overwhelms, delights, pleases the person and evokes an emotional response. Beauty transcends us, leading us to encounter something greater than ourselves and can pull us out of our mundane experience of life. Authentic beauty contributes directly to culture, because it inspires us to greater things. Being immersed in the great beauty of the Catholic tradition and faith plays a central role in teaching from a Catholic worldview. We think things are beautiful when they convey proportion and harmony, but also in a way that catches our attention, makes us stop in wonder, and inspires us. The artist does not simply reproduce nature but presents it to us in a new way to see more deeply into what we can take for granted. Great art combines this ability to see and perceive the inner nature of things with an objectively pleasing presentation.

Of all the creatures, human beings were made with the capacity for beauty, to be in awe and wonder of the created world. Human beings are made in the image and likeness of God as rational, free beings, ordered toward knowing the truth and loving what is good. This also means that human beings are made in the image of God the Creator, given a mission not just to perceive truth and choose goodness but also to extend the work of creation, making their own contribution to it. Human work, the taking up and fashioning of the goods of creation, expresses human creativity: our desire to express the interior life in exterior form. "Art" comes from "artifice," the making of things. The fine arts emerge when human work fashions something beautiful for enjoyment and edification. Human beings desire to make things, to make a contribution to the world through work; and art constitutes one of the highest ways of sharing in the creative work of God. He desires that his own hidden beauty be manifest outwardly in his creation. The created world illuminates his own truth, beauty, goodness, and love. He made human beings as sacraments of his own trinitarian communion and has called us to contribute to the work of creating beauty in the world.

The experience of beauty is integral to Catholic education, because beauty inspires us to seek the truth and to love the good. Art education in the Catholic school offers more than a cultural experience or an aesthetic moment. Catholic education finds its goal in the formation and transformation of the student himself. Experiences of beauty, therefore, are necessary to move the child towards the transcendent, opening up the mind, imagination, and soul to the sublime. Through this understanding of human anthropology, the Church has always recognized that an experience of beauty moves the human person towards the transcendent, towards God. This is why the arts have always found a home and flourished in the Church, with the Catholic faith inspiring the greatest art in human history. The notion of transcendent beauty marks a Catholic understanding of art as different than a secular notion of the arts.

The study of art complements other subjects as an expression of the human search for truth. It tells the human story through the concrete expression of what human beings have seen and dreamed throughout history. Art narrates the great unfolding of the inner life of humanity, giving witness to the hopes, aspirations, and fears of each age. By examining the unfolding of the many eras and movements of art history, we can find inspiration for answering these questions today. Nothing may transmit the human story as a whole better than art: the earliest traces of humanity can be discerned on the walls of caves, the first monumental architecture arose in the Ancient Near East, the Greeks and Romans captured the human figure in its perfection, the full blossoming of the arts unfolded in Christian Europe, and sadly we have experienced the slow demise into the abstraction of modernism. The great authors of this story have spoken to us through images and sounds, capturing the thrust of human aspirations and darkness. Their testimony speaks to us despite the efforts of iconoclasts, revolutionaries, and the avant-garde to silence them and undo beauty's role in lifting the human spirit.

Catholic art seeks the answer to the great questions of human life with the help of faith, pushing beyond the limits of sight to contemplate eternity. It first grew out of the realism of the Greco-Roman tradition but quickly developed its own iconographic style as a spiritual way of seeing, seeking a window into the life of Christ and the saints. In the Middle Ages the Church sought the impossible, to soar to the heavens, commissioning the great Romanesque and Gothic churches with their own lavish sculpture and painting. The Renaissance marked a creative explosion, bringing painting and sculpture to a new level of perfection, rooted in a humanistic vision that sought to express the perfection of life. This tradition was continued exuberantly in the drama of the Baroque period, full of energy and confidence. Like modern culture as a whole, this was followed by a great subjective turn in the Romantic and modern periods, making art into a personal interpretation of reality. Following this tradition, students can enter into conversation with the great masters of the past, contemplating Genesis with Michelangelo, the spiritual life with the sculpture of Bernini, or Dante's Inferno with the bronze gate of Rodin.

As we teach art in the Catholic schools, we must harness the unsurpassed Catholic artistic tradition as a treasure of inestimable worth. First, our students should come to know this tradition more deeply, becoming familiar with its great artists and masterpieces. How could a student graduate from Catholic school without exposure to the greatest accomplishments of the tradition? More importantly, they can experience the transcendent and transforming power of the beauty of Catholic art, which will enrich their lives and inspire them with the beauty of faith. This art does not just give us insight into the achievements of the past. It continues to serve its original function of leading us into the contemplation of our faith and assisting us in worshiping God. Finally, beyond a passive reception of this tradition, it can inspire students to answer the Lord's call to share in his work of creation, imitating this tradition in making beautiful things in whatever they do. Through this, they may come to see themselves in their studies and work more broadly as co-creators with God.

Teaching art forms important dispositions within students. First and foremost, it will inspire *wonder* in them, leading them to desire beauty. Looking at art and studying pictures fosters *attention*, which can then lead students to *imitate* the details they observe. This will build up their *imagination* in healthy ways, feeding their minds with beautiful things and the proper and proportional arrangement of objects. Building up their imagination will then lead to greater *inspiration*, which in turns fosters *creativity*. The process of making art will lead to *studiousness* in overcoming difficulties and also *docility* in accepting correction, building patience, and persevering to its completion. Finally, in engaging in the process of making art, students will strive for *excellence* in transmitting beauty through their work. Studying art contributes towards a contemplative approach to education, which teaches students to learn "how to look," to engage in silent reflection, to keep their attention engaged in thought, and to be drawn up into the realities conveyed by the art contemplated.

To give a practical example, perhaps the greatest pedagogical use of the arts came from theatrical productions in the early Jesuit schools. Dramatic performance reinforced fluency in Latin as well as moral lessons, and drew out a greater imaginative power when accompanied by elaborate sets, which even employed the greatest artists of the day such as Rubens and Bernini.[5] The Jesuit historian, John O'Malley,

---

5. See *The Jesuit Ratio Studiorum of 1599*, trans. and ed. Allan P. Farrell, SJ (Washington, D.C.: Conference of Jesuit Superiors, 1970), 122.

remarks, "the more I study the history of Jesuit education, the more integral to the program of the schools the arts seem to be, many of them consequences of the early Jesuit commitment to theater."[6] These performances were truly holistic experiences, accompanied by music, and sometimes even dance, reinforcing the overall aims of the curriculum outside of the classroom. Bruna Filippi describes how

> theatre was an integral part not only of the academic program but also of the students' daily lives and even of institutional social events. There were public performances during Carnival, improvised plays and contests between the various dormitories of the college, and private performances on the occasion of visits by important patrons or guests. The frequency and diversity of theatrical productions in Roman Jesuit circles demonstrates the key role of theatre, not only as a tool for training students in perfect eloquence, but also as a complement to the pedagogical program that, combining utility and recreation, became a characteristic feature of community life.[7]

When employed in this holistic way, the arts have the power to change lives and to make the curriculum come to life. The ideas we teach become alive when encountered in the flesh.

The fine arts provide an essential complement to the academic disciplines, drawing the principles of truth, goodness, and beauty to life, calling forth an active and more tactile response from the students, who are asked to step into the role of a protagonist. Whether through a performance or the creation of artistic works, the arts can draw together the school community in the appreciation and celebration of beauty as a lived reality.

---

6. John W. O'Malley, *Saints or Devils Incarnate?: Studies in Jesuit History* (Leiden: Brill, 2013), 212.

7. Bruna Filippi, "The Orator's Performance: Gesture, Word, and Image in Theatre at the Collegio Romano," in *The Jesuits II: Cultures, Sciences, and the Arts, 1540–1773*, ed. John W. O'Malley et al. (Toronto: University of Toronto Press, 2006), 514.

## The Glory of Our Musical Heritage

Like visual art, music education provides an opportunity for both appreciation and performance. The great heritage of Catholic music will enrich our students' minds, imaginations, and souls, leading them into the worship of God. Through musical studies, they can learn a new language, at once mathematical and poetic. Through their attention, they can build their own capacity to listen and appreciate. This formation, once again, cannot be seen as an "extra" or "special" added on to the curriculum, but essential to the proper and complete formation of the soul. After leaving off the visual arts with the example of the old Jesuit schools, we could open this section looking again to the history of that society. In the evangelization efforts in the New World, the Jesuits found music to provide an essential opening for inculturation and evangelization. They discovered immense musical talent in Native peoples, such as the Guaraní, who fashioned their own instruments and performed choral and operatic music. The power of musical performance proved an effective means of drawing peoples into the great tradition and the spiritual life of the Church, enabling them to make their own contributions within it.

We cannot underestimate the spiritual power of music, for both good and ill. Great music speaks to us and informs us, even when it is wordless. It communicates to us, regardless of words, through its powerful and complex melody, rhythm, and harmony, employing a beautiful and mathematical language that enchants, agitates at times, inspires, soothes, and stimulates. In contrast to the immediately pleasing and entertaining pop music, classical music opens up a new world of ideas and imagination, and leads us to spiritual depths of reflection, even when the music is not explicitly sacred.

Frodo Baggins describes such an experience, within J. R. R. Tolkien's *The Lord of the Rings*, when first hearing music within the elven realm of Rivendell:

At first the beauty of the melodies and of the interwoven words in elven-tongues, even though he understood them little held him in a spell, as soon as he began to attend to them. Almost it seemed that the words took shape, and visions of far lands and bright things that he had never yet imagined opened out before him; and the firelit hall became like a golden mist above seas of foam that sighed upon the margins of the world. Then the enchantment became more and more dreamlike, until he felt that an endless river of swelling gold and silver was flowing over him, too multitudinous for its pattern to be comprehended; it became part of the throbbing air about him, and it drenched and drowned him. Swiftly he sank under its shining weight into a deep realm of sleep.[8]

I will never forget the first time I attended a classical concert, a performance of Beethoven during a high-school study-abroad year in Poland. It was my first experience of musical ecstasy, like Frodo's experience in Rivendell. I liked classical music before that, but I loved it afterwards.

Sometimes spoken words are not enough. They cannot capture the grandeur, the mystery, or the solemnity of the occasion. During the first Mass at the Last Supper, we see Jesus singing with his disciples (Mt 26:30). Likewise, in the Middle Ages, priests did not "say" the Mass, they "sung" it. Singing is bound up with the sacred, expressing through its melody the joy and mystery of an encounter with the living God.

Human beings are made to sing. Regular speech is not profound or beautiful enough to express certain emotions and beliefs. Music creates joy and solemnity by adding melody, rhythm, and harmony to speech, elongating it, adding more expression, and making it beautiful. Some of the ancients, particularly Pythagoras, viewed the uni-

8. J. R. R. Tolkien, *The Fellowship of the Ring* (New York: Ballantine Books, 2018), 261.

verse itself as ordered by a musical harmony. Dante would later deepen this understanding, speaking of the "love that moves the spheres." We sing because we love, and God has established a cosmic harmony that we can perceive and imitate in our own music. St. Augustine said that "he who sings prays twice," because we do not simply articulate words in our mind but express them outwardly in a beautiful way, praising God publicly and giving witness to our belief.

Christian singing grew out of the Jewish chanting of the book of Psalms, the great, inspired hymnody that captures the soul's longing, anguish, and love as it reaches out to God. We know that Christians continued this practice, for St. Paul writes: "be filled with the Spirit, addressing one another in psalms and hymns and spiritual songs, singing and making melody to the Lord with all your heart, always and for everything giving thanks in the name of our Lord Jesus Christ to God the Father" (Eph 5:18–20). Christians began the practice of singing the three canticles of Luke's Gospel (*Benedictus*, *Magnificat*, and *Nunc Dimittis*), and the New Testament shows evidence of hymns, such as the "Christ Hymn" in Philippians 2. A little more than a hundred years ago, an Egyptian papyrus was discovered from the third century with a hymn to the Trinity along with ancient musical notation, known as the Oxyrhynchus hymn. It was in Syria, however, that a whole system of Church music developed in the early centuries of the Church, with great hymn writers, such as St. Ephrem the Syrian. Another Syrian monk, St. Romanus the Melodist, had a mystical experience in which Our Lady imparted a musical gift to him, enabling him to write the great liturgical hymns of the Byzantine tradition.

St. Ambrose brought the Syrian tradition of singing hymns to the Church of Milan, and himself wrote many beautiful hymns, some of which are still used today. St. Augustine and Boethius both wrote treatises on music, explaining it as one discipline of the liberal arts, examining its mathematical qualities as number in time, which gives audible expression to beauty. St. Gregory the Great organized the chant of the Church of Rome, giving his name to Gregorian chant, a reform needed because in the early Church and Middle Ages the Mass was always sung to show its unique and beautiful mode of speech to God. The Benedictine monks further developed Christian chant, especially in the Carolingian Empire, under the patronage of Charlemagne and his successors, expressing their unceasing work of praise, in the *opus Dei* (work of God) of the Liturgy of the Hours. It was during this time that monks initiated important developments in the history of music, because they needed to be able to share melodies with other monasteries.

In the ninth century, monks added *metrum*, time value for notes. In the eleventh century, Guido of Arezzo wrote many works in which he developed staff notation and the musical scale, employing "ut–re–mi–fa–sol–la" as a scale of rising notes (from the first words of Vespers for the feast of the Birth of John the Baptist). Other developments included accentuation (*ad cantus*) by placing emphasis on the right syllable, up or down, first shown by neums. They also developed punctuation in pausing and dividing, indicated by a point (*punctus*), and *jubilus* in bringing pure music into the articulation of the words, elaborating on the singing of certain syllables (syllabization). Originally the monks sang a capella (literally, in the chapel) and in unison as they prayed the psalms and other liturgical prayers. In the ninth century, we see the beginning of a further elaboration in adding additional lines of music, initially just a second bass voice in a practice called "organum" (or diaphony), the beginnings of further harmonization.

For these reasons, it is absolutely certain that the Church laid the foundations for Western music and the whole classical tradition. We see further contributions in the oratorio, a sung dramatization of Scripture, the lives of the saints, or a moral play (from which opera emerged as a secular version). As polyphony (the singing of many voices) further developed, initially from the cathedral school of Notre Dame in Paris, greater rules were developed for the harmonization of the voices. Palestrina, one the great masters of the Catholic musical tradition, developed strict rules for counterpoint, the harmonization of notes, that contributed to the Baroque style of music and were studied by J. S. Bach. Many of the great masters of the classical age, such as Mozart and Haydn, wrote many symphonic Masses, motets, sung Passion narratives, and other devotionals, such as the *Stabat Mater*, showing the ongoing power of sacred music. Classical composers continue to compose symphonic Masses even today (see Andrew Lloyd Webber and Arvo Pärt).

The Church's tradition of Gregorian chant underwent a major renewal in the nineteenth century. The Benedictine monks of Solesmes Abbey began compiling manuscripts and restoring older methods. Pope St. Pius X drew from Solesmes's work to provide new liturgical books for the entire Church in the early twentieth century, asking each parish to embrace the practice of singing Gregorian chant once again. The work of Solesmes and St. Pius was affirmed strongly by the Second Vatican Council: "The Church acknowledges Gregorian chant as specially suited to the Roman liturgy: therefore, other things being equal, it should be given pride of place in liturgical services."[9] After the council, the opposite happened, however, with most parishes abandoning the Church's tradition of chant and embracing hymns that took their inspiration more from contemporary music and Broadway musicals. Mundane, overly upbeat, and emotional music during the liturgy contributes to a loss of the sense of the sacred. The Church has a powerfully transcendent, mysterious, and sacred tradition that can draw students into an encounter with God that is otherworldly and sublime.

Music plays a unique role in Catholic education by guiding our students in prayer. Joseph Ratzinger spoke of the ability of sacred music to lead us into an encounter with God: "The mystery of infinite beauty is there and enables us to experience the presence of

---

9. Second Vatican Council, *Sacrosanctum concilium*, 116.

God more truly and vividly than in many sermons."[10] Music also forms their sensibilities in attending to beauty and harmony. It contributes to the fostering of a contemplative disposition of listening in silence and attending to the details of the music. The Benedictine monk, Dom Jacques Hourlier, reflects on the spiritual power of music:

> Music uplifts the soul. If we respond with even the bare minimum of sensitivity and understanding, our hearts immediately gladden and open up, making us feel more authentically ourselves. At the same time we become aware that we are entering into another world. Our spirits, indeed our spiritual lives, are enriched. . . . Only then do we become fully aware of what the ultimate goal of music really is: a return to uncreated Beauty.[11]

Music can inform our spiritual life and draw us into the worship of God.

In order to have this spiritual effect, music must communicate a transcendent beauty shaped by the Church's prayer, which has the power to lift us up to God. Catholic education would be incomplete without an immersion into this great tradition of musical prayer. Catholics have some of the most profound treasures in human history in their legacy, and many of them are not being appreciated by our students. Music has a natural power—rooted physically in the power of vibration and frequency and intellectually in its mathematical arrangement—that has been beautifully harnessed by the Church in order to move the soul spiritually.

Music, along with other expressions of art, forms an essential part of a sacramental approach to education. No education is

---

10. Joseph Ratzinger, *The Spirit of the Liturgy* (San Francisco: Ignatius Press, 2000), 148.

11. Dom Jacques Hourlier, *Reflections on the Spirituality of Gregorian Chant* (Orleans, Mass.: Paraclete Press, 1995), chap. 6.

complete without an immersion into the beauty of art and culture, which communicate truth and goodness in a way at once more rooted and more transcendent than mere words. The inspiration and love that flow from beauty will lead the way in drawing our students into a life of faith. For ideas on what to teach for the great artistic and musical tradition of the Catholic Church, see the appendix, which offers "A Guide to Building Catholic Literacy."

# 11 Responding to Technology: A Contemplative and Benedictine Approach

We might view technology primarily through the lens of convenience or entertainment, but it bears extraordinary influence on education. The constant interaction with screens, in particular, changes the way we think—literally altering how we process information, making it harder to concentrate and read for long periods because our brains have become accustomed to scrolling and jumping from one thing to the next in quick succession. This shift in thinking and reading clearly impacts the effectiveness of education, and, from a spiritual point of view, follows us into the chapel, making it harder to attend in silence to God, meditating on Scripture and spiritual works and embracing stillness.

Technology, therefore, presents us with an anti-sacramental threat to education. Sacramentality roots the ideas of education in concrete embodiment within the life of the community. Screens offer greater abstraction, pulling the communication of information out of an interpersonal context and hands-on experience. It hinders attention to people and to the realities we study. This matters, because, as Simone Weil argues, attention comprises the very essence of both prayer and school studies, showing how they reinforce one another. While prayer turns our attention completely to God, she points to how this can flow from study, as "the development of the faculty of attention forms the real object and almost the sole interest of studies."[1] One comes to the truth by waiting upon it, turning our desire toward it, and experiencing joy in its discovery.

---

1. Weil, *Waiting for God*, 62.

Technology poses a threat to learning by circumventing attention. Nicholas Carr has perhaps documented this better than anyone else in his book, *The Shallows: What the Internet Is Doing to Our Brains*. He relates, "What the Net seems to be doing is chipping away my capacity for concentration and contemplation. Whether I'm online or not, my mind now expects to take in information the way the Net distributes it: in a swiftly moving stream of particles. Once I was a scuba diver in the sea of words. Now I zip along the surface like a guy on a Jet Ski."[2] There is no waiting, no carefully attuned desire, and, therefore, no joy in learning. For the renewal of Catholic education, the fostering of attention must rise consciously to the surface of our efforts, employing a more contemplative approach to learning.

## Our Technological Problem

A frightening trend emerged when I was working in Catholic school administration. The acceleration of problems related to sexuality for young children was startling, beginning even with kindergarten. There was one common source: technology. Without a doubt, young children regularly using smartphones are frequently exposed to sexual images and messages that have led them to question their sexual identity. After hearing of problems week after week, I wanted to shout an SOS to every parent, "Please, take away devices from your children, because they are really wounding them." Parents and educators surely must exercise greater vigilance.

This is not just the overreaction of one Catholic educator. Even Denver public schools offered a workshop I attended on "Teens and Screens," speaking of a public health emergency due to the impact of social media on the mental health of teenagers. Coming under increasing scrutiny, in 2023 TikTok recently placed a 60 minute per

---

2. Carr, *The Shallows*, 7.

day limit on usage for those under 18 (although they can continue after entering a passcode). The Centers for Disease Control (CDC) found that nearly 60 percent of teen girls struggle with depression, and almost a third have considered suicide.[3] As technology use has increased each year, mental health difficulties have increased as well, with the introduction of the smartphone in 2012 as a turning point for the mental health crisis of youth.[4]

We cannot keep our heads in the sand while this major crisis unfolds. Young people are experiencing an identity crisis, inflamed by ideological forces using social media and entertainment to call their sexual identity in question at young ages. In a diocesan Catholic schools office, we had reports of kindergartners and first graders imitating inappropriate acts they had seen on screens. We heard from a third grader that she identified as asexual after she was groomed by an adult through an iPad, given to her by her parents. We often heard of bullying and sexting occurring over phones, even for elementary school students. These are the cases that make me repeat, "Parents, do not give your kids smartphones. Please take them away!"

As a father of six, including three teenagers, I try to be very vigilant. We use Gab phones and Light phones for our teenagers that prevent any direct Internet access. Our younger children have never needed a phone. In Catholic schools, we often had to remind parents that they could always call their children at school and their children would always be allowed to call them if there was a need. In their desire to protect their children by having constant access to them through a phone, parents are inadvertently harming them by giving them this constant exposure to negative influences on the web and

---

3. Centers for Disease Control, "Youth Risk Behavior Survey Data Summary & Trends Report: 2011–2021," https://www.cdc.gov/healthyyouth/data/yrbs/pdf/YRBS_Data-Summary-Trends_Report2023_508.pdf.
4. Ben Lovejoy, "Teen Girls' Mental Health Has Proven Link to Social Media Usage," February 23, 2023, *9TO5Mac*, https://9to5mac.com/2023/02/23/teen-girls-mental-health/.

social media. We have traded too much for the conveniences of its apps: namely peace of mind and space for others, including God! Change must begin with adults, because it is hard to protect our children if we are not protecting ourselves! We must regain the will-power to prioritize people before convenience.

The more normal the saturation of technology becomes the harder it will be to change. Jean Twenge's book *iGen: Why Today's Super-Connected Kids Are Growing Up Less Rebellious, More Tolerant, Less Happy—and Completely Unprepared for Adulthood* relates how the iGen, born between 1995 and 2009, marks a monument shift in development, growing up taking the Internet and social media for granted as an everyday experience. She reflects upon the individualism that has arisen in this generation based on how they spend their time in relation to technology:

> They socialize in completely new ways, reject once sacred taboos, and want different things from their lives and careers. They are obsessed with safety and fearful of their economic futures, and they have no patience for inequality based on gender, race, or sexual orientation. They are at the forefront of the worst mental health crisis in decades. . . . iGen'ers are growing up more slowly. . . . Teens are physically safer than ever, yet they are more mentally vulnerable.[5]

Parents should not remain passive before the great changes in child behavior shaped by technology. They can exercise loving control over how their children develop by encouraging them to rediscover person-to-person relationships, exercise discipline in using technology and in other areas, and by inspiring them to experience and cherish what is most important: a life rooted in truth, goodness, and beauty.

---

5. Jean Twenge, *iGen: Why Today's Super-Connected Kids Are Growing Up Less Rebellious, More Tolerant, Less Happy—and Completely Unprepared for Adulthood* (New York: Atria, 2017), 3.

## A Moral and Educational Emergency

When I voice concerns about technology, I often hear people respond emphatically that technology is neutral—simply a tool that can be used for good or ill. That may be true to an extent, but the invention of a tool and its systematic application are not neutral endeavors. The tool conditions its own use, shaping or enabling a particular action. More significantly, all things created by God have an intrinsic ordering toward him as their Origin and End—their purpose and goal. Human creations do not contain that same intrinsic ordering to God. A tree always bears the mark of its Creator and finds its purpose in glorifying him. We cannot say the same of a refrigerator, which was created for a limited and more utilitarian purpose. Technology depends upon human intentionality for its ordering and purpose. Unless we order it properly, it can easily disrupt the natural ordering of our lives to our true end.

Ultimately, technology is not neutral because its use requires human action, which itself is never neutral. If an action is freely chosen using our faculty of reason, then it must be good or evil based on the nature of the action. Aquinas relates this in the *Summa theologiae*: "Human action, which is called moral, takes its species from the object, in relation to the principle of human actions, which is the reason. Wherefore if the object of an action includes something in accord with the order of reason, it will be a good action according to its species" (I-II, q. 18, a. 8). Morally speaking, the use of technology constitutes a free choice, with its own particular object, intention, and circumstances, which render this choice either moral or immoral. When we use technology, we must ask: "What am I choosing to do, why, and in what way?" The object of an action employing technology would be determined generally by the nature of the technology itself. I conform to it by choosing to perform the action enabled by the tool, for the purpose I intend. The claim that technology is intrinsically neutral, or morally indifferent, can be used as an excuse which creates passivity. This allows technology to determine our action, rather than approaching it with clear deliberation and ordering it to its proper end: the true good of human life, which in turn is directed toward the glory of God. Technology is not good unless we use it well.

Furthermore, the Church teaches that technology is not neutral. In relation to biomedical technology, in particular, the Congregation for the Doctrine of the Faith asserted,

> It would on the one hand be illusory to claim that scientific research and its applications are morally neutral; on the other hand one cannot derive criteria for guidance from mere technical efficiency, from research's possible usefulness to some at the expense of others, or, worse still, from prevailing ideologies. Thus science and technology require, for their own intrinsic meaning, an unconditional respect for the fundamental criteria of the moral law: that is to say, they must be at the service of the human person, of his inalienable rights and his true and integral good according to the design and will of God.[6]

Pope Francis strongly repeated this principle: "We have to accept that technological products are not neutral, for they create a framework which ends up conditioning lifestyles and shaping social possibilities along the lines dictated by the interests of certain powerful groups. Decisions which may seem purely instrumental are in reality decisions about the kind of society we want to build."[7] Francis's insight reaches further to the use of technology to shape and control human behavior.

---

6. Congregation for the Doctrine of the Faith, *Donum vitae*, "Instruction on Respect for Human Life" (1987), 2, https://www.vatican.va/roman_curia/congre gations/cfaith/documents/rc_con_cfaith_doc_19870222_respect-for-human-life_en.html.

7. Pope Francis, encyclical letter *Laudato Si'*, "On Care for Our Common Home" (2015), 107, https://www.vatican.va/content/francesco/en/encyclicals/documents/papa-francesco_20150524_enciclica-laudato-si.html.

We have moved beyond the realm of technology as a tool. It forms an artificial environment and its use draws us into a web (if you will) of possibilities, conditions, demands, and restraints. It also subordinates us to a network of political, social, and economic controls and influences of large and increasingly domineering groups. To use technology rightly, in a human fashion, it must become a tool once again. We must withdraw ourselves from the technology that would make us into a tool of the new technocratic paradigm of an inhuman culture.

This requires limiting how much we make use of technology so as to create space for silence and relationships. It also means that we must make deliberate choices on when and how to use technology rather than become passive to its pervasive influence. We have to unplug—at least somewhat—or face the consequences of a negative, not neutral, technocracy over our thoughts, emotions, and life. Carr's follow-up book to *The Shallows*, titled *The Glass Cage: Automation and Us*, reflects on the unintended consequences of a digital culture. When we become overly reliant on technology, not only in our work but also in our personal life, we become less alert and attentive, less thoughtful and interactive with the world around us. After examining the effects of automation on aviation and medicine, among other things, he turns to agriculture at the conclusion of his work. Carr contrasts manual labor with an overreliance on technology. "Labor," he says, is "a way of seeing the world face-to-face rather than through a glass. Action un-mediates perception, gets us close to the thing itself. It binds us to the earth."[8] Contrast that with "the digital technologies of automation," which "pull us away from the world. That's a consequence not only of the prevailing technology-centered design practices that place ease and efficiency above all other concerns. It also reflects the fact that, in our personal lives, the computer has

---

8. Nicholas Carr, *The Glass Cage: Automation and Us* (New York: Random House, 2015), 213–14.

become a media device, its software painstakingly programmed to grab and hold our attention."[9] In anti-sacramental fashion, technology disengages us from others as well as our natural and cultural environment.

In our educational mission, the challenge of technology points us back to the need to foster attention in the middle of this distraction saturation. Pope Benedict XVI calls us to address this as an educational emergency, finding more human ways of communicating:

> Today many young people, stunned by the infinite possibilities offered by computer networks or by other forms of technology, establish methods of communication that do not contribute to their growth in humanity. Rather they risk increasing their sense of loneliness and disorientation. In the face of these phenomena, I have spoken on various occasions of an educational emergency, a challenge to which one can and should respond with creative intelligence, committing oneself to promote a humanizing communication which stimulates a critical eye and the capacity to evaluate and discern.[10]

Technology can and should serve our well-being, but many times it does just the opposite, by isolating us and drawing us into an artificial experience. Pope Benedict thinks education can respond by teaching young people how to use technology in a human way. We need to teach them how to preserve the legacy of our culture and to creatively and dynamically continue it today, with all of the opportunities and challenges that have been presented to us.

---

9. Carr, 219.
10. Benedict XVI, Address to Participants in the Plenary Assembly of the Pontifical Council for Culture, November 13, 2010, https://www.vatican.va/content/benedict-xvi/en/speeches/2010/november/documents/hf_ben-xvi_spe_2010 1113_pc-cultura.html.

## Cultivating Freedom from Technological Dominance

Catholic education entails handing down a way of thinking and living within the community of the Church. This requires a certain level of literacy of the Catholic tradition, as well as formation of practices and habits that root us within the community. We could say that the Catholic tradition and communion continue to live in the world through the members of the Body of Christ. It is through their faith, their love, and their life that it continues from one generation to the next. When a breakdown in transmission occurs, the community itself faces a life-and-death crisis. It is no exaggeration to suggest that technology poses just such a disruption of the traditional modes of education, offering a seemingly more compelling source of information and values for young people.

Examining this crisis from a different perspective, Carr recognizes a breakdown in the transmission of culture as a whole in the outsourcing of thought and practices to devices. "Culture is sustained in our synapses," he relates. "It's more than what can be reduced to binary code and uploaded onto the Net. To remain vital, culture must be renewed in the minds of the members of every generation. Outsource memory, and culture withers."[11] There are things we can do, however, to reverse this trend, offering a more contemplative experience of life, found in unplugging, attending to reality, and embracing the silence of prayer. Once again, from a more secular perspective, Carr points to a stronger immersion in the reality of nature over and against our artificial world: "A series of psychological studies over the past twenty years has revealed that after spending time in a quiet rural setting, close to nature, people exhibit greater attentiveness, stronger memory, and generally improved cognition. Their brains become both calmer and sharper."[12] Unplugging from a technology-saturated world elevates our mental, and one must

---

11. Carr, *Shallows*, 197.
12. Carr, 219.

surmise, spiritual life. Our students need to find such calmness and sharpness in their lives.

Grace builds upon nature, according to the scholastic adage. By "nature," we mean the natural foundation of human life—our ability to think, make free choices, and order our lives through good habits. Even more foundationally, nature refers to the basic soil of human potential that God uses to draw forth his divine fruit. But how would we describe the "state of nature" today? It is not a stretch to say that the soil of human life has worn thin through the saturation of technology and a fundamental change in the way we understand and relate to one another, mediated by a screen with less interpersonal contact.

Just as grace builds upon nature, so faith builds upon culture. In fact, Pope St. John Paul II declared faith to be "incomplete" without a culture that enables one to live it out faithfully.[13] Culture is a shared way of life, one that is necessary because Christians need to live out their faith in communion with others. As we know from our own experience, it can be quite difficult to live the Christian life when swimming against the cultural currents. Perhaps our religious education has fallen short because we have not attended closely enough to the cultural dynamics of faith. Right thinking, healthy living, rightly ordered work, and robust community all contribute to building the soil needed to support the Christian life.

Education can no longer presuppose sufficient natural and cultural soil to understand and receive the faith fully. In our efforts to evangelize, we will have to humanize at the same time as as we Christianize. Because grace builds upon nature, we now must help those we catechize to rediscover nature—their own identity as made in the image and likeness of God and how the beauty of the world itself points to its source. Learning from God's creation and listening to how it points to the Creator provide an important foundation for

---

13. See John Paul II, Address to Plenary Assembly of the Pontifical Council for Culture.

the Gospel. Pope Francis, in *Laudato Si'*, acknowledges that a barrier has arisen from our culture's lack of organic contact with nature: "We were not meant to be inundated by cement, asphalt, glass and metal, and deprived of physical contact with nature" (44). We can learn from approaches to evangelization and catechesis that engage nature, as seen in ministries such as Creatio, COR Expeditions, JPII Outdoor Lab, and Camp Wojtyla, all of which are based in the Rocky Mountains.[14] Could schools provide youth and families with outdoor experiences of the beauty of God's creation as a better setting for evangelization?

If we were not meant to be inundated by concrete, we were also not meant to be saturated by a constant barrage of manufactured, artificial images and sounds. This unceasing distraction makes it difficult to concentrate and think deeply, creating another obstacle for the message of catechesis. How much harder has it become for students to sit alone for extended periods of silence in prayer? Furthermore, ideas contrary to the Gospel flow into the imagination through media, forming a largely undetected but persuasive resistance to the Christian life. Teaching silence and providing opportunities to unplug may be difficult, but doing so would till the soil of the soul by creating more opportunities for God to speak and act. Forming the imagination with good images and sounds promotes a right order and harmony in the mind.

Faith needs to be put into practice to shape how we live. An often overlooked complement to instruction, work provides a needed outward expression for students to engage their desire to make and to serve. Integrating work with education will help overcome the secular divide that keeps faith from influencing daily life. This work can consist in service, with projects around the school and parish or for those in need. Common effort creates stronger

---

14. See their websites at https://creatio.org, https://www.corexpeditions.org/, https://annunciationheights.org/outdoor-lab, and https://www.camp-w.com.

bonds of friendship and community and starts to put faith in action. Setting aside time for hard work would also present opportunities to engage with nature, spend time away from technology, exercise creativity, and build stronger relationships.

## Teaching Silence

Recovering stronger relationships and attention to the realities of nature, culture, and faith will require sacrifice, giving up some of the conveniences of technology. Almost no one would willingly give up a smartphone or return to our pre-wifi days, even though we are beginning to feel unsettled in our new digital landscape. We want peace and quiet, even as we are addicted to our devices. In fact, our tools increasingly govern our life. We cannot drive anywhere without them. They now manage our houses and information. We constantly receive new alerts and notifications. Everything is at the tip of a finger—everything except peace.

Even young people who have grown up in this saturation are looking for something else. For instance, *TIME Magazine* featured Professor Constance Kassor for running Lawrence University's most popular class: "Doing Nothing." This is how she describes the course:

> One of the things that we really want students to get out of this class is that we want them to have a space where they can be fully themselves, where they can be present—not just physically, but also mentally and emotionally. Because I think this is kind of anti-thetical to what's being asked of them a lot of the time. It's really designed as a way to give students the space to slow down a little bit. . . . And that'll make them better people, more empathetic people, more creative people, deeper thinkers.[15]

---

15. Katie Reilly, "This Professor Teaches a Class on 'Doing Nothing.' It's the Most Popular One on Campus," *TIME*, October 5, 2022, https://time.com/6219696/doing-nothing-college-class/.

The class's success points to something that we have lost in education and life more broadly.

Even as technology dominates the day for so many young people, some are looking for something more. For example, a group of high schoolers formed what they called a Luddite Club, describing the liberation that comes with abandoning a smartphone: "We've all got this theory that we're not just meant to be confined to buildings and work.... [but] experiencing life. Real life. Social media and phones are not real life." One student, Lola, reported on giving up her smartphone: "I started using my brain. It made me observe myself as a person."[16] We can no longer take such simple things for granted. These high schoolers, even though a minority, have realized something necessary in guarding our humanity against too much noise and the intrusion of technology.

Rather than taking a course on doing nothing, Catholics have ready answers to the domination of technology. We do not seek silence for its own sake (even if that is a start), but as an opportunity to encounter God. Cardinal Robert Sarah's important book, *The Power of Silence*, teaches us that silence is the language of God, which we need in order to learn to converse with him:

> At the heart of man there is an innate silence, for God abides in the innermost part of every person. God is silence, and this divine silence dwells in man. In God, we are inseparably bound up with silence.... God carries us, and we live with him at every moment by keeping silence. Nothing will make us discover God better than his silence inscribed in the center of our being. If we do not cultivate this silence how can we find God?[17]

---

16. Avery Hartmans, "Why Teens Are Giving Up Their Smartphones and Joining the 'Luddite Club,'" *Insider*, October 24, 2022, https://www.businessinsider.com/teens-ditching-smartphones-social-media-to-become-luddites-2022-10?op=1.
17. Robert Cardinal Sarah, *The Power of Silence: Against the Dictatorship of Noise* (San Francisco: Ignatius Press, 2017), 22.

We have to learn the practice of silence, although it will not come from a course as much as time spent before the Blessed Sacrament.

Students will balk at silence initially. It must be cultivated through practice, helping them to enter into a greater peace over time. At first, the mind wanders, the body fidgets, and, in extreme cases, panic sets in. After a couple of weeks, however, the mind and body calm down, and can begin learning how to focus on God and to listen to his voice. Even young children can learn this through regular times of silence. It does entail a battle, but one worth fighting. Cardinal Sarah explains that, "Noise is a deceptive, addictive, and false tranquilizer. The tragedy of our world is never better summed up than in the fury of senseless noise that stubbornly hates silence. This age detests the things that silence brings us to: encounter, wonder, and kneeling before God."[18] Noise or silence—frenetic activity or leisure—this choice will shape the state of our soul.

Silence may save our souls because it will enable us to pull back from the craziness of life, gain peace, become reflective, and make space for God. We may realize that we need it but do not want to accept it because the sacrifice of time and convenience that comes from putting down technology may be painful. If we are overwhelmed by the noise of life, it is possible to find healing and peace. God can repair the damage of modern culture within us, but we need to turn to him ardently in prayer. This healing may come to us most fully in the silence of adoration and the encounter with Christ the healer in confession. There he gives us his peace and makes us new once again. He can help us to overcome our dread of silence by making us whole with his saving presence.

---

18. Sarah, 56.

## Creating Space for Contemplation: A Benedictine Approach

In seeking greater attention for God and studies, the Catholic tradition has a model tradition, the Benedictines, who St. John Henry Newman called "poetic" for their concrete contemplation of the everyday realities of nature and grace. St. Benedict specifically dubbed the monastery a place dedicated to leisure: "a school of the Lord's service" (*dominici scola servitii*). The word "school" itself indicates a place of leisure (*skole* means "leisure" in Greek), precisely the kind of escape from the normal world of drudgery that grinds the person down and leaves little time for contemplation. The monks created a school to learn the Christian life, not simply in a theoretical way—even though the monks did study and create schools for outside pupils—but to learn how to live a life dedicated to Christ, the true teacher.

Benedictine monasteries model Christian culture in their integration of prayer, work, and study. Educators always squabble about the goal of education, whether it is theoretical or practical, but the monks cut through this argument by showing how the two aspects of life necessarily relate. The monks dedicate their lives to the work of God, the *opus Dei* of daily prayer, but they must also eat, be clothed, and have shelter. The monks, therefore, also work as an extension of their primary *opus*, sanctifying the world itself through their labor. As Pieper explained about the relationship of work and leisure, we work so as to be able to create the conditions to enter into higher things. We must care for the body and its needs, serve our family and society, and enjoy the rest that comes from accomplishing these goals. Pieper locates worship as the highest act of leisure as we stop our mundane tasks and engage in public ceremony to praise and thank God and affirm the goodness of the life he has given us.[19] We can also understand personal prayer as an expression of the leisure needed for contemplation.

---

19. Pieper, *Leisure the Basis of Culture*, 65ff.

The monastery aims to draw its monks into contemplation, as the school can do for its students. This is not simply the meditation that arises from our own efforts to think about the realities of faith. Contemplation comes from fixing the attention on God in love, allowing him to transport us into the divine realities of our faith. Contemplation is the goal of both the Christian life and Catholic education because through it we come into communion with what we study. By fostering attention and forming desire, study should dispose us toward contemplation, removing the obstacles that keep us from this union. Aquinas recognizes how contemplative prayer lifts us above our common distractions, if only briefly before we are pulled back again: "The human mind is unable to remain aloft for long on account of the weakness of nature, because human weakness weighs down the soul to the level of inferior things: and hence it is that when, while praying, the mind ascends to God by contemplation, of a sudden it wanders off through weakness."[20] In both ways—public worship and private prayer—we see how leisure enables us to pause from the mundane course of things to participate in higher realities. Work done well enables us to devote time to the most important things, the things of truth, beauty, and goodness.

Education is an expression of leisure, and the monasteries model how leisure immerses us into the highest goods. Students, like monks, have been given time to pursue goods that often get squeezed out of the busyness of life. In school, students have the freedom to immerse themselves in truth, goodness, and beauty. We have to make use of this leisure so that it is not wasted simply on the practical things that will be picked up in the world. Pope Benedict XVI noted that our use of time should not be directionless, but truly focused on encountering the Lord: "Leisure time is something good and necessary, especially amid the mad rush of the modern world; each of us knows this. Yet if leisure time lacks an inner focus,

---

20. Thomas Aquinas, *Summa theologiae*, II-II, q. 83, a. 13, ad 2.

an overall sense of direction, then ultimately it becomes wasted time that neither strengthens nor builds us up. Leisure time requires a focus—the encounter with him who is our origin and goal."[21] Students often view school as a waste of time, even as if it were a prison. Instead, more like a monastery, they need rightly ordered leisure to give purpose to their study and to make space for God in prayer.

Imitating the monastery, the school can teach an entire way of life that is modeled by the daily rhythm of the community. As faith continues to decline, it could be tempting to insist simply upon teaching more doctrine, but this would overlook a more fundamental problem. What is education really about? It is not simply about knowledge of the faith, but knowledge of the living God, a knowledge that includes and goes beyond information, as it must reach to a complete transformation of life. We are not simply missing knowledge of the faith but the entire structure of life and culture that should undergird and support this knowledge.

A Benedictine approach to education can help us to attend to both soul and body with its fusion of *ora et labora*. It models how we must keep firmly rooted in the reality of our nature in order to be elevated to what is highest. John Senior's teaching inspired many Benedictine vocations because he recognized the power of the poetic and holistic experience within the monastery: "Senior had found a deep and healthy Realism in Benedictine life, rooted in the soil and pointing to the stars."[22] The Benedictines embody the sacramental mission of education by sustaining a life of contemplation in the concrete embodiment of the work needed to uphold community life. One need not be a monk to appreciate and enter into a more contemplative approach to education, rooted in daily prayer, silence, the

---

21. Benedict XVI, homily, September 9, 2007, https://www.vatican.va/content/benedict-xvi/en/homilies/2007/documents/hf_ben-xvi_hom_20070909_wien.html.
22. Bethel, *John Senior*, 79.

engagement of the body, the discipline of community, and the search for God in contemplation.

In what follows, I will provide ten ways in which the Benedictine tradition can inspire renewal in Catholic schools.

### Ora: The Inner Center of the Monastery and School

1. *Liturgy.* The monastery becomes a school of the Lord's service primarily through the liturgy. Liturgy offers the greatest expression of leisure, and leisure is what makes a school a school through its time devoted to the most important things. Monks dedicate their lives to learning how to live in the highest sense, and students have a gift of many years to do the same. Monks order their lives to what is highest, and Catholic education is successful when students learn to live for God. The Eucharist is the heart of the school, because it is the moment of encounter with the *Logos* who made the world and who invites us to be his disciples.

2. *Contemplation.* Pope Benedict XVI said that more than anything else monks are marked by the great *quaerere Deum*, the search for God. They center their life on contemplation, studying the Scriptures and praying through them in *lectio divina*, an important practice for our students to learn. A contemplative approach to education does not simply strive to gain knowledge but to seek God, who teaches us how to approach the whole of things and fit them together in him. We cannot truly understand ourselves and the world without coming to know him. The monks show us how to attend him in silence, to receive the truth from him. "Study" comes from the Latin word for effort and zeal, and the monks' dedication models the effort of waiting upon the truth in loving patience.

3. *Prayer.* The monks demonstrate how prayer and learning are connected. They do not learn out of curiosity, which is a vice identified by St. Thomas Aquinas. Distraction is another way of describing this vice, when the mind jumps from thing to thing and goes after information it does not need. Study forms discipline and focus.

Just as the monks devote their lives to the great effort of prayer throughout the day and even in the night, so coming to know the truth entails an ordered effort of attention. The mind's ability to know the truth will expand through the development of intellectual virtues, inflamed by the love of prayer.

4. *Words*. Monks focus on the Word, seeking him in contemplation but also through their attention to the meaning of words. Through the centuries they have toiled at mastery of grammar, logic, and rhetoric in order to approach God's revelation with greatly clarity and understanding. This is why monks formed libraries and preserved ancient, pagan literature, which they used to master facility with language. The monks need books for their life, because it stimulates their contemplation of the faith, and their mastery of language provides a model for students who employ this mastery in all of their subjects.

5. *Interior Order*. The dispositions of the monastic life model the virtues of the students. Students, like monks, need stability, constant growth (called conversion of life by the Benedictines), humility to learn, obedience to the truth, and direction by a guide and mentor. The Benedictines strive for a life ordered to the truth and should inspire us to seek the truth not just with the mind but with the heart. If a life becomes disordered morally, this will darken the mind as well. We need to give our lives over to the truth to be transformed by it.

### *Labora: Exterior Expression in the Community*

6. *Culture*. We find in the monastery a complete culture, where we can see how the major elements of the Christian life fit together as a whole. A community becomes rightly ordered when it is built around the proper ordering of the soul in relation to God. Christian culture seeks to embody exteriorly what has been received from Christ through the grace of the sacraments. Christian culture orders life through faith and the good habits that flow from it.

7. *Work*. The monks teach us that work has an important role in the Christian vocation. Catholic schools may focus on the highest things, but they also inspire vocations in the world, forming graduates who are willing to sacrifice to enact what they have received in formation. The work of God, the *opus Dei*, informs all the work that is done by the Christian, who ideally will merge all work into one, doing all for God's glory. Through work, the Christian changes the world, drawing out its potential and ordering it to God.

8. *The Arts*. The monastery builds up the arts to attune the mind to divine realities. This is part of the Benedictine attention to the body and the poetic, which recognizes that an outward expression of faith is needed for human life. The monks laid the foundation for the whole Western musical tradition through their development of liturgical chant. The monastery forms the soul through the beauty of its chanted prayer, and adorns the chapel with a dignity to match their vocation in seeking God. The Benedictine life fosters wonder in the mystery of God's presence and engages all of the senses in its prayer and work.

9. *Memory*. The monastery is a place of preservation for culture and learning, as we have seen throughout history. Therefore, the monastery fosters memory of who we are and how we continue the great search of human history. We have received a great legacy of Christian culture, which the monks painstakingly have preserved and continue to pass on. The monks model for teachers and students how to remember as a channel for the tradition that will bring about a new springtime of Christian culture.

10. *Hospitality*. Finally, the monastery is a place of hospitality. Many secular people visit them because they find in them an oasis of peace and tradition in a barbaric age. Should not our schools offer the same sense of relief and security? St. Benedict says that all must be received at the monastery as Christ himself. The school too should serve as a sign of Christian love to all students, families, parishioners, and visitors. They can become centers of culture to

begin rebuilding, fostering relationships, support, and inspiration for parishes and families.

The ultimate answer to the problem of technology cannot be found in simple avoidance alone. Its lure will remain too strong if nothing counters its influence. The Benedictine tradition points us in a more positive direction. We must live for God bolstered by the concrete life of a community expressed in daily routines of prayer and work. We must counter the abstraction of technology with a sacramental approach that prioritizes people, the reality of creation, and an embodiment of the truths we learn within education.

# 12 Sacrifice for Community:
## How the Vision Takes Flesh

It is one thing to wax eloquently about the tradition of Catholic education and another to do something about it. American Catholics built up the largest parochial school and Catholic university system in the world. And then, in the last five decades, it largely became secular. More recently, we have seen another great expansion within Catholic education, largely led by the laity, working to reform Catholic institutions and to found new ones when necessary. Change is possible, so long as we have courage and are willing to put forth the effort to accomplish it.

The words "reform" and "renewal" both point to a preexisting reality that needs to be brought back to its true form or made new again. We have received the mission of Catholic education from Jesus himself. The Church has perfected her pedagogy through the centuries. We have been experimenting with modern methods, with mixed results. We do not have to reject anything of value out of hand, but we do need a deep evaluation through the lens of faith. Renewal is not simply taking material from the past and bringing it into the present. It is more personal than that. We need people to allow themselves to be enriched by the great tradition, to synthesize its fruit with our contemporary possibilities, and to take up the great work of Catholic education today.

A sacramental approach to education prioritizes the concrete embodiment of our beliefs. This includes prioritizing the life of the community, which becomes the means for receiving and living out the great tradition we inherit from the Church. We must avoid abstraction here as well, as a school does not exist as an institution apart from people. The school community comes alive through the faith and charity of the people called to the work of that particular place. They are the ones who must realize the mission of Catholic education for a particular parish and region. The personal realization of our renewal efforts will bear fruit in discovering the great vocation to teach, stepping forward to lead, and making necessary changes, both within schools and also dioceses. The work of renewal happens within the faithful, who then shape institutions in accord with the Lord's truth and grace, as well as the great legacy of our tradition.

## The Vocation to Teach

The Lord has gifted me with many wonderful opportunities in my life: great schools where I have studied and taught, impactful teachers, study abroad experiences, rewarding friendships, and a prolific writing career. When I look back over the past two decades, however, one thing stands out: my students. I am humbled by their profound influence over me, becoming some of my closest friends and collaborators. Many have gone on to teach and found successful apostolates of their own. Teaching entails a shared pursuit of the good, linking students and teachers together in one of the highest and most significant of human actions. I cannot think of a better apologetic for teaching than my own gratitude to my teachers, who set me on my course, and for my students, who embraced a common vision and purpose in education.

When I am asked about the most important priority for renewal, my answer is clear and emphatic: teachers. Even with a great leader and curriculum, a school will be only as good as its teachers, because they are the ones who unfold the mission of the school. They spend the most time with students, making them the ones who can most substantially pass on the school's spiritual mission and educational vision. They should embody the educational philosophy of the school and model its fruits for the student. John Senior called the school "a faculty of friends,"[1] and the culture of the school will be built around not only the competence of teachers, but also their shared commitment to the school's mission, which becomes enacted in their lives and the community of the school that they form through their shared work.

And yet, we now face a serious teacher shortage. Many young people ask why they should teach when many seemingly better options abound. It certainly is true that being a teacher will not prove lucrative and, in fact, requires much hard work. On the other hand, it is important work, and rewarding as well. I often wonder why we generally would say that we value education highly and yet are not willing to reward it. What is more impactful for the future of our country: trading stocks on Wall Street or teaching second grade at St. Mary's parochial school? You often hear of a teacher changing a student's life. The renewal of Catholic education requires the next generation of young people to grasp its transforming mission and to commit to it.

Teaching is not the best path for anyone whose primary intention consists in getting ahead in life. Rather than a job, teaching is a vocation, one imbued with spiritual significance. Jesus told his disciples to make disciples, a word that means "students," and to teach them (see Matthew 28). Education stands at the center of the Church's mission to form followers of Jesus Christ. Nonetheless, we often reduce education to utilitarian means. We expect teachers to sacrifice their own career potential in order to help their students prepare for college and find high paying jobs. No wonder we need more teachers. Perhaps we are missing the real purpose of education.

Why do we spend so much time in school? Is it simply to pick up useful skills for the future? We have heard, or possibly even

---

1. Quoted in Bishop James Conley, "Friendship: A Pillar of Catholic Education," *Crisis Magazine*, February 19, 2016, https://crisismagazine.com/opinion/friendship-a-pillar-of-catholic-education.

repeated, the common complaint of students, "I will never use this again." Education is not simply a matter of skills, because human beings have to learn how to be human. Unlike animals, who just know what to do through instinct, as free rational beings we have to shape our minds and freedom, discovering what is good and dedicating our lives to realizing it. Work is one part of our lives, but education more broadly helps students to learn how to think, what they should value, how to form their character, and to discover their own vocation.

Looked at from that perspective, the vocation of teaching takes on much more significance. If we really understand education in this way, we can see why it is worth the sacrifice and comprises a more important profession than almost anything else. It makes an investment in the very souls of our children, and the future of the Church and our society depends fundamentally on its success. The call to teach should be received as a great gift, which, like any vocation, requires sacrifice. Moreover, the benefits are immense. To teach means to be dedicated to the truth, to seek it, and to share it with others. What a privilege! More than any method or curriculum, teaching constitutes a shared pursuit of the truth, no matter the topic; and the search enriches the soul of teacher and student alike.

Teachers may envy their friends in business, who do not have the same concerns about covering bills and getting their children through Catholic school. It can be easy to second guess oneself. The practical difficulties, however, can be offset by the joys of leisure. The teaching vocation enables leisure by focusing on reading, thinking, and discussing with colleagues and students. Of course, this life devoted to leisure is still full of the "busyness" of lesson plans and grading, which accompany the joy of leading students into what matters most. This leisure—a life dedicated to truth—reflects a higher road, a choice for "the better part" as a kind of spiritual investment. At the moment of death, when money no longer matters, when all of our comforts and pleasures have passed, what will bring us comfort? Now is the time to invest in what is most important and what will endure. Sacrificing a materially rewarding career requires faith, believing that the eternal benefits will outweigh the competing offers of this world.

The Lord hopes that we will respond to his call. And we, for our part, want to hear him say, "Well done, good and faithful servant" (Mt 25:21). He has made an investment in us and wants a return, making good use of the gift of our life and the talents we have received to spread his kingdom. In our individualistic culture, we do not tend to think about work in terms of this kind of stewardship. Only in heaven can we truly see, with the audience of God and our friends, the fruit of the seed that has been tilled in the souls of our students. With this goal in mind, it is much harder to turn down St. Thomas More's excellent advice, given to Richard Rich in *A Man for All Seasons*: "Why not be a teacher?"

## Leadership for Renewal

Although teachers enact the mission of Catholic education in the classroom, the renewal of schools certainly requires strong leadership. Most fundamentally, transformative leadership flows from conviction about the nature of Catholic education and the ability to guide communities in embracing a vision for renewal within that distinctive identity. Proverbs tells us that "without a vision, the people perish" (Prv 29:18). The future growth and survival of Catholic education depend upon a strong articulation of a vision of renewal within the Church's unique approach to education. This vision must be communicated to the broader community in a compelling way, and formation must be offered to all members of the community within it.

What does it mean to be a leader? In general, a leader unites people in working together to achieve a common goal and provides practical support to accomplish it. This definition applies to anyone, although, from a Christian perspective, we possess a supernatural vision to evaluate the true purpose and success of leadership. It is not enough merely to oversee the exterior functioning of the school, as Catholic leadership fulfills a mandate given from above.

The leader acts as steward of this mission. We cannot judge success simply based on exterior elements such as enrollment and fundraising, because the mission of the school is spiritual: to form disciples and to teach them everything that the Lord has commanded (cf. Matthew 28). The school arises not simply from a need for education on a practical or societal level. The Church runs schools to form the person in a way much deeper than a secular approach can do. A leader must take a sacramental approach, allowing the very purpose of Catholic education in its interior mission to shape and guide the necessary exterior elements that instantiate it.

Not everyone can lead. It requires a certain competency, as well as conviction. Christian leadership cannot be reduced to bureaucratic effectiveness because it must flow from a genuine vocation of service. There is a calling from God to enter school leadership, to which one must respond in prayer. Christian leadership also requires virtue, as it entails guiding others in a spiritual mission. First and foremost, Christian leadership flows from the theological virtues, which provide a supernatural vision in faith, confidence in God's help through hope, and a focus on others before self in charity. The theological virtues direct leadership toward God and others, rather than toward any egoism and careerism. Christian leadership also flows from the human virtues of prudence, justice, courage, and temperance, which shape character toward the good.

Vocation and virtue, however, must be followed by skill, knowing how to do the work of school leadership effectively. Faith cannot compensate for mediocrity. Vocation, conviction, and character need competency to bring the mission to life in a school. What are the skills and formation needed to be a Catholic school leader? Leading a school requires understanding the nature of education, the Church's own educational tradition, knowledge of effective curriculum and instruction, the ability to offer teachers coaching and mentoring, effective communication skills, competency in balancing a budget, and technological know-how. Leading a school requires a broad skill set, combined with much patience and charity.

Leadership focuses on one thing more than any other: helping others to fulfill their role within the community. The school's mission largely unfolds in the classroom through the work of the teacher. The effective administrator must recruit the proper candidate to make this mission come alive for the students. Teachers also must balance interior dispositions and exterior skills, and the principal must mentor them in developing both aspects of their vocation. Like a shepherd, the Catholic school leader knows his or her flock well, establishes a rapport with each teacher, and spends time offering constructive advice on improving the craft of pedagogy. School leaders mentor teachers so that they in turn can mentor their students effectively.

It would be hard to fulfill the many aspects of Catholic school leadership without a deep spiritual life. To fulfill a supernatural mission of forming disciples, the school leader must take time for prayer on a daily basis, receive spiritual guidance, and continue to learn about the Catholic faith and tradition. In the spiritual life, the leader can not only strive to be like Jesus but also can experience an inner conformity to him, as he lives more and more within the soul. Jesus is our model, as we strive to lead like him and for him, always in charity and ordered toward what is most important. With Jesus, anything is possible, although without him we will experience difficulties as burdens that can lead to anxiety and even burnout. Knowing that Jesus is the true leader of the Church and of the school helps us to trust in his grace in all things.

By being rooted in the school's ultimate mission and prayer, it becomes easier to acquire the prudence needed in decision making. Difficult decisions must be made and, as they are deliberated, mission must remain in the forefront. Whether it concerns personnel, discipline, communication with parents, or curriculum, the end must be kept in mind. What is the goal toward which we are aiming? How do we judge effectiveness and success? Keeping the true spiritual, moral, and intellectual good of our students in mind, leaders will find the courage to make the right decisions. Although charity should guide all of our actions, we cannot allow a desire to be charitable to prevent difficult, though necessary, decisions. In terms of personnel decisions in particular, it is not charitable to retain a teacher who is not suited to the mission or will not truly help the students in the way they need. We also cannot ask someone to perform a task for which they are not suited or adequately formed. In charity, however, we must always guide people to see the true goal and give them time to make adjustments. Effective leadership knows when a change is needed and also recognizes potential in someone who simply needs more time and mentorship.

Transformative leadership places Christ at the center and through faith and prayer finds inspiration for the difficult work of the distinct educational tasks of the school. The leader plays an essential role in helping everyone in the community to embrace a shared mission and to work cooperatively towards it. In this shared pursuit, not only will students come to know Jesus more deeply, they will also come to know themselves and the true happiness they can find in God when they embrace a life in him. The same can be said for all teachers and staff, who by living the mission can deepen their own spiritual and intellectual lives, while also inviting parents to do the same. In living out this beautiful mission, the school leader becomes an instrument for transformation in the Church and society more broadly.

### Renewal within a Diocese

Renewing a school offers a difficult enough project. Uniting a diocese with many different schools of various sizes and with their own distinct approaches may appear daunting. It is possible, however, with strong leadership, beginning with the bishop, supported by a strong schools office, and uniting a dedicated group of principals. I worked in the Office of Catholics Schools in the Archdiocese of Denver from 2018 to 2022, focusing particularly on the areas of mission and formation. Our efforts of renewal were particularly successful due to a staff that shared a common vision and complemented one another in strengths and approaches. In terms of the renewal of our Catholic mission, we had a few major goals:

1. Make the mission of the Catholic school clear to all constituencies, including its application to all areas of the school.
2. Help our principals and teachers to grow in their spiritual and intellectual life through stronger formation.
3. Recruit mission-aligned principals and teachers.
4. Strengthen curriculum in alignment to a Catholic worldview.

Many other dioceses asked us to describe how we went about our work of renewal. Here is a timeline of efforts, while I was still a member of the team.

### Summer of 2018

Under the leadership of our faith-filled, new superintendent, we held multi-day sessions within the Catholic Schools Office to establish clarity about our mission rooted in the Church's teaching. The documents we read included Pope Benedict XVI's address at The Catholic University of America (which proved the most important document for us), Pius XI's *Divini illius magistri*, the opening of *Renewing the Mind* by Ryan Topping, Stratford Caldecott's *Beauty for Truth's Sake*, and, of course, Archbishop Miller's *The Holy See's Teaching on Catholic Schools*. Spending time together reading these documents and praying through them (we cannot skip this step), our team became aligned on the purpose of Catholic education which enabled us to build a cohesive team within the office. We then began sharing this vision for renewal, rooted in the Church's teaching, with principals during regular meetings and held a one-day retreat on relational prayer for them.

### 2018–2019 School Year

One of my first steps was to establish a new, two-year "Leadership Formation Program" for prospective principals focused on areas of mission, catechesis, Christian leadership, school culture, curriculum, pedagogy, and operations. The previous program lasted a few months and focused overwhelmingly on the practical tasks of administration. We also revamped our formation for new principals to include much more time for intellectual and spiritual formation.

We began overhauling the curriculum standards revision process ordered toward forming in students a Catholic way of seeing. This included offering intellectual formation for teachers to support the implementation of the new standards. We incorporated many of the Cardinal Newman Society standards (offered for the areas of math, science, literature, and history), as well as dispositional standards to form a child in attending, thinking deeply, considering, and contemplating truth. We included text selections ordered toward these aims, a recommended literature list, and pedagogical principles for content area. We revised standards for math (2018), English (2019), science (2019), catechesis (2020), history (2021), and art and music (2022).

### Summer of 2019

Another major initiative of my role entailed establishing a four-day "Catholic Worldview Seminar," a requirement for new teachers. This restructured the previous program, which consisted of lectures on the *Catechism*, making it into an interactive seminar that drew themes from the *Catechism* into relation with different areas of the curriculum. We began each day with a selection from the *Catechism*, readings from the liberal arts on our topic, and then applications to particular areas of the curriculum. The first day, "The Logic of Creation" focused on a fuller approach to math; the next day "The Sacramental Imagination" engaged beauty and literature; day 3, "The Human Person in the World," related science to a spiritual understanding of human life; and the last day, "The Mission of Catholic Education," showed how Catholic schools can teach the great inheritance we have received from history.

We also hosted the eight-day *Fides et Ratio* seminar for Office of Catholic Schools staff, principals, and teachers (with about thirty in attendance). This provided further impetus to renew the liberal arts in our schools by creating a shared experience of the power of truth to awaken our minds and to draw us into deeper community. This intense resident experience provides enough time and depth to make a lasting difference for those attending, showing them how a liberal arts education can impact us.

### 2019–2020 School Year

We changed the name our monthly principal meetings to "Leadership Learning Days" to emphasize the centrality of ongoing formation, and started monthly Zoom call for communicating logistical information. We announced that one of our diocesan high schools would embrace a stronger humanities core curriculum, after seeing fruits of a classical approach at Our Lady of Lourdes and Frassati Catholic Academy. Another parochial school also decided to move in a classical direction at this time to improve literacy for its largely minority population (which has been initially successful). Four Chesterton Academy high schools also have opened in Colorado.

### Summer of 2020

As we were revising our catechesis/theology standards, we created a framework for forming disciples, *School of the Lord's Service: A Framework for Forming Disciples in Catholic Education*. We led a full day workshop on the document in the fall and asked schools to make concrete goals for its implementation. The Institute for Catholic Liberal Education (ICLE) led its "Spirit and Craft of Teaching" seminars for some of our teachers, and we began sending principals to their annual conference.

### 2020–2021 School Year

We intensified our formation for principals, beginning to read more substantial material, such as the book *From Christendom to Apostolic Mission* published by the University of Mary. As the priests from the archdiocese were reading that book together as well, we had fruitful conversations about it.

We released new catechesis and theology standards (formerly "religion"), which included a stronger emphasis on discipleship and prayer, as well as the theology of the body, by adopting the Ruah Woods/Cardinal Newman Society Christian Anthropology standards. We also released new history standards from a Catholic worldview in place of social studies. As a follow up to our document on discipleship, we released *Splendor of the Human Person*, a document on human sexuality to give parishes and schools a brief overview of the Church's teaching. The archdiocese partnered with the apostolate Acts 29 to offer a three-day retreat on the kerygma for archdiocesan employees with principals in attendance.

In a major move, we established a new partnership with the ICLE for credentialing new teachers through a year and a half program that meets for two weeks in the summer and two days each month. This credential is now accepted in place of a state license.

### 2021–2022 School Year

To continue our reading with principals, we began the Habiger Institute's *The Heart of Culture* on the history of Catholic education. To deepen our discussion, we offered a multi-day principal retreat on beauty, prayer, and suffering. We also used the synod process to engage school leaders and communities in reflecting on the apostolic nature of our schools. We released a new contract for principals that includes a multi-page overview of beliefs related to Catholic mission and identity. This will be given to teachers for the fall of 2023.

In my own last major contribution within the archdiocese, I created a new mission assessment process for schools, and made a visit to the first two pilot schools. This assessment sends out surveys to teachers and parents before the visit, as well as a questionnaire for the principal and pastor. A site visit is conducted with interviews with all of these groups and also students, while observing classrooms. Finally, a report is offered with affirmations and suggestions for improvement.

Everything did not go smoothly, of course, and we did face challenges. Certainly, there were principals and teachers who were not mission aligned, and, therefore, resisted renewal efforts or even refused to implement certain aspects. Many people have seen the renewal of Catholic education as a "new thing" or a "switch to classical" rather than seeing the renewal as becoming more what our schools were established to be and always should have been. Many teachers or leaders see this as something new rather than an invitation to recapture our own identity. It is hard for experienced teachers to think differently about how to teach and the goals of education. Many teachers sought practical workshops and resisted intellectual formation, as they had been trained in a more pragmatic approach. Newer teachers often come out of college steeped in identity politics. There have been moments when we did not have enough candidates for a particular position who were aligned to our mission. Sometimes, however, by simply building strong relationships and showing good faith in these efforts we were able to win over some leaders who seemed skeptical at first.

Overall, we saw consistent growth in mission throughout the archdiocese each year. We focused on recruiting mission-focused principals, when possible, and saw that these principals did the same in their own hiring of teachers. We noticed that the consistency of our message began to sink in, as we heard it repeated by principals and teachers. We also saw fruit from formation efforts, such as the "Catholic Worldview Seminar," which offered teachers a deeper perspective on the curriculum.

## To Renew or to Found

Parents, perceiving that education has fallen under the control of experts, often feel left out of the work of renewal. Perhaps they experienced the power of a Catholic liberal arts education in college and see a disparity with their children's education; or they may recognize that formation in the Catholic faith is not being emphasized by the school. They may bring these concerns to the principal and pastor without being taken seriously. What should they do? They could home school, but not every family can do that or desires to do it.

They may find a principal or priest, even if at a neighboring school, who shares their vision of education. They might gather a group of like-minded parents together to support renewal at that institution, making a longer commute to support the work of renewal there. I have seen this happen many times. It can work, especially if there is an alignment between the pastor, the principal, and a group of parents, who are willing to take a number of years to work slowly through the steps of strengthening the curriculum, recruiting teachers with a liberal arts background or who are open to learn, and raising the necessary funds to support growth. Any renewal project will face challenges. Putting the Catholic faith and liberal arts at the forefront of a school's priorities will drive away families who are looking for the college prep focus that has come to represent the norm for Catholic education. There are parents who will view this approach as "too Catholic." On the other hand, there will be families who are drawn to it, looking for a stronger Catholic vision and community. Generally speaking, Catholic schools that embrace a stronger emphasis on faith and the liberal arts tend to experience growth.

There is another possibility, however, if parents cannot find a sympathetic priest and principal. Without a willingness to change, a new institution may need to arise. Groups of parents have founded independent Catholic schools across the country, either with the blessing of the diocese or completely independent while working in the Catholic tradition. This option requires much effort, but it is possible. I helped to found two high schools working within the Chesterton Schools Network and sat on the steering committee of a third fully independent school. All three opened with the blessing of the local bishop. I was most involved with the founding of the Chesterton Academy of Our Lady of Victory, where I served as the school's first president, on a volunteer basis.

This new school began following years of discussion among parents about the need for a robustly Catholic and classical high school in the south Denver metro area. We had been very blessed by a strong liberal arts education at our parochial school in Denver and, at the time, there were no high schools where our children could continue not only with a traditional liberal arts education but also formation in a strong Catholic culture. We wanted a holistic formation that embraced the spiritual life, fine arts, outdoor adventure, service, and serious academics from a Catholic worldview. If it was going to happen, we knew we were going to have to get something started ourselves. My wife, Anne, and I began talking to other parents at our school and then joined up with some others from a neighboring parish who had started a men's group called the "First Educators" to promote solid educational principles. Working with them, we invited people to a discussion to gauge interest, with fifty people attending. The next week we held a follow-up meeting with thirty parents seriously interested in sending their incoming high schoolers to a new school.

We had clearly touched upon a pressing need, but we had to decide if it was realistic to start a new high school in just six months. Even though it was not practically realistic in such a short time, we sensed God's will guiding the group and also the profound desire of families, so we took a leap of faith and rallied a small group of committed people to launch the school. It was truly a talented group who had assembled, with backgrounds in education, law, technology, marketing, accounting, and fundraising. Many of our founding board members did not even have children coming into the school initially, but they wanted to build for the future. The archdiocese, surrounding parishes and religious groups, and many others supported our efforts at key moments. We also partnered with the Chesterton Schools Network, adopting their curriculum and formation because they matched our goals exactly and enabled us to draw upon an existing structure. Looking back, it was a stressful six months, but we fought through many logistical problems with the help of God's grace and Our Lady's intercession! The school began with twenty students in the freshman class in rented space in a beautiful school building, and six dedicated teachers, most of whom began part-time. We believed in the model of education, saw the desire for it from committed families, and assembled a talented group who dedicated a great deal of time and effort to make the vision a reality.

Although we have seen a strong renewal of Catholic higher education, the same kind of renewal has taken longer to trickle down to the K–12 level. This renewal, however, has begun in earnest and just in the last ten years has grown significantly stronger. I sought to bring the principles of the Catholic liberal arts, which my children had experienced at their parochial, classical school to the high-school level, working with a great community of families and the help of the Chesterton Schools Network. If we are to experience a renewal of Catholic education, it will require many more lay people to step forward and to take a similar leap of faith to found other desperately needed schools.

The renewal of Catholic education will require action on many fronts. Dioceses, parishes, and groups of parents can all contribute to the work of aligning our schools and founding new ones in accord with the Church's rich educational heritage, plotting a new course that draws from the past to prepare our students for their vocation in a secular age.

# Conclusion
## Building Culture in the School

"Where should we begin?" school leaders often ask.[1] There is no simple or uniform answer. Each community is different, with a different history, community makeup, current practices, faculty, and families, all of which make for different possibilities. What should students study? In some ways, my answer might surprise you. It does not matter that much. How should they be assessed? Here too, it does not matter that much. It does not matter, *so long as* they are doing something worthwhile. That is a significant if.

I am not saying that content does not matter. Quite the contrary. What I am saying is that the actual choice of which books to read or what topics to teach does not matter very much, because there are so many good things to study. A school could never go through all of the great or good books that could be read. There are so many wonderful things to learn about throughout history. Simply do something worthwhile. Teachers will ask me what to do if they feel stuck within a curriculum or environment that does not seek renewal. My answer is to do anything—in prayer, in what you read, in the activities you choose—that will engage what is true, good, and beautiful. If a single activity draws students into an encounter with the higher things, we can be happy. If students read a good book, which leads to a rich conversation, and inspires them to write something in response to it, then that book, even if there are count-

1. For practical suggestions on getting started, I would also point to the book I edited in collaboration with the Institute for Catholic Liberal Education, *Renewing Catholic Schools: How to Regain a Catholic Vision in a Secular Age* (Washington, D.C.: Catholic Education Press, 2020).

less others better than it, proved a success. Too often, however, we have students read texts that are not worthwhile, and engage in activities that are not formative. I hope this book has provided some inspiration for choosing things to study that would be worthwhile.

Choosing good texts to teach may be the easy part. It is more difficult to complement instruction with lived experience, helping it to take root within the student, who is prepared to live it out. In this conclusion, I will give some further actions to consider in order to implement a more sacramental approach to education. The beautiful ideas of Catholic education must be translated into action, taking flesh within the community: forming teachers, informing students, and flowing over into the life of the family.

## The School as a Builder of Culture

Education drives culture, truly forming students in an entire way of thinking and living. The architects of modern, secular education knew this, and have put us in the position we are in today because of the education young people have received for decades. Relativism and materialism have turned them away from the pursuit of truth and virtue. Young people have been initiated into a culture that is materialistic in its epistemology and aspirations. Nothing in contemporary education has inspired young people to break out of an individualistic and horizontal view of life or to sacrifice their lives for others in the context of family life and service.

The best response to our culture, however, stems from a truly Christian education, which initiates students into a Christian culture that teaches them how to think and live as followers of Christ in the modern world. In what Pope Benedict XVI called an "educational emergency,"[2] it is no longer a valid option to supplement a secular

---

2. Benedict XVI, Address to Participants in the Plenary Assembly of the Pontifical Council for Culture.

education with one hour of religious education a week. Parents might counter that the home can balance the influence of secular education, but students spend far too much time at school and among peers with this formative experience going against the values of the family and Church. This creates a conflict within the student that tends to undermine faith in the long run. The school, Church, and home must align to form a partnership for the formation of children.

Catholic education is worth the sacrifice for parishes and families because it is an investment in our children. If we are unsatisfied with the state of society and the Church, then prioritizing the education of our children is the best way to make an impact for the future. Even more important, however, is simply the everlasting worth of each child. Catholic education aims at the complete formation of the person—body, mind, and soul—and no education could be complete that forms only a part of the person. We are investing not simply in the future of society and the Church; we are investing in the eternal vocation of each Christian. It is incumbent on Christian parents and pastors to do all that they can for the souls that have been entrusted to them.

Forming culture through the school means building relationships and practices that instantiate the faith concretely. The foundation may be a shared vision of faith and reason, which sees the cosmos as created by God and human life as destined for an eternal good which transcends it. The realization of this vision within the community has been the missing aspect of Catholic education. Forming a Christian way of life entails mentorship in the virtues, praying together, being prepared for mission. It means more than simply learning about the meaning of human life, for this meaning must be experienced.

Students will be confirmed in their identity as children of God, learning what it truly means to be a human being by entering more deeply into communion with God and others. They will find meaning through communication, unlocking the power of language to enliven the mind, memory, and imagination, which opens up a great tradition. This education will inspire students to love what is truly beautiful and be willing to give their lives for this beauty in love. This kind of education will enact change, forming students in what matters most and enabling them to shape culture beyond the school by living out this vision.

The school has its own culture within its daily rhythms and shared practices. It is not a complete culture, of course, as it extends the culture of the family by assisting parents in the formation of their children and generally exists within the broader culture of the parish. The school's own culture will impact students in an enduring way more easily if it aligns with the family and parish. It can become a place for families to form relationships with other families to support one another in faith, as they continue to learn and live the faith. It can also become a means for the parish to express its mission for the salvation of souls through the points of contact it has with students and families through the school community. Parishes often are too large to engage all their parishioners effectively, but the school can become a means of drawing families into the life of the Church. This can happen through forming small groups of families, meeting for meals and conversation related to the faith but also the curriculum of the school so that they can enter more directly into the mission. School culture becomes a median point of contact between the family and the Church.

## The Eucharistic Heart of Education

The sacramental mission of the school can be found most directly at the altar. It is here that the general sacramental approach, looking at how every created reality can point us to God, becomes sacramental in actuality. The *Logos*—the Word of God, Truth itself, the Creator—entered into his creation to save it. For Catholic school students, he continues to enter it at Mass. He makes himself available to be seen, touched, and tasted. In encountering him, we do not simply learn about the truth; we enter into Truth. He enlightens us from within and draws us into his goodness to transform us from the inside out. In the Eucharist, the *Logos* empties himself for each student, drawing them into the communion, which is the very purpose of their lives.

The Mass offers us the most significant solution for the renewal of Catholic education. As I have written elsewhere, the Eucharist can save our civilization, and, all the more, therefore, it can save Catholic education.[3] The Lord's sacramental presence provides all that we need to overcome any difficulty within the parish, school, and family. The answer is waiting for us on the altar and in the tabernacle, but too often we overlook Jesus' presence there and do not prepare ourselves well enough to receive the graces he desires to give us.

The Blessed Sacrament anchors the culture of the entire school, making it a place where God dwells and where all things are ordered to the glory of God. I would tell any school: go to Mass more often. If you go to Mass once a month, start going once a week. If you go once a week, go at least twice a week. Try to get the students into church every single day, for Mass if possible but at least for prayer before the tabernacle. Schools should not view time at Mass as wasted time out of the classroom. Nothing could be more important. Here stands the goal of everything we do. With Jesus, everything will go better. Students will learn better, behave better, and grow in virtue more easily, if they walk around school as tabernacles of the Lord's presence.

The Mass creates Christian culture in the school by drawing the entire community together and uniting all in the highest good. It becomes a source of grace that animates all that happens within the school community, providing it with a supernatural culture.

---

3. See my book *How the Eucharist Can Save Civilization* (Charlotte, N.C.: TAN Books, 2023).

Many teachers lament that students are not going to Sunday Mass. The Mass stands at the very center of Catholic culture, the Catholic way of life. If students are going to learn how to live as Catholics in the world, the Catholic school should show them the sacrament's central importance in their lives. Even if it does not occur in every case, many students encourage their parents to begin attending Mass on Sunday. It also teaches students how to pray at Mass and sets the expectation that the Eucharist stands at the center of the Christian life.

The Eucharist makes Catholic education sacramental in a more complete sense, truly forming soul and body at once. The Creator comes into us to remake us. The Word by whom all was created enlightens us with his presence within us. In the Blessed Sacrament, we come to the source of all truth and the true fulfillment of every genuine desire. Students should become tabernacles of Christ, carrying his presence within them as they study and interact with one another. If the curriculum seeks to provide students with access to what is true, good, and beautiful, these will be found in the full in Christ, not to be studied as an object from without, but to be experienced from within. The goal of Catholic education does not await far off in the future. The goods for which it strives are given to students during the holy sacrifice of the Mass.

## Implementing a Sacramental Approach in Education

There is no one way to pursue renewal. We must prioritize anything that will help us build a culture centered on truth, goodness, and beauty. Nonetheless, it can be helpful to form clear goals to focus on the practical steps of implementation. The following points summarize the chapters of this book, phrased concisely as action points:

1. Embrace the Church's vision as a necessary path to reach the true ends of education, spending time explicating this vision and applying it in all aspects of school culture.

2. Offer Mass more frequently as the center of school culture, prioritizing it in the school schedule.

3. Form a community rooted in conviction flowing from the Catholic faith, ensuring that all employees and volunteers understand, embrace, and live in accord with the school's mission.

4. Prioritize discipleship (becoming a student of Christ) in all aspects of education, inviting teachers and students to grow in faith and to live it out in the school community.

5. Ensure, through concrete steps of cooperation, that parents exercise their essential role in education, especially in matters of faith.

6. Encourage parents to take up their formative role through hands-on action with their children.

7. Form a Catholic worldview by integrating all that is studied in a coherent vision of the whole of reality.

8. Make intellectual formation a priority for teachers, reading and discussing impactful books as a faculty.

9. Choose student books carefully, emphasizing those that are truly worthy of being read and inspire a healthy imagination and moral sense.

10. Help students to engage nature, embrace physical activity, and experience the beauty of the arts to welcome them into the adventure of learning and to foster a poetic encounter with reality in wonder.

11. Increase student literacy in Catholic history and cultural achievements, unfolding the great treasury of the tradition.

12. Restore history to its rightful place in the liberal arts, helping students to discover their own place within the narrative of salvation history and the mission of the Church.

13. Teach the universal story of the Church that touches all peoples and continents, drawing out diverse contributions of cultures within the unity of faith.

14. Teach grammar and Catholic heritage through the Latin language, drawing out its contribution in divine worship, music, and literature.

15. Integrate the fine arts as an essential element of formation, drawing forth wonder, refining sensibilities, and eliciting a creative response.
16. Limit the use of technology to foster a contemplative spirit in learning.
17. Hire for mission and form a community of teachers who embrace the ongoing pursuit of truth.
18. Be bold in reforming and building programs that fully embrace the Church's teaching on education.
19. Allow faith to take flesh in education by being lived out in a community centered around shared daily practices and especially devotion to the Blessed Sacrament.

## Inflaming the Divine Fire

Catholic education stands at a key moment of renewal. We have so many tools at our disposal: inspiring content and holy role models within a strong global communion. There are also many obstacles: financial strain, the legacy of scandals, internal divisions, secularism, doubt, and lack of vision. If we really seek God before all else and strive to bring our children before him, then he will help us in our work of renewal.

It is customary to start the academic year with a votive Mass to the Holy Spirit. Jesus said that the Spirit would lead us to all truth, bringing to mind all that he taught and guiding our understanding of it. Jesus baptizes us with the Spirit and fire (Mt 3:11) and the Letter to the Hebrews calls God himself a "consuming fire" (Heb 12:29). This divine fire burns away all that stands in the way of his most holy will, purifying and refining us, transforming us ever more into the image of Christ. God wills that "all will be saved and come to a knowledge of the truth" (1 Tim 2:4) and when we are truly inflamed by the Spirit, this fire becomes contagious, reaching others and spreading into the world itself.

Pope Benedict described the relation of Christ to fire both within us and surrounding us at the Easter vigil: "Christ, the light, is fire, flame, burning up evil and so reshaping both the world and ourselves."[4] And speaking to the Catholic University of the Sacred Heart, he connected this image to education, noting how this fire helps us to see the true transcendent vocation of humanity: "The light of the gospel is a source of true culture able to spark energies of a new, integral, and transcendent humanism."[5] Although our culture has grown further away from God, we should not lose hope.

We discover a powerful source of inner renewal through faith, which provides the true source for transformation. Catholic education can keep this flame alive, preserving it, and passing it on to the next generation. Speaking at Christmas, Pope Benedict prayed that we do this: "May that inner brightness spread to us, and kindle in our hearts the flame of God's goodness; may all of us, by our love, bring light to the world! Let us keep this light-giving flame, lit in faith, from being extinguished by the cold winds of our time!"[6] Having received this divine fire, we have the privilege of sharing it with others within the great mission of Catholic education.

Being made in the image and likeness of God is a spark that too often seems to smolder. Christ came to set the world on fire, kindling that spark with the fire of the Holy Spirit. This is the true goal of Catholic education: to inflame mind and heart with the divine life, which will then enliven the world. Catholic education will be successful when our hearts are inflamed with the fire of God's love, purifying God's image within us and enabling us to embrace the mission

---

4. Benedict XVI, homily, April 7, 2012, https://www.vatican.va/content/benedict-xvi/en/homilies/2012/documents/hf_ben-xvi_hom_20120407_veglia-pasquale.html.

5. Benedict XVI, Address to the Catholic University of the Sacred Heart, May 21, 2011, https://www.vatican.va/content/benedict-xvi/en/speeches/2011/may/documents/hf_ben-xvi_spe_20110521_sacro-cuore.html.

6. Benedict XVI, homily, December 24, 2005, https://www.vatican.va/content/benedict-xvi/en/homilies/2005/documents/hf_ben-xvi_hom_20051224_christmas.html.

he has given us. Each student has a spark of the divine within, created in the image and likeness of God; and education seeks to draw out this flame so that it will become a fire of God's life within.

To embrace this mission of inflaming souls and culture alike, we can pray daily the Prayer to the Holy Spirit, asking to be refined and equipped for the great work ahead:

> *Come, Holy Spirit, fill the hearts of your faithful and kindle in them the fire of your love. Send forth your Spirit and they shall be created. And you shall renew the face of the earth.*
>
> *O God, who by the light of the Holy Spirit, did instruct the hearts of the faithful, grant that by the same Holy Spirit we may be truly wise and ever enjoy his consolations. Through the same Christ Our Lord. Amen.*

# Appendix
## A Guide for Building Catholic Literacy

As Catholics, we have inherited a great cultural legacy, but, unfortunately, much of it has been forgotten. This appendix offers ideas for growing in fluency in the Catholic tradition. Catholic school students generally focus more on the doctrinal, moral, and sacramental elements, which we emphasize currently in Catholic education. This Guide offers an aspirational goal for recovering missing elements of the Catholic tradition that can enrich our curriculum, especially in history, culture, and the arts. Some of it will seem obvious, but we should not take anything for granted in our secular culture.[1] Other elements will seem impossibly advanced but will become more realistic as we gain familiarity with the tradition. Simply viewing the achievements of the Church as a whole can help shape a vision of all that our heritage offers and how it can weave together the curriculum in an interdisciplinary fashion.

Teachers can use this list for their own research and edification, finding nuggets to incorporate in the classroom. This guide should not be approached as abstract information to be memorized, but as offering material to be employed according to the poetic, sacramental, and narrative-based approaches outlined in this book. It is not simply a list of the greatest accomplishments in any of these areas, because it provides an overview of the Catholic tradition as a whole, detailing historic milestones for each area. It does include the achievements of some non-Catholics when they touch on the

---

1. Publisher's note: One resource on the history and meaning of many words on Dr. Staudt's lists below is Anthony Lo Bello, *Origins of Catholic Words: A Discursive Dictionary* (Washington, D.C.: The Catholic University of America Press, 2020). It is "unlike any dictionary you have ever read" (Joseph Pearce), "a treasure trove of Catholic history and culture" (Fr. Uwe Michael Lang).

Catholic tradition, such as Bach's great Catholic Mass in B Minor and T. S. Eliot's play about the death of St. Thomas Becket. No list could be perfect and will always reflect the sensibilities of the compiler, but I hope it provides a good starting point for building Catholic literacy.

## I. Catholic Belief

### Doctrine

One God
    Pure Act
    Eternity
    Simplicity
    Perfection
    Omnipotence
    Omniscience
Trinity
    Divine Persons
    Processions
    Eternally Begotten
    Consubstantial
    Spiration
    Circumincession
    Divine missions
    Divine economy
Creation
    Free gift, no necessity
    *Ex Nihilo*
    Goodness of creatures
    Dominion, stewardship
Angels
    Angelic nature
    Choirs of angels
    Guardian angels
    Demons, devil, Satan

Jesus Christ
    Logos
    Son of God, Son of Man
    Incarnation
    Hypostatic union
    Savior
    Salvation, redemption, atonement
Holy Spirit
    Procession of love
    Filioque
    Mission of sanctification
Divine Revelation
    Sacred Scripture
    Inspiration and inerrancy
    Old Testament
    New Testament
    Sacred tradition
    Dogma
    Development of doctrine
    Hierarchy of truths
    Heresy
Grace
    Actual
    Sanctifying
    Cooperation with
    Deification
    Created, uncreated
    Divine indwelling
    Merit

Church
Mystical Body of Christ
Marks: One, Holy, Catholic,
Apostolic
Communion of Saints
Laity
Hierarchy
Apostolic succession
Episcopate
Teach, sanctify, govern
Infallibility in faith and morals
Ordinary Magisterium
Papacy, pope, Holy See
Papal infallibility
Ecumenical council
Diocese
Synods
Encyclical
Excommunication
Last Things
Eschatology
Eternal life
Death
Judgment, particular and final
Resurrection of the dead
Heaven
Hell
Purgatory
Temporal punishment
Indulgences
Beatific Vision
Mary/Our Lady/Blessed Mother
Immaculate Conception
Virgin birth
Perpetual virginity
Assumption
Queen of Heaven and Earth

*Salvation History*

God's free creation
Creation and fall of angels
Two creation stories
Made in God's Image and
Likeness
Immortal soul
The Garden of Eden
The Fall, Original Sin
Cain and Abel
Noah
Abraham, Isaac, and Jacob
Covenant
Joseph
Moses and the Exodus
Covenant at Sinai
Wandering in the desert
Joshua and conquest of Canaan
Judges
Ruth
Samuel
David
Solomon
Major prophets
Minor prophets
Babylonian Exile
Maccabees
Birth of the Messiah
Holy Family
Childhood of Jesus
Preaching of John the Baptist
Baptism of Jesus
Public ministry
Twelve Apostles
Transfiguration
Last Supper
Paschal Mystery

Passion
Crucifixion (the Cross)
Resurrection
Ascension
Pentecost
Mission of the Church
Evangelists
Church in Acts
Conversion of Paul
Letters of Paul
Book of Revelation
Second Coming
Last Judgment

### Sacraments

Sacrament
Sacramental character
*Ex opere operato*
Efficacious sign
Matter and form
Minister
Effects
Baptism
    Water
    Infusion or immersion
    Grace of adoption
    Original sin
    Sanctifying grace
    Godparent
Confirmation
    Laying on of hands
    Anointing with chrism
    Completing baptism
    Soldier of Christ
Eucharist
    Bread and wine
    Words of institution

Mass
True presence
Transubstantiation
Communion
Confession/Penance/
Reconciliation
    Sin, mortal and venial
    Concupiscence
    Examination of conscience
    Contrition
    Oracular confession
    Absolution
    Remission of sins
    Penance and reparation
Anointing of the Sick
    Viaticum
    Apostolic pardon
Marriage/Matrimony
    Vows
    Permanence, fidelity, openness
      to life
    Domestic Church
Holy Orders
    Ordination
    Bishop
    Priest
    Deacon
    *In Persona Christi*
    Celibacy

## II. Catholic Prayer

### Liturgy

Mass
Liturgy of the Word
Liturgy of the Eucharist
Homily/sermon

Offertory
Eucharistic canon/anaphora
Epiclesis
Consecration, words of institution
Communion
Altar
Altar cloth
Cruets
Chalice
Paten
Vestments
    Chasuble
    Stole
    Alb
    Cincture
    Cassock
    Miter
    Crosier
    Cope
    Dalmatic
    Surplice
Incense
Censer/thurible
Reliquary
Exorcism
Blessing
Genuflection
Kneeling
Bowing, prostration
Consecration and blessing of
    objects
Divine Office/Liturgy of the Hours
Matins—Office of Readings
Lauds—Morning Prayer
Prime
Terce—Midmorning Prayer
Sext—Midday Prayer

None—Midafternoon Prayer
Vespers—Evening Prayer
Compline—Night Prayer
Propers of the Mass
    Introit—Entrance Antiphon
    Collect
    Offertory
    Communion Antiphon
Ordinary of the Mass
    Kyrie
    Gloria
    Sanctus, Benedictus
    Agnus Dei
Byzantine Divine Liturgy
Traditional Latin Mass
Liturgical reform of Paul VI
Latin as sacred language
Vernacular language
Sacramentary
Lectionary
Lector
Altar Server/acolyte
Sacramentals
Scapular
Miraculous Medal
Blessing of home

### *Liturgical Calendar*

Liturgical seasons
Liturgical colors
Feast day
Memorial
Solemnity
Holy day of obligation
Octave
Season
Advent

Christmas day, octave, season
Epiphany
Lent
Ash Wednesday
Holy Week
Good Friday
Easter Sunday and octave
Easter season
Pentecost
Ordinary Time (Sundays after
    Pentecost)
Corpus Christi
Assumption
Exaltation of the Cross
Nativity of Mary
Allhallowtide
    All Hallows Eve
    All Saints Day
    All Souls Day
Presentation of Mary
Immaculate Conception
Ember days
Rogation days
Michaelmas Day (Archangels)
Martinmas Day (St. Martin of
    Tours)
Annunciation (Lady Day)
Candlemas Day (Presentation)
Birth of John the Baptist
    (Midsummer's Day)

### Church Building

Parish
Cathedral
Chapel
Crypt

Consecration of church and altar
Crucifix
Stations of the Cross
Baldacchino
Tabernacle
Monstrance
Candelabra
Pulpit/ambo
Cathedra
Altar
Altar stone
Sanctuary
Altar rail
Nave
Narthex, vestibule
Spire
Bell tower
Stations of the Cross
Mary, Joseph altars
Transepts
Apse
Vaulted ceiling
Pews
Eastern orientation
Candles
Processional Cross
Sanctuary lamp
Chrism
Baptismal font
Dome/copula
Sacristy
Rectory
Cemetery
    Consecrated ground
    Columbarium

*Prayers and Devotions*

Sign of the Cross
Our Father
Hail Mary
Glory Be
Act of Contrition
Hail Holy Queen
*Memorare*
Rosary
Twenty Mysteries of the Rosary
Seven Sorrows of Mary
Divine Mercy Chaplet
Stations of the Cross
Prayers before and after
    Communion
Spiritual Communion
Mass responses
Apostles Creed
Nicene Creed
Vocal prayer
Meditation
Contemplation
Adoration of the Blessed
    Sacrament
Benediction
Divine Praises
*Lectio divina*
Spiritual Exercises
Examen
Prayer for the Faithful Departed
Grace before and after meals
Morning Offering
Bedtime prayers
Litany of the Saints
Litany of the Sacred Heart
Litany of the Blessed Virgin Mary
    (Loreto)

Litany of Humility
Novena
*Sub tuum praesidium*
Acts of Faith, Hope, and Love
*Anima Christi*
St. Michael Prayer
Guardian Angel Prayer
*Suscipe*
St. Patrick's Breastplate
Marian Consecration
Deliverance prayers

## III. Catholic Life

### *Moral and Spiritual Life*

Virtue
Sin and vice
Evil as privation of good
Happiness
Conscience
Ten Commandments
Beatitudes
Natural law
Divine Law
    Old Law (Law of Moses)
    New Law of the Holy Spirit
Precepts of the Church
Theological Virtues
    Faith
    Hope
    Love
Cardinal Virtues
    Prudence
    Justice
    Fortitude
    Temperance

Gifts of the Holy Spirit
   Knowledge
   Understanding
   Wisdom
   Counsel
   Fortitude
   Piety
   Fear of the Lord
Humility
Religion
Evangelical Counsels
   Poverty
   Chastity
   Obedience
Stages of the Spiritual Life
   Purgative Way
   Illuminative Way
   Unitive Way
Dark night of the senses
Dark night of the soul
Penance
Mortification
Fasting
Abstinence from meat
Seven Deadly Sins (capital sins)
Spiritual direction

### Community and Catholic Social Teaching

Almsgiving
Tithing
Corporal Works of Mercy
Spiritual Works of Mercy
Confraternities
Guilds
Religious drama
Pilgrimage

Catholic social teaching
   Common Good
   Subsidiarity
   Solidarity
   Socialism, Church's teaching
      against
   Universal Destination of Goods
   Care of the environment
   Just War Theory
   Theology of the body
   Complementarity of man and
      woman
   Preferential Option for the Poor
   Human Dignity
   Life issues
      Contraception
      Abortion
      Euthanasia
      Assisted suicide
      IVF/ART
      Adoption
   Religious liberty
   Catholic approach to bioethics
   Principle of double effect
   Morality of medical treatment
      Ordinary and extraordinary
         means
      Refusing treatment
      Ability to prepare for death
      Brain death and organ donation
Ecumenism

### Mission and Education

Catechesis
Baptismal catechumenate
Catechumen
Rite of Election

Purification and enlightenment
Initiation
Easter Vigil
Mystagogy
Evangelization
New Evangelization
Disciple
Discipleship
Mission
Conversion
Interior growth in virtue and
    holiness
Universal Call to Holiness
Liberal arts
Philosophy
Importance of philosophy for
    theology
Scholasticism
Humanism
Monastery and cathedral schools
Founding of universities
Teaching orders
Parochial schools
Trivium
Quadrivium
Vocation
Faith and reason
Catholic contribution to science
*Ex corde ecclesiae*
Apologetics
Proofs for the existence of God

### Religious Orders and Monastic Life

Evangelical counsels
Religious vows
Religious life

Consecrated Virginity
Discernment
Monk
Friar
Nun
Brother
Sister
Hermit
Anchor/anchoress
Canon
Monastery
Convent
Cloister
Enclosure
Rule
Habit
Scapular
Cowl
Tonsure
Benedictines
Cistercians (and Trappists)
Norbertines
Augustinians
Carthusians
Knights of Malta
Carmelites
Franciscans
Capuchins
Poor Clares
Dominicans
Jesuits
Piarists
Oratorians
Vincentians
Lasallians
Visitation Sisters
Basilians

Holy Cross Fathers
Salesians
Passionists
Redemptorists
Claretian Sisters
Little Sisters of the Poor

Paulists
Opus Dei
Missionaries of Charity
Sisters of Life
Daughters of St. Paul
Third orders and oblates

---

# IV. Catholic History

## Ages of the Church (general timeline)

I.    Witness: Apostolic Age
II.   Teaching: Age of the Fathers
III.  Building: Eastern and Western Christendom
IV.   Living: Christian Culture in the Middle Ages
V.    Division: Decline of Christendom and Reformation
VI.   Secularism: New Age of Persecution and Witness

## Church Fathers

St. Ignatius of Antioch (d. early 2nd c.)
St. Justin Martyr (100–165)
St. Irenaeus of Lyon (130–202)
St. Cyprian (210–58)
St. Athanasius of Alexandria (296–373)
St. Cyril of Jerusalem (313–86)
St. Cyril of Alexandria (376–444)
St. Basil the Great and his family (330–79)
St. Gregory Nazianzus (329–90)
St. Ambrose (339–97)
St. Jerome (342–420)
St. John Chrysostom (347–407)
St. Augustine of Hippo (354–430)
St. Leo the Great (400–461)
St. Gregory the Great (540–604)
St. Maximus the Confessor (580–662)
St. John Damascene (675–749)

## *Saints*

Beatification
Canonization
Intercession
Patron saints
Incorruptibility
Doctors of the Church
Martyrs
Virgins
Confessors
Oblates
Missionaries
Founders
Stigmata
Sts. Felicity and Perpetua (182–203)
St. Agnes (291–304)
St. Cecilia (200–235)
St. Sebastian (255–88)
St. Antony of the Desert (251–356)
St. Nicholas of Myra (270–343)
St. Monica (332–87)
St. Martin of Tours (316–97)
St. Patrick (5th c.)
St. Benedict of Nursia (480–547)
St. Columba (521–97)
St. Columban (543–615)
St. Augustine of Canterbury (d. 604)
St. Isidore of Seville (560–636)
St. Venerable Bede (673–735)
St. Boniface (675–754)
St. Bernard (1090–1153)
St. Hildegard of Bingen (1098–1179)
St. Anselm (1033–1109)
St. Thomas Becket (1119–70)
St. Francis of Assisi (1181–1226)
St. Anthony of Padua (1195–1231)
St. Dominic (1170–1221)

St. Louis IX, king of France (1214–70)
St. Thomas Aquinas (1225–74)
St. Bonaventure (1221–74)
St. Catherine of Siena (1347–80)
St. Bridget of Sweden (1303–73)
St. Joan of Arc (1412–31)
St. Thomas More (1478–1535)
St. Ignatius of Loyola (1491–1556)
St. Francis Xavier (1506–52)
St. Charles Borromeo (1538–84)
St. Robert Bellarmine (1542–1621)
St. Philip Neri (1515–95)
St. Francis de Sales (1567–1622)
St. Teresa of Ávila (1515–82)
St. John of the Cross (1542–91)
St. Edmund Campion (1540–81)
St. Margaret Clitherow (1556–86)
St. Vincent de Paul (1581–1660)
St. Louis de Montfort (1673–1716)
St. Bernadette Soubirous (1844–79)
St. Thérèse of Lisieux (1873–97)
St. Josephine Bakhita (1869–1947)
St. Jacinta, St. Francisco, and Ven. Lucia (Fatima children; 1910–20,
    1908–19, and 1907–2005)
St. Faustina Kowalska (1905–38)
St. Maria Goretti (1890–1902)
St. Maximilian Kolbe (1894–1941)
Bl. Pier Giorgio Frassati (1901–25)
St. Teresa of Calcutta (1910–97)
St. Gianna Beretta Molla (1922–62)
Bl. Carlo Acutis (1991–2006)

### Saints of the Americas

St. Louis Bertrand, OP (1526–81), Apostles of the Americas
St. Toribio Alfonso de Mogrovejo (1538–1606), first bishop of Lima,
    first seminary
St. Francis Solanus, OFM (1549–1610), missionary in Peru

St. Martin de Porres, OP (1579–1639), Dominican brother, first black saint of New World

St. Peter Claver, SJ (1580–1654), slave of slaves

St. Rose of Lima (1586–1616), Third Order Dominican

St. Mariana de Jesús de Paredes (1618–45), Third Order Franciscan

St. Marie of the Incarnation (1599–1672), religious life in Quebec, education

St. Francois de Laval (1623–1708), first bishop of Quebec

North American martyrs (1642–49)

Bl. Eusebio Kino (1645–1711), Apostle of the Southwest, linguist

St. Kateri Tekakwitha (1656–80), Lily of the Mohawks

St. Junipero Serra (1713–84), Apostle of California

St. Elizabeth Ann Seton (1774–1821), convert, educator

St. Rose Philippine Duschene (1769–1852), missionary to American frontier

Ven. Frederic Baraga (1797–1868), missionary, bishop in Michigan's upper peninsula

St. Théodore (Anne Thérèse) Guerin (1798–1856), established schools in Indiana

St. John Neumann (1811–60), bishop of Philadelphia, founder of the Catholic school system

Bl. Francis Xavier Seelos (1819–67), missionary in American West

St. Narcisa de Jesús (1832–69), laywoman in Ecuador

St. Marianne Cope (1838–1918), founded hospitals, work with lepers in Hawaii

St. Damian Molokai (1840–89), mission to lepers in Hawaii

St. José Gabriel del Rosario Brochero (1840–1914), gaucho priest of Argentina

Bl. Andre Bessette, CSC (1845–1937), Holy Cross brother, St. Joseph Shrine in Montreal

St. Francis Xavier Cabrini (1850–1917), served immigrants in US

Bl. Michael McGivney (1852–90), founder of Knights of Columbus

St. Katharine Drexel (1858–1955), founded schools for minority children

Bl. Solanus Casey, OFM Cap. (1870–1957), ministry to sick, healer

Bl. Miguel Pro (1891–1927), martyr during Mexican persecution

Ven. Fulton Sheen (1895–1979), bishop, media apostolate

Servant of God Dorothy Day (1897–1980), convert, Catholic Worker
   Movement
St. Teresa of the Andes (1900–2000), Carmelite nun in Chile
Bl. Teresa Demjanovich (1901–27), young teacher and Sister of Charity
Ven. Patrick Peyton, CSC (1909–92), Apostle of the Rosary
St. José Luis Sánchez del Rio (1913–28), young solider in Cristero War,
   martyr
St. Óscar Romero (1917–80), archbishop of San Salvador, martyr
Bl. Stanley Rother (1935–81), missionary to Guatemala, martyr
Bl. James Miller, FSC (1944–82), teaching brother, martyred in Guatemala

### Historical Events

| | |
|---|---|
| 67 | Martyrdom of Peter and Paul |
| 112 | Pliny the Younger writes to the Emperor Trajan about Christians |
| 155 | Justin Martyr writes public appeal to Emperor Antoninus Pius |
| 199 | Establishment of the Catacombs of St. Callixtus |
| 250–51 | Decian Persecution, followed by "lapsed" controversy |
| 303–13 | Diocletian or Great Persecution |
| 312 | Battle of Milvian Bridge |
| 313 | Constantine Legalizes Christianity in Edict of Milan |
| 325–787 | Christological controversies |
| | 325 Arianism, Council of Nicaea |
| | 381 Semi-Arianism, Council of Constantinople |
| | 431 Nestorianism, Council of Ephesus |
| | 451 Monophysitism, Council of Chalcedon |
| | 680–81 Monothelitism, Third Council of Constantinople |
| | 787 Iconoclasm, Nicaea II |
| 380 | Emperor Theodosius's Edict of Thessalonica |
| 410 | Sack of Rome, leads to Augustine's *City of God* |
| 476 | Fall of Roman Empire in the West |
| 496 | Conversion of King Clovis of the Franks |
| 535–54 | Justinian's Gothic War |
| 596 | Augustine of Canterbury begins mission to Anglo-Saxons |
| 627 | Battle of Nineveh, Heraclius defeats Persians, recovers True Cross |

636        Battle of Yarmouk, Byzantines defeated by Arabs in Syria
718        Boniface begins mission to Germans
732        Battle of Tours/Poitiers stops Muslim invasion of France
793        Vikings sack Lindisfarne, beginning raids
800        Crowning of Charlemagne as Roman emperor
829        Ansgar begins mission to Scandinavia
863        Cyril and Methodius begin mission to Slavs
878        Alfred the Great defeats the Great Heathen Army
910        Founding of Cluny
962        Otto the Great crowned emperor
966        Miesko I of Poland accepts Catholic faith
1000       Conversion of St. Stephen of Hungary
1050–80    Gregorian reform
1054       Great Schism with Orthodox
1071       Battle of Manzikert, Turks defeat Byzantines
1098       Cistercian Reform
1095–1291  Crusades in Holy Land
        1099       Crusaders capture Jerusalem
        1187       Jerusalem falls
        1204       Sack of Constantinople
1170       Martyrdom of St. Thomas Becket
1209       Founding of Franciscans
1215       Fourth Lateran Council; *Magna Carta*
1216       Founding of Dominicans
1229       Founding of Inquisition in response to Catharism
1231       Charter of the University of Paris
1241       Battles of Legnica and Mohi, Mongols defeat Poles and
        Hungarians
1245       First Council of Lyon excommunicates Frederick II
1337–1453  Hundred Years War
        1431       Joan of Arc executed
1378–1417  Great Western Schism
1410       Battle of Grunwald, Jagiełło defeats Teutonic Knights
1445       Attempted reunion with Orthodox in Florence
1453       Fall of Constantinople
1492       End of *Reconquista* in Spain; Columbus lands in America
1521       Conquest of Tenochtitlan

| | | |
|---|---|---|
| 16th c. | Reformation and Counter-Reformation | |
| | 1517 | Luther's "95 Theses" |
| | 1531 | Henry VIII breaks with the Church |
| | 1545–63 | Council of Trent |
| | 1547 | Battle of Muhlburg, Charles V defeats Protestant Schmalkaldic League |
| | 1562–98 | French Wars of Religion |
| | 1572 | St. Bartholomew's Day Massacre |
| 1527 | Sack of Rome | |
| 1540 | Founding of Jesuits | |
| 1571 | Battle of Lepanto | |
| 1582 | Gregorian Calendar introduced | |
| 1618–48 | Thirty Years War | |
| 1633 | Trial of Galileo | |
| 1683 | Turkish Siege of Vienna | |
| 1685 | Louis XIV revokes the Edict of Nantes | |
| 1713 | Pope Clement XI condemns Jansenism | |
| 1773 | Suppression of the Jesuits | |
| 1789 | John Carroll named first bishop of United States | |
| 1789 | French Revolution | |
| | 1793 | Reign of terror, martyrs |
| | 1801 | Concordat with Napoleon |
| | 1804 | Coronation of Napoleon |
| | 1806 | Dissolution of Holy Roman Empire |
| | 1814, 1815 | Downfall of Napoleon |
| 1803 | Louisiana Purchase brings more Catholics into United States | |
| 1829 | Catholic Emancipation in Great Britain | |
| 1846–48 | Mexican-American War | |
| 1854 | Dogma of Immaculate Conception proclaimed by Pius IX | |
| 1865 | African missions gain momentum | |
| 1869–70 | Vatican I and Declaration of Papal Infallibility | |
| 1873 | Kulturkampf in Germany | |
| 1891 | Leo XIII's encyclical *Rerum novarum*, Catholic social teaching | |
| 1917 | Our Lady of Fatima; October Revolution in Russia | |
| 1926–29 | Cristeros Uprising | |
| 1929 | Lateran Treaty | |
| 1936–39 | Spanish Civil War | |

| 1937 | Pope Pius XI condemns Naziism |
|------|------|
| 1940–45 | Auschwitz camp: death of nearly one million Jews including St. Teresa Benedicta of the Cross (Edith Stein); also St. Maximilian Kolbe |
| 1945 | Atomic bomb dropped on Urakami, Catholic suburb of Nagasaki |
| 1950 | Proclamation of dogma of the Assumption |
| 1962–65 | Vatican II and new pastoral approach |
| 1969 | New Roman Missal |
| 1989–91 | Fall of Berlin Wall and Soviet Union, influenced by Pope John Paul II |
| 2000 | Great Jubilee Year |

## Political Figures

Emperor Constantine the Great (272–337), conversion led to freedom for the Church

Emperor Theodosius I (347–95), Catholic faith made religion of Roman Empire

King Clovis (466–511), Frankish leader who embraced Catholic faith

Emperor Justinian I (482–565), reestablished Roman Empire in West

Emperor Heraclius (575–641), defeated Persians, defeated by Arabs

Emperor Charlemagne (747–814), Father of Europe

King Alfred the Great (848–99), defended England from Vikings

Emperor Otto the Great (912–73), established empire in Germany

Emperor Otto III (980–1002), international vision for empire

Emperor Basil II (958–1025), height of Macedonian Renaissance in East

Vladimir the Great (958–1015), brought Christianity to the Rus

Emperor St. Henry II (973–1004), bolstered Church as Benedictine oblate

St. Stephen of Hungary (975–1038), brought Hungary to Catholic faith

St. Edward the Confessor (1003–66), holy king of England, his death led to Norman conquest

St. Ladislaus I of Hungary (1040–95), model of chivalry

Baldwin I (c. 1060–1118), king of Jerusalem during First Crusade

Emperor John II Komnenos (1087–1143), strengthened Byzantium, allied with West

King Henry II of England (1133–89), conflict with Thomas Becket,
    father of Richard the Lionhearted and King John
St. Louis IX of France (1214–70), model king and crusader
Emperor Frederick II (1194–1250), height of empire in Europe, conflict
    with Church
Władysław II Jagiełło (c.1352–1434), drew Lithuania and Poland into
    union after marrying St. Jadwiga
Emperor Sigismund (1368–1437), led Council of Constance to end
    Great Western Schism
St. Thomas More (1478–1535), chancellor of England, martyr
Emperor Charles V (1500–58), opposed Reformation in Germany
Queen Mary Tudor (1516–58), restored Catholic Church in England
King Philip II (1527–98), high point of Spanish Empire
Henry IV of France (1553–1610), ended French Wars of Religion
Jan III Sobieski (1629–96), Polish king, lifted Siege of Vienna
King Louis XIV (1638–1715), height of royal power, Grand Siècle
James II (1633–1701), last Catholic king of England
Bonnie Prince Charlie (1720–88), Catholic pretender to British throne
Miguel Hidalgo (1753–1811), priest who led Mexican independence
Daniel O'Connell (1776–1847), leader of Catholic emancipation in
    Britain
Gabriel García Moreno (1821–75), devout president of Ecuador,
    assassinated
Bl. Giuseppe Toniolo (1845–1918), inspired Catholic political
    movements in Italy
Fr. Luigi Storzo (1871–1959), cofounded Italian People's Party based on
    Catholic social teaching
Bl. Karl von Habsburg (1887–1922), last emperor of Austria-Hungary
Ven. Robert Schumann (1886–1963), founder of European Union
John Wu (1889–1986), Chinese jurist, drafted constitution for Republic
    of China
Ngo Dinh Diem (1901–63), Catholic president of Vietnam, assassinated
President John F. Kennedy (1917–63), first Catholic president of US,
    assassinated
Lech Wałęsa (1943– ), leader of Polish Solidarity Movement

## Global and Diverse Church

Eastern Catholic Churches
    Byzantine Churches, Rite
    Syriac Churches, Rites
    Chaldean Catholic Church
    Coptic Church, Rite
    Ethiopian Church, Geʿez Rite
    Armenian Church
    Syro-Malabar and Syro-Malankara Churches in India
    Maronite Church
Reunion of Orthodox Christians

| | |
|---|---|
| 1182 | Maronites affirm union with Catholic Church |
| 1595–96 | Union of Brest (Ruthenian) |
| 1599 | Syro-Malabar Union |
| 1623 | Martyrdom of St. Josaphat |
| 1646 | Union of Uzhhorod (Ruthenian) |
| 1729 | Melkite reunion with Church |
| 1830 | Chaldeans/East Syriac reunion |

Growth of the Church in Asia
    Thomas Christians in India

| | |
|---|---|
| c. 301 | Conversion of Armenia |
| 431–1360 | Syriac Missions to Asia |
| 1501 | Matteo Rici enters China's Forbidden City |
| 1521 | Catholic faith in the Philippines |
| 1541–52 | Missionary journeys of St. Francis Xavier |
| 1597–1639 | Japanese martyrs |
| 1752 | Martyrdom of St. Devasahayam Pillai, a layman in India |
| 1801 | Martyrs of Korea |
| 1900 | Martyrs of Boxer Rebellion, China |

    Servant of God Takashi Nagai (1908–51), layman, survivor of
    Nagasaki bombing
Growth of the Church in Africa

| | |
|---|---|
| 68 | Death of the Evangelist Mark in Alexandria, Egypt |
| 3rd c. | Development of Latin theology in North Africa |
| c. 325 | Conversion of Aksum (Ethiopia) |
| 6th c. | Conversion of Nubia |
| 1485 | Kingdom of Kongo begins embrace of faith |

19th c.        Growth of Catholic Church in Sub-Saharan Africa
1885–87        Ugandan martyrs
1981-89        Marian apparitions in Kibeho, Rawanda

Missions in the United States

1565        Mission at St. Augustine, Florida
1598        Missions in New Mexico
1609        First Jesuit mission in Canada
1632        Missions in Texas
1667        Jesuit mission near Green Bay, Wisconsin
1769        St. Junipero Serra founds San Diego mission

Native American Saints

St. Juan Diego (1474–1548)
Martyrs of Tlaxcala: Cristobal (1527), Antonio and Juan (1529)
Apalachee Florida martyrs (d. 1704, cause for beatification opened)
St. Kateri Tekakwitha (1656–80)
Servant of God Nicholas Black Elk (1863–1950)

African-American Causes for Sainthood

Ven. Pierre Toussaint (1766–1853), born a slave in Haiti, hairdresser
    in New York
Servant of God Mary Elizabeth Lange (1789–1882), founded first
    congregation of Black Sisters
Ven. Henriette Delille (1812–62), founded sisters in New Orleans
Servant of God Julia Greeley (mid-19th. c.–1918), former slave,
    laywoman in Denver
Ven. Augustus Tolton (1854–97), first black priest
Servant of God Thea Bowman (1937–90), Franciscan Sister of
    Perpetual Adoration

## Popes

*Listed with years of reign.*

Peter (33–68)
Clement I (92–99), Letter to the Corinthians
Victor I (186/189–197/201), North African, Easter controversies
Sylvester I (314–35), built Roman basilicas
Damasus (366–84), commissioned Vulgate, Council of Rome
Leo the Great (440–61), great teacher, meeting with Attila the Hun
Gregory the Great (590–604), liturgy, father of Western Christendom

Martin I (649–55), died in exile for the faith

Sergius I (687–701), Syrian, conflict with Byzantium, Lamb of God

Zachary (741–52), peace with Lombards, established Pepin as king of Franks

Nicholas I (858–67), strengthened papacy in West, conflict with Greeks

Sylvester II (999–1003), promoter of math and science

Leo IX (1049–54), German, initiated great reform movement in Church

Gregory VII (1073–85), Gregorian reform, investiture controversy with Roman Empire

Urban II (1088–99), called First Crusade

Innocent III (1198–1216), height of papal power, Lateran Council IV, mendicant orders

Gregory IX (1227–41), Inquisition, Northern Crusade, canon law, conflict with Frederick II

Boniface VIII (1294–1303), followed resignation of Celestine V, conflict with Philip the Fair, *Unam sanctam*

Clement V (1305–14), brought papacy to Avignon, suppressed Knights Templar

Martin V (1417–31), his papacy ended the Great Western Schism

Nicholas V (1447–55), founded the Vatican Library, rebuilding Rome, patron of arts, Portuguese conquests

Julius II (1503–13), warrior pope, great patron of arts, design for new St. Peter's Basilica

Paul III (1534–49), reforming pope, convoked Council of Trent

Pius V (1566–72), implemented Council of Trent, excommunication of Elizabeth I, Battle of Lepanto

Benedict XIV (1740–58), learned, promoted seminary education, academies, museums

Pius VII (1800–23), concordat and conflict with Napoleon

Pius IX (1846–78), Syllabus of Errors, Immaculate Conception, Vatican Council I, loss of Papal States

Leo XIII (1878–1903), father of Catholic Social Teaching, promoter of the Rosary, St. Michael prayer

Pius X (1903–14), earlier First Communion, promoter of Gregorian chant, condemned Modernism

Pius XII (1939–58), dogma of the Assumption, opposed Nazism and Communism

John XXIII (1958–63), called the Second Vatican Council, opening
windows of the Church
Paul VI (1963–78), implemented the Second Vatican Council, *Humanae
vitae*, evangelization
John Paul II (1978–2005), reinvigorated Church, fall of Communism,
Great Jubilee
Benedict XVI (2005–13), great theologian and teacher
Francis (2013– ), witness to the poor and marginalized

### Catholic Scientists and Mathematicians

Gerbert of Aurillac/Pope Sylvester II (c. 946–1003), introduced Arabic
numerals, abacus, and armillary sphere
St. Hildegard of Bingen (1098–1179), botany, herbal medicine
Bishop Robert Grosseteste (c. 1175–1253), first articulation of scientific
method, optics, color
Albertus Magnus (c. 1206–80), natural sciences, first study of minerals
Fr. Roger Bacon (c. 1214–94), optics, scientific method
Abbot Richard of Wallingford (1292–1336), clocks, trigonometry
Jean Buridan (c. 1300–58), theory of impetus
St. John Cantius (1390–1473), furthered theory of impetus
Nicolaus Copernicus (1473–1543), heliocentric solar system
Fr. Luca Pacioli (c. 1446–1517), Franciscan, father of accounting
Ven. Matteo Ricci (1552–1610), bringing Western science to Chinese
imperial court
Galileo (1564–1642), astronomy, physics, advanced scientific method
Fr. Francesco Maria Grimaldi (1618–63), Jesuit who discovered the dif-
fraction of light
René Descartes (1596–1650), mathematics, method
Fr. Giovanni Battista Riccioli (1598–1671), acceleration, selenograph
Fr. Athanasius Kircher (1602–80), first to observe microbes, father of
Egyptology
Pascal (1623–62), probability, calculator, vacuum
Bl. Nicholas Steno (1638–86), bishop, father of geology, stratigraphy
Maria Angesi (1718–99), calculus
Laura Bassi (1711–78), first woman with a doctorate in and professor of
science
Fr. Roger Joseph Boscovich (1711–87), atomic theory, astronomy

Louis Braille (1809–52), education of the blind, Braille system
Fr. Eugenio Barsanti (1821–64), first combustion engine
Louis Pasteur (1822–95), microbiology, pasteurization
Fr. Gregor Mendel (1822–84), father of genetics
Bl. Francesco Faà di Bruno (1825–88), mathematician
Fr. Giuseppe Mercalli (1850–1914), seismology, Mercalli scale
Fr. Georges Lemaitre (1894–1966), father of the Big Bang theory
Ven. Jerome Lejeune (1926–94), chromosomes, Down syndrome
Sr. Miriam Michael Stimsom (1913–2002), structure of DNA

## V. Written Works

### *Theological Works*

St. Irenaeus of Lyon, *Against Heresies*, 175
Origen, *On First Principles*, 220
St. Athanasius, *On the Incarnation*, 335
St. Basil the Great, *On the Holy Spirit*, 375
St. Augustine, *City of God*, 420; *On the Trinity*, 400
Dionysius the Areopagite (pseudonym), *On the Divine Names*, ca. 5th–6th c.
St. John Damascene, *On the Orthodox Faith*; *On Holy Images*, 8th c.
St. Anselm, *Proslogion*, 1077; *Why God Became Man*, 1095
St. Bonaventure, *The Mind's Ascent to God*, 1259
St. Thomas Aquinas, *Summa theologiae*, 1273; *Summa contra Gentiles*, 1260
St. Robert Bellarmine, *Controversies of the Christian Faith*, 1586–93
St. John Henry Newman, *Essay on the Development of Christian Doctrine*, 1845; *Apologia pro vita sua*, 1864
Matthias Scheeben, *The Mysteries of Christianity*, 1865
Joseph Ratzinger, *Introduction of Christianity*, 1968; (as Pope Benedict XVI) *Jesus of Nazareth*, 2007

### *Spiritual Works*

St. Augustine, *Confessions*, late 4th c.
*Lives and Saying of the Desert Fathers*, 5th c.
St. Patrick, *Confessions*, 5th c.
St. Benedict, *Rule*, 530

St. Gregory the Great, *Pastoral Care*, 590; *Dialogues*, 593
St. John Climacus, *Ladder of Divine Ascent*, 600
St. Bernard, *On Loving God*, 12th c.
St. Hildegard of Bingen, *Scivias*, 1151
St. Bonaventure, *Life of St. Francis*, 1263
Julian of Norwich, *Revelations of Divine Love*, ca. 14th–15th c.
St. Bridget of Sweden, *Revelations*, 14th c.
St. Catherine of Siena, *Dialogues*, 1370
*Ars moriendi* (The Art of Dying Well), mid-15th c.
St. Thomas à Kempis, *Imitation of Christ*, 15th c.
St. Teresa of Ávila, *Autobiography*, 1565; *The Way of Perfection*, 1566;
   *Interior Castle*, 1588
St. John of the Cross, *The Ascent of Mount Carmel*, 1579
Dom Lorenzo Scupoli, *The Spiritual Combat*, 1589
St. Francis de Sales, *Introduction to the Devout Life*, 1609
St. Alphonsus Liguori, *Uniformity with God's Will*, 1755
St. Louis de Montfort, *True Devotion to Mary*, 1863
St. Thérèse of Lisieux, *Story of a Soul*, 1898
St. Faustina Kowalska, *Diary of Divine Mercy*, 1938
Walter Ciszek, *He Leadeth Me*, 1973
Robert Cardinal Sarah, *The Power of Silence*, 2017

## Literary Works (prose and verse)

Prudentius, *Crown of Martyrs*; *Psychomachia*, 5th c.
Boethius, *Consolation of Philosophy*, 523
Arthurian Legend
   Chretien de Troys, *Lancelot*, *Perceval*, 12th c.
   Vulgate Cycle (Lancelot-Grail), 13th c.
   Wolfram von Eschenbach, *Parzival*, 13th c.
   Sir Gawain and the Green Knight, 14th c.
   Sir Thomas Malory, *Morte d'Arthur*, 15th c.
*The Song of Roland*, 1040–1115
*The Song of the Nibelungs*, ca. 1200
Jacobus de Voragine, *The Golden Legend*, 1266
Dante Alighieri, *Divine Comedy*, 1321
Geoffrey Chaucer, *Canterbury Tales*, late 14th c.
William Langland, *Piers Plowman*, late 14th c.

Thomas More, *Utopia*, 1516

Marco Girolamo Vida, *Christiad*, 1536

Torquato Tasso, *Jerusalem Delivered*, 1581

Cervantes, *Don Quixote*, 1605, 1615

John Dryden, *The Hind and the Panther*, 1687

Alessandro Manzoni, *The Betrothed*, 1827

Adam Mickiewicz, *Pan Tadeusz*, 1834

Henry Wadsworth Longfellow, *Evangeline: A Tale of Arcadie*, 1847

Henryk Sienkiewicz, *Quo Vadis*, 1895

Robert Hugh Benson, *Lord of the World*, 1907

G. K. Chesterton, *Ballad of the White Horse*, 1911

Sigrid Undset, *Kristin Lavransdatter*, 1920–22

Willa Cather, *Death Comes to the Archbishop*, 1927

Gertrud von Le Fort, *The Song at the Scaffold*, 1931

François Mauriac, *The Vipers Tangle*, 1932

Georges Bernanos, *Diary of a Country Priest*, 1936

Graham Greene, *The Power and the Glory*, 1940

Evelyn Waugh, *Brideshead Revisited*, 1945

J. R. R. Tolkien, *The Lord of the Rings*, 1954–55

Walter Macken, *Seek the Fair Land*, 1959

Walter M. Miller, *A Canticle for Leibowitz*, 1960

Edwin O'Connor, *The Edge of Sadness*, 1962

Shusaku Endo, *Silence*, 1966

Rumer Godden, *In This House of Brede*, 1969

Flannery O'Connor, *The Complete Stories*, 1971

Michael O'Brien, *Father Elijah: An Apocalypse*, 1996

Steven Faulkner, *The Image: A Novel in Pieces*, 2021

### Children's Literature (ascending by age)

Tomie dePaola, *The Clown of God*, 1978; *The Lady of Guadalupe*, 1980; and others

Margaret Hodges, *St. George and the Dragon*, 1984

Josephine Nobisso, *The Weight of a Mass: A Tale of Faith*, 2002; *Take It to the Queen: A Tale of Hope*, 2008

Anna Egan Smucker, *Brother Giovanni's Little Reward: How the Pretzel Was Born*, 2015

Sylvia Dorham, *The Monks' Daily Bread*, 2015

Paolo Guarnieri, *A Boy Named Giotto*, 1998

Benedictines of Mary Queen of Apostles, *Brides of Christ*, 2023

Brothers Grimm, *Fairy Tales*, 1812

Charles Perrault, *Fairy Tales*, 1697

Mother Mary Loyola, *The King of the Golden City*, 1921

Susan Helen Wallace, *Saints for Young Readers for Every Day*, 1995

Mary Fabyan Windeatt, *The Lives of the Saints* (twenty story books), 1941

Raissa Maritain, *St. Thomas Aquinas*, 1934

Andrew and Nora Lang, *The Book of Saints and Heroes*, 1912

Henri Daniel-Rops, *Golden Legend of Young Saints*, 1960

J. R. R. Tolkien, *The Hobbit*, 1937

Carlo Collodi, *Adventures of Pinocchio*, 1883

Marion Florence Lansing, *Barbarian and Noble*, 1911

Barbara Willard, *Augustine Came to Kent*, 1963

C. S. Lewis, *The Chronicles of Narnia*, 1950–56

Marguerite de Angeli, *The Door in the Wall*, 1949

Madeleine Polland, *Beorn the Proud*, 1961

Aloysius Roche, *Christians Courageous*, 2009

Susan Peek, *Crusader King: A Novel of Baldwin IV and the Crusades*, 2004

J. Walker McSpadden, *Robin Hood*, 1921

Sr. Imelda Wallace, *Outlaws of Ravenhurst*, 1923

Barbara Willard, *Son of Charlemagne*, 1959

Elizabeth George Speare, *The Bronze Bow*, 1961

Donal Foley, *The Secret of Glastonbury Tor*, 2015

Mark Twain, *Joan of Arc*, 1896

Alexander Dumas, *The Three Musketeers*, 1844

Walter Scott, *The Talisman*, 1825

Louis de Wohl, *The Spear*, 1955; *The Joyful Beggar*, 1959; *The Golden Thread*, 1953; *Citadel of God*, 1959; others

Evelyn Waugh, *Helena*, 1950

G. K. Chesterton, *The Man Who Was Thursday*, 1908

## Poems[2]

St. Ephrem the Syrian (206–73), *Hymns on Faith; Hymns on Paradise*
St. Gregory Nazianzus (329–90), "To His Own Soul"
St. Ambrose (339–97), Ambrosian Hymns
St. Paulinus of Nola (354–431), "Another Year Completed"
Coelius Sedulius (5th c.), "From the Pivot of the Sun's Rising"
Venantius Fortunatus (530–609), "Sing, O Tongue, of the Glorious
    Struggle"; "The Royal Banners Forward Go"
Old English Poet (ca. 8th c.), "Dream of the Rood"
St. Gregory Narek (ca. 951–1011), *Lamentations*
St. Bernard of Clairvaux (1090–1153), "The Sweet Memory of Jesus"
Bernard of Cluny (12th c.), "On Contempt for the World"
St. Francis (1181–1226), "Canticle of the Creatures" ("Canticle of the
    Sun")
Arnulf of Leuven (1200–1250), "*Membra Jesu nostri*"
St. Thomas Aquinas (1225–74), "*Adoro te devote*"
Jacopane da Todi (1230–1306), "The Highest Wisdom"
Petrarch (1304–74), "To the Virgin Mary"
Luis de Leon (1527–91), "The Life Removed"
St. John of the Cross (1542–91), "The Spiritual Canticle"; "The Dark
    Night of the Soul"
St. Robert Southwell (1561–95), "The Burning Babe"
Richard Crashaw (1612–49), "The Flaming Heart"
Angelus Silesius (1624–77), "The Soul Wherein God Dwells"
Jean de La Ceppède (1550–1623), *Theorems*
Alexander Pope (1688–1744), "The Dying Christian to His Soul"
St. John Henry Newman (1801–90), "The Pillar of the Cloud"; *The
    Dream of Gerontius*
Coventry Patmore (1823–96), "*Magna est veritas*"
Charles Warren Stoddard (1843–1909), "The Bells of San Gabriel"
Gerard Manley Hopkins (1844–89), "God's Grandeur"; "Pied Beauty"
St. Thérèse of Lisieux (1873–97), "My Song of Today"

---

2. I recommend Thomas Walsh's *The Catholic Anthology: The World's Great Catholic Poetry* (New York: MacMillan, 1939). Many of my recommended poems can
be found within it.

Émile Verhaeren (1855–1916), "The Cathedral of Rheims"
Francis Thompson (1859–1907), "Hound of Heaven"
José Asunción Silva (1865–1896), "First Communion"
Paul Claudel (1868–1955) "The Shadows"
Joseph Mary Plunkett (1887–1916), "I See His Blood Upon the Rose"
T. S. Eliot (1888–1965), "Ash Wednesday"
Hilaire Belloc (1870–1953), "To Dives"
G. K. Chesterton (1874–1936), "Lepanto"
Joyce Kilmer (1886–1914), "Trees"
Dame Edith Sitwell (1887–1964), "Still Falls the Rain"
Pope John Paul II (1920–2005), *Roman Triptych*
Dana Gioia (1950– ), "The Angel with the Broken Wing"

## Drama

*The Mystery of Adam*, 1150
Hildegard of Bingen, *Ordo Virtutum* (*Order of the Virtues*), 1151
Beauvais Cathedral School, *Play of Daniel*, early 13th c.
York Cycle of Mystery Plays (48 plays), 15th c.
*Everyman*, 15th c.
Gil Vicente, *Auto da Alma* (*The Soul's Journey*), 1518
Shakespeare, *Works*
Pedro Calderon de la Barca, *The Purgatory of St. Patrick*, 1635
Pierre Corneille, *Polyeucte*, 1643
Joost van den Vondel, *Lucifer*, 1654; *Adam in Exile*, 1664; *Noah*, 1667
Jean Racine, *Athalie*, 1691
Alexander Pushkin, *Boris Godunov*, 1831
G. K. Chesterton, *Magic*, 1913
T. S. Eliot, *Murder in the Cathedral*, 1935
Dorothy Sayers, *The Zeal of Thy House*, 1936
Georges Bernanos, *Dialogue of the Carmelites*, 1949
Robert Bolt, *A Man for All Seasons*, 1960
John Paul II, *The Jeweler's Shop*, 1960

## Historical Accounts and Narratives

Eusebius, *Church History*; *Life of Constantine*, 4th c.
Athanasius, *Life of St. Antony*, 360

Jerome, *Lives of Illustrious Men*, 393
Egeria, *Diary of a Pilgrimage*, 4th c.
Gregory of Tours, *Ten Books of History* (*History of the Franks*), 6th c.
Venerable Bede, *Ecclesiastical History of the English People*, 731
Einhard, *Life of Charlemagne*, early 9th c.
Bishop Otto of Freising, *The Two Cities*, 1146
Anna Comnena, *Alexiad*, 1148
Jordan of Saxony, *Libellus* (*History of the Beginnings of the Order of Preachers*), 1233
John of Joinville, *Chronicle of the Crusades*, 13th c.
*The Little Flowers of St. Francis*, late 14th c.
Bartolomé de las Casas, *Conquest of the Indies*, 1542
Bernal Díaz de Castillo, *The True History of the Conquest of New Spain*, 1568
Cardinal Baronius, *Ecclesiastical Annals*, 1588–1607
Antonio Ruiz de Montoya, SJ, *The Spiritual Conquest*, 1639
Jacques-Bénigne Bossuet, *A Universal History*, 1681
St. John Henry Newman, *Historical Sketches*, 1897
François-Auguste-René, vicomte de Chateaubriand, *The Genuis of Christianity*, 1802
Count de Montelambert, *The Monks of the West from St. Benedict to St. Bernard*, 1861
Francis Parkman, *The Jesuits in New France: An Outline, 1611–1847*, 1867
Sr. Blandina Segale, *At the End of the Santa Fe Trail*, 1932
Hilaire Belloc, *The Great Heresies*, 1938; *Characters of the Reformation*, 1936
Henri Daniel-Rops, *The History of the Church of Christ*, 1960–65
Gereon Goldmann, OFM, *The Shadow of His Wings*, 1964
Christopher Dawson, *The Formation of Christendom*, 1967; *The Dividing of Christendom*, 1965
Eamon Duffy, *The Stripping of the Altars: Traditional Religion in England, 1400–1580*, 1992
Warren Carroll, *Christendom* series, 1985–2013

# VI. Catholic Art

## *Art Terms*

Periods
- Roman techniques, adoption of
- Byzantine art and architecture
- Romanesque art and architecture
- Gothic art and architecture
- Renaissance art and architecture
- Baroque art and architecture
- Romantic and Neoclassical art and architecture
- Modern art and architecture

Beauty
Proportion
Harmony
Clarity
Perspective
Vanishing point
Naturalism
Stylization
Abstraction
Chiaroscuro
Icon
Statue
Mosaic
Tesserae
Relief sculpture
Historiated capital
Gospel cover
Illumination
Vellum
Pigment

Stucco
Stained glass
Fresco
Tempera
Oil paint
Wood panel
Canvas
Polychrome
Rounded versus pointed arch
Tympanum
Altarpiece
Triptych
Vault
Pillar
Pier
Portal
Ambulatory
Clerestory
Rose window
Lancet window
Gable
Pinnacle
Spire
Crocket
Embroidered vestments
Buttress, flying buttress
Archivolt
Jamb and trumeau statuary
Portal
Porch
Labyrinth
Iconostasis

# Images

Shroud of Turin as model

St. Luke, icon of Our Lady as model

Frescoes of Dura Europas house church, early 3rd c.

Catacomb paintings: Callixtus, Priscilla, Domitilla, Marcellinus, and Peter

*Sinai Pantocrator*, 6th c., other encaustic images of St. Catherine's Monastery at Sinai

Red Monastery of St. Pishay, Sohag, Egypt, 5th–7th centuries

Frescoes of Christ, St. John's Abbey, Müstair, ca. 800

Frescoes of Christ, St. George at Oberzell, ca. 1000

*Deesis*, Hagia Sophia, 1261

Stained glass at Augsburg, Chartres, Paris, Sainte Chapelle, York

*Life of St. Francis* cycle, Assisi Basilica, 1260–1320

Giotto, *Arena Chapel*, 1305

Duccio, *Maestà*, 1311

*Wilton Diptych*, late 14th c.

*Apocalypse Tapestries of Angers*, 1377–82

Andrei Rublev, *Trinity*, 1425

Jan van Eyck, *Altarpiece of Ghent*, 1432

Rogier van der Weyden, *Deposition*, 1435

Hugo van der Goes, *Monteforte Altarpiece*, 1440

Fra Angelico, frescoes at the Convent of San Marco, 1438–50

Masaccio, *Holy Trinity*, Santa Maria Novella, 1425–27

Stefan Lochner, *Dombild Altarpiece (Last Judgment)*, mid-15th c.

Piero della Francesca, *Legend of the True Cross*, Arezzo, 1452–66

Andrea Mantegna, *San Zeno Altarpiece*, 1457–60

Hans Memling, *Last Judgment*, 1460s

*Lady and the Unicorn Tapestries*, 1500

Sandro Botticelli, *Madonna of the Magnificat*, 1483; *Madonna of the Book*, 1480–83

Pietro Perugino, *Delivery of the Keys*, 1482

Gentile Bellini, *Procession of the True Cross in Piazza San Marco*, 1496

Leonardo DaVinci, *The Last Supper*, 1498; *Virgin and Child with St. Anne*, 1519

Vittore Carpaccio, *Legend of St. Ursula*, 1498

Luca Signorelli, Frescoes of Orvieto Cathedral, early 16th c.

Hieronymus Bosch, *Garden of Earthly Delights*, 1505
Albrecht Dürer, *Feast of the Rose Garlands*, 1506; Woodcuts of the
　Apocalypse, 1498
Giovanni Bellini, *Madonna of the Trees*, 1510
Grünewald, *Isenheim Altarpiece*, 1512–16
Michelangelo, Sistine Chapel ceiling, 1512; *Last Judgment*, 1541
Titian, *Assumption*, 1518
Raphael, Raphael Rooms in the Vatican Apartments, ca. 1520;
　*Transfiguration*, 1520
Hans Holbein the Younger, *Body of the Dead Christ in the Tomb*, 1522;
　*Sir Thomas More*, 1527
Juan de Juanes, *Last Supper*, 1562
Paolo Veronese, *Wedding at Cana*, 1563
Pieter Bruegel the Elder, *The Procession to Calvary*, 1564
Tintoretto, paintings of the Scuola di San Rocco, 1565–88
El Greco, *Burial of Count Orgaz*, 1586; *Resurrection*, 1595
Caravaggio, *Calling of St. Matthew*, 1600; *The Crucifixion of Peter*, 1602;
　*Entombment of Christ*, 1603
Annibale Carracci, *Pieta with St. Francis*, 1602–7
Peter Paul Rubens, *Descent from the Cross*, 1612; *Triumph of the Eucharist*
　series, 1620s
Gerard van Honthorst, *Adoration of the Shepherds*, 1622
Francisco de Zurbarán, *Saint Francis Contemplating a Skull*, 1635
Guido Reni, *St. Michael Archangel*, 1636
Diego Velázquez, *Christ in the House of Mary and Martha*, 1618;
　*Coronation of the Virgin*, 1644
Rembrandt, *100 Guilder Print*, 1649; *Return of the Prodigal Son*, 1669
Georges de la Tour, *Joseph the Carpenter*, 1642
Phillipe de Champaigne, *St. Augustine*, 1650
Nicholas Poussin, *Annunciation*, 1655–57
Bartolomé Esteban Murillo, *The Annunciation*, 1660
Jan Steen, *Supper at Emmaus*, 1668
Johannes Vermeer, *Allegory of Faith*, 1672; *Woman Holding a Balance*,
　1664
Pompeo Batoni, *Sacred Heart*, 1767
Giovanni Battista Tiepolo, *Immaculate Conception*, 1768
Friedrich Overbeck, *Triumph of Religion in the Arts*, 1840

Peter von Cornelius, *Last Judgment*, 1840
Jean-Auguste-Dominique Ingres, *Virgin Adoring the Host*, 1852; *Joan of Arc*, 1854
Ary Scheffer, *Augustine and Monica*, 1854
Gustav Doré, Divine Comedy engravings, 1857–67
Jean-François Millet, *The Angelus*, 1859
Eugène Delacroix, Angel murals of St. Sulpice, 1861
Joseph von Führich, *Rudolf von Habsburg and the Priest*, 1870
William Adolphe Bouguereau, *Pietà*, 1876
St. Adam Chmielowski, *Ecce Homo*, 1881
William Hunt, *Triumph of the Holy Innocents*, 1884
Jacques Joseph Tissot, Bible illustrations, 1886–1902
Maurice Denis, *Le Mystère Catholique*, 1889
Claude Monet, Rouen Cathedral painting series, 1890s
Ludwig Seitz, *Life of Mary* series; Modesto Faustini, *Life of Joseph* series at Holy House at Loretto, late 19th c.
Marie Alain Couturier, OP, *Pieta*, mid-20th c.
Georges Rouault, *Ecce Homo*, 1952
Salvador Dalí, *Sacrament of the Last Supper*, 1955
Nielson Carlin, *Communion of Saints*, Epiphany Catholic Church, 2015

### Illuminated Manuscripts

Rabbula Gospels, 6th c.
Rossano Gospels, 6th c.
St. Augustine Gospels, 6th c.
*Codex Amiatinus*, c.700
Lindisfarne Gospels, 715–20
Book of Kells, ca. 800
Lorsch Gospels, 778–820
Ebbo Gospels, 816–35
Sacramentary of Charles the Bald, 870
Utrecht Gospels, 9th c.
Etchmiadzin Gospels, 10th c.
Paris Psalter (Byzantine), 10th c.
Joshua Roll, 10th c.
Morgan Beatus, Apocalypse, 10th c.
Gospels of Otto III, 1001

Hitda Codex, 1020
Psalter of St. Louis, mid- to late 13th c.
The Hours of Jeanne d'Evreux, 1328
Visconti Hours, late 14th–early 15th c.
Very Rich Hours of the Duc de Berry, 1416
Hours of Mary of Burgundy, 1477
Black Hours, 1480
Grandes Heures of Anne of Brittany, 1508
Rothschild Prayerbook, 1520
Farnese Hours, 1546
St. John's Bible, 2011

## Sculpture, Carving, and Metal Work

Santa Maria Antiqua Sarcophagus, ca. 270
Sarcophagus of Jonah, ca. 300
Good Shepherd Statue of Catacomb of St. Domitilla, ca. 325
Junius Basso Sarcophagus, 359
Brescia Casket, ivory reliquary, late 4th c.
Doors of Santa Sabina, 432
Throne of Maximian, ivory panels, 6th c.
Bewcastle and Ruthwell Crosses, late 7th or early 8th c.
Holy Face of Lucca, late 8th c.
Medieval Gospel covers: Lorsch Gospels, ca. 800; Lindau Gospels, 9th
    c.; Codex Aureus of St. Emmeram, 870; Gospel Book of Otto III, ca.
    1000; Codex Aureus of Echternach, 1030–50; Gospels of Judith of
    Flanders, late 11th c.
Golden Altar of Sant'Ambrogio, 825–59
Cross of Desiderius, mid-9th c.
Lothair Crystal, mid-9th c.
Gero Cross, 965–70
Pala d'Oro Altar, San Marco, 976–1345
Jelling Stones of Harald Bluetooth, Denmark, 10th c.
Limburg Staurotheke (Cross container), Reliquary of True Cross, 10th c.
Cross of Lothair, ca. 1000
Bishop Bernward, bronze doors and column, St. Michael's Hildesheim,
    1015–20
Triumphal Arch, Santa Maria Ripoll, 12th c.

Romanesque tympana at Santiago de Compostela, Vézelay, Autun,
    Conques, Toulouse
Gothic statuary at Cathedrals of Chartres, Amiens, Rheims, Strasbourg,
    Magdeburg
Nicola Pisano, pulpit of Siena Cathedral, 1268
Benedetto Antelami, figures of the Parma Baptistery, early 13th c.
*Le Beau Dieu*, Amiens Cathedral, early 13th c.
*Smiling Angel*, Rheims Cathedral, 1245
*Pillar of Angels* (or *Judgment*), Strasbourg, 1235
Arnolfo di Cambio, statue of St. Peter in the basilica; first carved nativity,
    St. Mary Major, mid-13th c.
Lorenzo Maitani, "Scenes from Genesis," "Last Judgment" Orvieto
    Cathedral, 1331
Röttgen Pietà, 1330s
Giovanni di Balduccio, *Arc of Peter Martyr*, Milan, 1339
Lorenzo Ghiberti, *Gates of Heaven*, 1452
Hans Multscher, *Man of Sorrows*, Ulm Cathedral, ca. 1429
Lucca della Robbia, *Madonna and Child*, ca. 1475
Niccolò dell'Arca, *Lamentation over Dead Christ*, 1463
Retables of Spanish cathedrals: Seville, Toledo, Coimbra, late
    15th–16th c.
Donatello, statues in Basilica of St. Anthony, Padua, 1450; *Magdalene
    Penitent*, 1455
Bernt Notke, *St. George*, 1487
Veit Stoss, altarpiece of St. Mary's, Cracow, 1489
Michelangelo, *Pietà*, 1499; *David*, 1504; *Moses*, 1513
Tilman Riemenschneider, Altar of the Holy Blood, 1505
Bramante, design for the Marble Encasing of Holy House, Loretto,
    16th c.
Germain Pilon, *Resurrection*, 1572
Giacomo Serpotta, stucco of the Oratory of the Rosary in Santa Cita,
    Palermo, 1685–90
Gian Lorenzo Bernini, *Ecstasy of St. Teresa*, 1752; statuary, baldacchin,
    and altar of the Chair in St. Peter's
Giuseppe Sanmartino, *Veiled Christ*, 1753
Antonio Canova, *Penitent Magdalene*, 1796; funerary monuments of
    Clement XIII and Clement XIV

Pierre Le Gros the Younger, *St. Ignatius*, 1699; *Religion Overthrowing Heresy and Hatred*, 1695–99

Auguste Rodin, *The Gates of Hell*, 1880–1917; *The Hand of God*, 1898

Lello Scorzelli, *Crocefisso* (used by Paul VI, John Paul II), 1963

Pericle Fazzini, *La Resurrezione*, 1977

George Carpenter, Clear Creek Abbey's Tympanum, 2020

## Architecture: Great Churches

Church of the Holy Sepulcher, Jerusalem, 335

St. Peter's Basilica, Rome, Constantinian church, 333; dedication of new basilica, 1626

St. Paul's Outside the Walls, Rome, 4th c., restored 1840

San Ambrosio, Milan, 379

Etchmiadzin Cathedral, Armenia, 5th c.

Santa Sabina, Rome, 422

Santa Mara Maggiore, Rome, 432

San Vitale, Ravenna, 6th c.

Hagia Sophia, Constantinople, 6th c.

The Monastery of St. Catherine, Mt. Sinai, 6th c.

Skellig Michael, Ireland, 6th c.

San Pedro de la Nave, Spain, 8th c.

Cordoba Cathedral, 785 (oldest part of structure)

Charlemagne's chapel, Aachen, 800

Cathedral of the Holy Cross, Lake Van, Turkey (Armenian), 10th c.

Hosios Loukas Monastery, Greece, 10th c.

Cave Churches of Göreme, Cappadocia, 9th–11th c.

Westminster Abbey, London, 960

Mont Saint-Michel Abbey, Normandy, 966

Bamberg Cathedral, 1002

St. Michael's, Hildesheim, 1010

St. Sophia, Kiev, 1037

Cluny, third church (now destroyed), Burgundy, 1095

Speyer Cathedral, 1030

Abbey aux Hommes (St. Etienne), Caen, 1065

Fontenay Abbey, France, 1147

Italian cathedrals: Venice, 1094; Monreale, 1172; Pisa, 1064; Siena, 1215; Orvietto, 1290; Florence, 1436

Gothic cathedrals of France: St. Denis, 1140; Chartres, 1194; Paris,
1163; Amiens, 1220; Beauvais, 1225; Reims, 1211; Strasbourg, 1439
English cathedrals: Durham, late 11th c.; Canterbury, 1070; Wells, 1175;
Lincoln, 1092; Ely, 1083; Lichfield, 1085; Peterborough, 1118;
Salisbury, 1220
Cathedrals of Spain: Burgos, 1221; Leon, 1302; Seville, 1401; Toledo,
1493; Cadiz, 1635; Salamanca, 1733
Frari Church, Venice, 1250
Santa Croce, Florence, 1294
Lalibela Rock Churches, Ethiopia, 13th c.
Chora Church, Constantinople, 14th c.
San Giorgio Maggiore, Venice, 16th c.
San Miguel at Huejotzingo, Mexico, 1550
Chapel of the Rosario, Puebla, Mexico, 1550
El Escorial Monastery Palace, Spain, 1563
Church of the Gesù, Rome, 1568
Cathedrals of Latin America: Santo Domingo, 1504; Mexico City, 1573;
Lima,1540; Cusco, 1539
San Pedro Apóstol de Andahuaylillas, Peru, 16th c.
Churches of Quito: Convent of San Francisco, 1673; La Merced, 1749;
La Compañía 1605
Santa Maria della Salute, Venice, 1631
Sant'Ivo alla Sapienzia, Rome, 1660
San Xavier del Bac, Arizona, 1692
Melk Abbey, Austria, 1702
Ottobeuren Abbey, Germany, 1711
St. Sulpice, Paris, 1725
Asam Church, St. Nepomuk, Munich, 1733
Karlskirche, Vienna, 1737
Church of the Fourteen Holy Helpers (Vierzehnheiligen), Bavaria, 1743
Weis Church, Bavaria, 1745
San Francisco Convent, Salvador, Brazil, 1755
Miagao Church, Philippines, 1787
Notre Dame de Montréal, Canada, 1829
La Madeleine, Paris, 1837
St. Patrick's Cathedral, New York, 1858
Leeds Cathedral, 1904

Sacre Coeur Basilica, Paris, 1914
Cathedral Basilica of St. Louis, Missouri, 1926
Basilica of Sainte-Thérèse, France, 1951
National Basilica of the Immaculate Conception, Washington, D.C., 1959
St. Joseph Oratory, Montreal, 1967
Basilica of Our Lady of Peace, Ivory Coast, 1989
Shrine of the Most Blessed Sacrament, Alabama, 1999
Basilica of Our Lady of Lichen, Poland, 2004
Sagrada Família, Barcelona, 1886–2026

## Film

Carl Theodor Dreyer, *The Passion of Joan of Arc*, 1928
Henry King, *The Song of Bernadette*, 1943
Maurice Cloche, *Monsieur Vincent*, 1947
Victor Fleming, *Joan of Arc*, 1948
Roberto Rossellini, *The Flowers of St. Francis*, 1950
Robert Bresson, *Diary of a Country Priest*, 1951
Alfred Hitchcock, *I Confess*, 1953
Robert Hamer, *Father Brown (The Detective)*, 1954
Ladislao Vajda, *Miracle of Marcellino*, 1956
Ralph Nelson, *Lilies of the Field*, 1963
Fred Zinnemann, *A Man for All Seasons*, 1966
George Schaefer, *In this House of Brede*, 1975
Ermanno Olmi, *The Tree of Wooden Clogs*, 1978
Michael Lindsay-Hogg and Charles Sturridge, *Brideshead Revisited*, 1981
Jerry London, *The Scarlet and the Black*, 1983
Josefina Molina, *Teresa de Jesús*, 1984
Roland Joffé, *The Mission*, 1986
Alain Cavalier, *Thérèse*, 1986
Gabriel Axel, *Babette's Feast*, 1987
Michael Anderson, *The Jeweller's Shop*, 1988
John Duigan, *Romero*, 1989
Mel Gibson, *The Passion of the Christ*, 2004
Volker Schlöndorff, *The Ninth Day*, 2004
Philip Gröning, *Into Great Silence*, 2005
Alejandro Gomez Monteverde, *Bella*, 2006

Xavier Beauvois, *Of Gods and Men*, 2010
Martin Scorsese, *Silence*, 2016
Terrence Malick, *A Hidden Life*, 2019

## VII. Catholic Music

### *Music Terms*

Acapella
Chant
Organ
Choir
Polyphony
Chanting of Mass and Divine
Office
Ordinary and proper parts of the
Mass
Mass setting
Orchestral Mass
Hymn
Antiphons
Motet

Oratorio
Monks' musical contributions
Musical notation
Mode
Keys
Melody
Harmony
Rhythm
Organum
Melisma
Counterpoint
Chant modes
Consonance
Dissonance

### *Classic Hymns*[3]

Marian Antiphons
   *Salve Regina*
   *Ave Regina Caelorum*
   *Alma Redemptoris Mater*
   *Regina Caeli*

---

3. I recommend the following hymnals for use in schools: *Source and Summit Missal* (https://www.sourceandsummit.com/missal), the hymnals and missals from Corpus Christi Watershed (https://www.ccwatershed.org/), the *Adoremus Hymnal* (San Francisco: Ignatius Press, 1997), and the *Ignatius Pew Missal* (http://www.pewmissal.com/brand_new/).

Aquinas's Eucharistic Hymns
  *Pange Lingua Gloriosi* (Sing My Tongue)
  *O Salutaris* (O Saving Victim)
  *Tantum ergo* (Down in Adoration Falling)
  *Lauda Sion Salvatorem* (Laud, O Sion)
Praise to God
  *Te Deum*
  Of the Father's Love Begotten
  Sing Praise to Our Creator
  Holy God We Praise Thy Name
  Be Thou My Vision
  O Trinity of Blessed Light
  All Creatures of Our God and King
  All Hail Adored Trinity
Advent
  *Vox Clara Ecce Intonat*
  O Come, O Come Emmanuel
  Creator of the Stars of Night
  Lo How a Rose E'er Blooming
  On Jordan's Bank
  People Look East
  O Come Divine Messiah
  The Angel Gabriel from Heaven Came
  Come Thou Long-Expected Jesus
  *Rorate Coeli*
Christmas
  *Puer Natus in Bethlehem*
  O Come All Ye Faithful (*Adeste Fideles*)
  Silent Night
  *Puer Nobis Nascitur*
  Angels We Have Heard on High
  Come All Ye Shepherds
  For Love of Me
  *In Dulci Jubilo*
  Holiest Night
  From Lands that See the Sun Arise

Lent

The Glory of These Forty Days
Lord, Who Throughout These Forty Days
*Parce Domine*
O Sacred Head Surrounded
Again We Keep This Solemn Fast
O Merciful Creator, Hear Our Prayer
In Prayer Together Let Us Fall
*Stabat Mater*
All Glory, Laud, and Honor (Palm Sunday)
*Ubi Caritas* (Holy Thursday)
The Royal Banner Forward Goes (Good Friday)

Easter

*Victimae Paschali Laudes*
Jesus Christ Is Risen Today
O Sons and Daughters
All Creatures of Our God and King
At the Lamb's High Feast We Sing
*Salve Festa Dies*
Ye Watchers and Ye Holy Ones
Alleluia! Sing to Jesus
The Lamb's High Banquet We Await
Morning Spreads Her Crimson Rays

Eucharistic Hymns

*Adoro Te Devote*/Godhead Here in Hiding
*Panis Angelicus*
Soul of My Savior
At That First Eucharist
Sweet Sacrament Divine
*Adoremus in Aeternum*
O Lord, I Am Not Worthy

Hymns to Christ

*Christus Vincit*
All Hail the Power of Jesus' Name
Glory Be to Jesus (*Viva! viva! Gesù*)
*Iesu Dulcis Memoria*
Jesus Splendor of the Father

Christ Is Made the Sure Foundation
Jesus in Your Heart We Find
All Who Seek a Comfort Sure
Hymns to Mary
   *O Sanctissima*
   Immaculate Mary
   Hail Holy Queen Enthroned Above
   Mary Immaculate, Star of the Morning
   Thou Lady Bright
   *Concordi Laetitia*/Sounds of Joy Have Put to Flight
   Bring Flowers of the Rarest
   On This Day O Beautiful Mother
   Hail, O Star of Ocean
   The God whom Earth and Sea and Sky
Holy Spirit/Pentecost
   Come Down, O Love Divine
   Come Holy Ghost
   *Veni Creator Spiritus*/Creator Spirit by Whose Aid
Eternal Life/Saints
   *Dies Irae*
   *In Paradisum*
   For All the Saints
   With Souls Alert for Happiness
   Holy Patron, Thee Saluting (to St. Joseph)
   *Tu Es Petrus* (to St. Peter)
Fr. Frederick Faber's Hymns
   Sweet Sacrament, We Thee Adore
   Faith of Our Fathers
   There Is a Wideness in God's Mercy

## Musical Pieces

Romanos the Melodist, *Kontakion of the Nativity*, 6th c.
St. Kassiani, *The Hymn of Kassiani* (The Hymn of the Fallen Woman), 9th c.
St. Hildegard of Bingen, *Symphony of the Harmony of Celestial Revelations*, mid-12th c.
Pérotin, *Viderunt omnes*, 1198

Guillaume de Machaut, *Christe qui lux est*, 14th c.

Red Book of Montserrat (*Llibre Vermell de Montserrat*), 14th c.

Guillaume Du Fay, *Nuper rosarum flores*, 1436

Josquin des Prez, *Inviolata*, 1519

Tomás Luis de Victoria, *Tenebrae Responsories*, 1585; Lamentations of Jeremiah, 1585

Orlando di Lasso, *Tears of Peter*, 1594

Giovanni Gabrieli, *Sacrae Symphoniae*, 1597, 1615

Giovanni Pierluigi da Palestrina, *Sicut Cervus*, 1608

Claudio Monteverdi, *Vespers of the Blessed Virgin Mary*, 1610

Gregorio Allegri, *Miserere*, 1638

Heinrich Ignaz Franz von Biber, *Rosary/Mystery Sonatas*, 1676

Jean-Baptiste Lully, *Dies Irae*, 1683

Henry Purcell, *Te Deum; Jubilate Deo*, 1694

Marc-Antoine Charpentier, *Te Deum*, 1690s

Domenico Zipoli, SJ, music for Jesuit reductions, early 18th c.

Antonio Vivaldi, *Judith Triumphant*, 1716; Gloria in D Major, early 18th c.; *Stabat Mater*, 1712

Johann Sebastian Bach, *St. Matthew's Passion*, 1727

Giovanni Battista Pergolesi, *Stabat Mater*, 1736

Giovanni Battista Sanmartino, *Pianto di Maddalena al Sepolchro*, mid-18th c.

Joseph Haydn, *Seven Last Words of Christ*, 1785; Creation, 1798

Wolfgang Amadeus Mozart, *Laudete Dominum*, 1680; Ave Verum Corpus, 1791

Franz Schubert, *Ave Maria*, 1825

Gioachino Rossini, *Stabat Mater*, 1841

Gaetano Donizetti, *Poliuto*, 1848

Charles Gounod, *Ave Maria*, 1853

Hector Berlioz, *The Infancy of Christ*, 1854

Franz Liszt, *Dante Symphony*, 1857

César Frank, *Panis Angelicus*, 1872

Antonín Dvořák, *Stabat Mater*, 1880

Richard Wagner, *Parsifal*, 1882

Edward Elgar, *Dream of Gerontius*, 1900

Francis Poulenc, *Dialogue of the Carmelites*, 1953

Henryk Górecki, *Totus Tuus*, 1987

Libera, *Adoramus*, 2004
Arvo Pärt, *In Principio*, 2006
Lucio Mosè Benaglia, *Stabat Mater für Mariupol*, 2023

## Mass Settings

Plain Chant
Gregorian Chant Masses, *Missa de angelis; Missa orbis factor*; others
Guillame de Machaut, *Messe de Nostre Dame*, mid-14th c.
Guillaume Du Fay, *Missa se la face ay pale; Missa L'Homme armé*,
    mid-15th c.
Josquin des Prez, *Missa de Beate Virgine*, late 15th c.; *Missa Pange
    Lingua*, 1515
Giovanni Pierluigi da Palestrina, *Missa Papa Marcelli*, 1562
Orlando di Lasso, *Missa Venatorum (Jägermesse)*, 1577
Thomas Tallis, *Mass for Four Voices*, 1575
William Byrd, *Mass for Five Voices*, 1594
Alessandro Scarlatti, *St. Cecilia Mass*, 1721
Bach, *Mass in B Minor*, 1749
Mozart, *Great Mass*, 1783; *Requiem*, 1791
Haydn, *Nelson Mass/Missa angustiis*, 1798
Ludwig van Beethoven, *Mass in C Major*, 1807; *Missa Solemnis*, 1823
Franz Schubert, *Mass No. 2*, 1815
Gaetano Donizetti, *Requiem in D Minor*, 1835
Hector Berlioz, *Grande Messe des Morts*, 1837
Anton Bruckner, *Mass No. 3 (Great Mass)*, 1872
César Frank, *Mass in A Major*, 1860
Giuseppe Verdi, *Requiem*, 1874
Gabriel Fauré, *Requiem*, 1890
Antonín Dvořák, *Mass in D Major*, 1892
Maurice Duruflé, *Requiem*, 1947
Andrew Lloyd Webber, *Requiem*, 1985
Arvo Pärt, *Berliner Messe*, 1990
Zbigniew Preisner, *Requiem for My Friend*, 1998
Frank La Rocca, *Mass of the Americas*, 2018

# Bibliography

Adler, Eric. *The Battle of the Classics: How a Nineteenth-Century Debate Can Save the Humanities Today*. New York: Oxford University Press, 2020.

Alvaré, Helen. *Religious Freedom after the Sexual Revolution: A Catholic Guide*. Washington, D.C.: The Catholic University of America Press, 2022.

Aquila, Samuel. "Discipleship Beyond the First Encounter." February 9, 2017.

Aquinas, Thomas. *De Veritate*. Vol. 2, *Questions 10–20*. Translated by James V. McGlynn, SJ. Chicago: Henry Regnery Company, 1953.

———. *Commentary on John's Gospel*. Vol. 1, *Chapters 1–5*. Translated by Fabian Larcher, OP, and James A. Weisheipl, OP. Albany, N.Y.: Magi Books, 1998.

———. *Summa theologiae*. Translated by English Dominican Province. London: Burns, Oates, and Washbourne, 1927.

Aristotle. *The Basic Works of Aristotle*. Edited by Richard McKeon. New York: Modern Library Classics, 2001.

Archdiocese of Denver. *School of the Lord's Service: A Framework for Forming Disciples*. Edited by R. Jared Staudt. 2020. http://archden.uberflip.com/i/1312720-school-of-the-lord-s-service/0?.

Augustine. *Selected Sermons*. Edited by Q. Howe Jr. New York: Holt, Rinehard and Winston, 1966.

Baars, Conrad W. *Feeling and Healing Your Emotions: A Christian Psychiatrist Shows You How to Grow to Wholeness*. Gainesville, Fla.: Bridge-Logos, 2003.

Barron, Robert. *Catholicism: A Journey to the Heart of the Faith*. New York: Image Books, 2011.

Benedict XVI. Presentation of the *Compendium of the Catechism of the Catholic Church*. June 28, 2005. https://www.vatican.va/content/benedict-xvi/en/speeches/2005/june/documents/hf_ben-xvi_spe_20050628_compendium.html.

————. Address to the Participants in the Convention of the Diocese of Rome. June 11, 2007. https://www.vatican.va/content/benedict-xvi/en/speeches/2007/june/documents/hf_ben-xvi_spe_20070611_convegno-roma.html.

————. Address at a Meeting with Catholic Educators at The Catholic University of America. April 17, 2008.

————. Address to Participants in the Plenary Assembly of the Pontifical Council for Culture. November 13, 2010. https://www.vatican.va/content/benedict-xvi/en/speeches/2010/november/documents/hf_ben-xvi_spe_20101113_pc-cultura.html.

————. Address to the Catholic University of the Sacred Heart. May 21, 2011. https://www.vatican.va/content/benedict-xvi/en/speeches/2011/may/documents/hf_ben-xvi_spe_20110521_sacro-cuore.html.

Bethel, Francis. *John Senior and the Restoration of Realism*. Merrimack, N.H.: Thomas More College Press, 2017.

Bowman, Thea. "Black History and Culture." In *Black Catholic Studies Reader: History and Theology*, edited by David J. Endres, 19–26. Washington, D.C.: The Catholic University of America Press, 2021.

Burkey, Blaine. *In Secret Service of the Sacred Heart: The Life and Virtues of Julia Greeley*. Denver: Julia Greeley Guild, 2012.

————. *An Hour with Julia Greeley*. Liguori, Mo.: Liguori Publications, 2020.

Caldecott, Stratford. *Beauty for Truth's Sake: On the Reenchantment of Education*. Grand Rapids, Mich.: Brazos, 2009.

————. *Beauty in the Word: Rethinking the Foundations of Education*. Brooklyn, N.Y.: Angelico Press, 2012.

Carr, Nicholas. *The Shallows: What the Internet Is Doing to Our Brains*. New York: W. W. Norton, 2010.

————. *The Glass Cage: Automation and Us*. New York: Random House, 2015.

Congregation for Catholic Education. "The Catholic School." 1977. https://www.vatican.va/roman_curia/congregations/ccatheduc/documents/rc_con_ccatheduc_doc_19770319_catholic-school_en.html.

————. "The Religious Dimension of Education in a Catholic School." April 7, 1988. https://www.vatican.va/roman_curia/congregations/

ccatheduc/documents/rc_con_ccatheduc_doc_19880407_catholic-school_en.html.

Craig, Jason. *Leaving Boyhood Behind: Reclaiming Catholic Brotherhood.* Huntington, Ind.: Our Sunday Visitor Books, 2019.

Crawford, Matthew B. *Shop Class as Soulcraft: An Inquiry into the Value of Work.* New York: Penguin Books, 2009.

D'Arezzo, Leonardo. "Concerning the Study of Literature: A Letter Addressed to the Illustrious Lady, Baptista Malatesta." In *Vittorino da Feltre and Other Humanist Educators,* edited by W. H. Woodward, 119–33. Cambridge: Cambridge University Press, 1912. https://history.hanover.edu/texts/bruni.html.

Dawson, Christopher. *The Crisis of Western Education.* Washington, D.C.: The Catholic University of America Press, 2003.

———. *Understanding Europe.* Washington, D.C.: The Catholic University of America Press, 2008.

De La Salle, John Baptiste. *The Conduct of the Christian Schools.* Translated by F. de La Fontainerie and Richard Arnandez, FSC. Edited by William Mann, FSC. Landover, Md.: Lasalian Publications, 2007.

Dewey, John. "My Pedagogic Creed." *School Journal* 54 ( January 1897): 77–80.

———. *Democracy and Education.* New York: The Free Press, 1916.

———. *Experience & Education.* New York: Touchstone, 1938.

Drane, Augusta Theodosia. *Christian Schools and Scholars or Sketches of Education from the Christian Era to the Council of Trent.* New York: E.G. Stechert & Co., 1907.

Egan, Kieran. *Getting It Wrong from the Beginning: Our Progressivist Inheritance from Herbert Spencer, John Dewey, and Jan Piaget.* New Haven, Conn.: Yale University Press, 2002.

Farrell, Allan P., ed. *The Jesuit Ratio Studiorum of 1599.* Washington, D.C.: Conference of Jesuit Superiors, 1970.

Filippi, Bruna. "The Orator's Performance: Gesture, Word, and Image in Theatre at the Collegio Romano." In *The Jesuits II: Cultures, Sciences, and the Arts, 1540–1773,* edited by John W. O'Malley, Gauvin Alexander Bailey, Steven J. Harris, and T. Frank Kennedy, 512–29. Toronto: University of Toronto Press, 2006.

Finkenstaedt, Thomas, and Dieter Wolff. *Ordered Profusion: Studies in Dictionaries and the English Lexicon*. Germany: C. Winter, 1973.

Flores, Daniel. "The Synthetic Impulse in Catholic Life." Lecture at the University of Mary. February 24, 2017. https://www.primematters. com/perspectives/synthetic-impulse-catholic-life.

Francis. *Scripturae sacrae affectus*. Apostolic letter. September 30, 2020. https://www.vatican.va/content/francesco/en/apost_letters/ documents/papa-francesco-lettera-ap_20200930_scripturae-sacrae-affectus.html.

———. *Patris corde*. Apostolic letter. December 8, 2020. https://www. vatican.va/content/francesco/en/apost_letters/documents/papa-francesco-lettera-ap_20201208_patris-corde.html.

Gilby, Thomas. *Poetic Experience: An Introduction to Thomist Aesthetic*. New York: Sheed & Ward, 1934.

Gregg, Samuel. *Reason, Faith, and the Struggle for Western Civilization*. Washington, D.C.: Regnery Gateway, 2019.

Guroian, Vigen. *Tending the Heart of Virtue: How Classic Stories Awaken a Child's Moral Imagination*. New York: Oxford University Press, 2002.

Habiger Institute for Catholic Leadership. *The Heart of Culture: A Brief History of Education in the West*. Providence, R.I.: Cluny Media, 2020.

Hasson, Mary Rice, and Theresa Farnan. *Get Out Now: Why You Should Pull Your Child from Public School Before It's Too Late*. Washington, D.C.: Regnery Gateway, 2018.

Haug, Werner, Paul Compton, and Youssef Courbage, eds. *The Demographic Characteristics of National Minorities in Certain European States*. Volume 2. Strasbourg: Council of Europe Directorate General III, Social Cohesion, 2000.

Hirsch, E. D., Jr. "Cultural Literacy." *The American Scholar* 52, no. 2 (Spring 1983): 159–69.

———. *Cultural Literacy: What Every American Needs to Know*. New York: Vintage Books, 1988.

Hourlier, Dom Jacques. *Reflections on the Spirituality of Gregorian Chant*. Orleans, Mass.: Paraclete Press, 1995.

Jain, Ravi Scott, Robbie Andreasen, and Chris Hall. *A New Natural Philosophy: Recovering a Natural Science and Christian Pedagogy*. Camp Hill, Penn.: Classical Academic Press, 2021.

John Paul II. Address to the Italian National Congress of the Ecclesial Movement for Cultural Commitment. January 16, 1982. https://www.vatican.va/content/john-paul-ii/it/speeches/1982/january/documents/hf_jp-ii_spe_19820116_impegno-culturale.html.

————. Address to the Plenary Assembly of the Pontifical Council for Culture. March 18, 1994. http://www.vatican.va/content/john-paul-ii/en/speeches/1994/march/documents/hf_jp-ii_spe_18031994_address-to-pc-culture.html.

————. Address to the Catholic University of the Sacred Heart. November 9, 2000. https://www.vatican.va/content/john-paul-ii/en/speeches/2000/oct-dec/documents/hf_jp-ii_spe_20001109_gemelli.html.

————. "Letter to Artists." April 4, 1999. https://www.vatican.va/content/john-paul-ii/en/letters/1999/documents/hf_jp-ii_let_23041999_artists.html.

La Salle, St. John Baptiste de. *The Conduct of the Christian Schools*. Edited by William Mann, FSC. Translated by F. de La Fontainerie and Richard Arnandez, FSC. Landover, Md.: Lasallian Publications, 2007.

Leclercq, Jean. *The Love of Learning and the Desire for God: A Study of Monastic Culture*. New York: Fordham University Press, 1982.

Lev, Elizabeth. *How Catholic Art Saved the Faith: The Triumph of Beauty and Truth in Counter-Reformation Art*. Manchester, N.H.: Sophia Institute Press, 2018.

Lewis, C. S. "Bluspels and Flalansferes: A Semantic Nightmare." In *Rehabilitations and Other Essays*. Oxford: Oxford University Press, 1939.

Maritain, Jacques. *Creative Intuition in Art and Poetry*. New York: Pantheon Books, 1953.

————. *The Education of Man*. Edited by Donald and Idella Gallagher. Garden City, N.Y.: Doubleday & Company, Inc., 1962.

McInerny, Daniel. "Poetic Knowledge and Cultural Renewal." *Logos* 15, no. 4 (2012): 17–35.

Miller, J. Michael. *The Holy See's Teaching on Catholic Schools*. Manchester, N.H.: Sophia Institute Press, 2006.

Montessori, Maria. *The Montessori Method*. Translated by Anne E. George. New York: Frederick A. Stokes Company, 1912.

Morey, Melanie M., and John J. Piderit. *Catholic Higher Education: A Culture in Crisis*. New York: Oxford University Press, 2006.

Newman, John Henry. *Historical Sketches*. Vol. 2. New York: Longmans, Green, and Co., 1906.

O'Malley, John W. *Saints or Devils Incarnate?: Studies in Jesuit History*. Leiden: Brill, 2013.

Paul VI. *Sacrificium laudis*. Apostolic letter. August 15, 1966.

Pestalozzi, Johann Heinrich. *The Education of Man: Aphorisms*. New York: Philosophical Library, 1951.

Pieper, Josef. *Leisure, The Basis of Culture*. San Francisco: Ignatius Press, 2009.

Plato. *The Complete Works*. Edited by John Cooper. Indianapolis: Hackett, 1997.

Postman, Neil. *Amusing Ourselves to Death: Public Discourse in the Age of Show Business*. 2nd ed. New York: Penguin, 2005.

Prather, Anika, and Angel Adams Parham. *The Black Intellectual Tradition: Reading Freedom in Classical Literature*. Camp Hill, Penn.: Classical Academic Press, 2022.

Ratzinger, Joseph. *Introduction to Christianity*. San Francisco, Ignatius Press, 1990.

———. *The Spirit of the Liturgy*. San Francisco: Ignatius Press, 2000.

———. *On the Way to Jesus Christ*. San Francisco: Ignatius Press, 2005.

———. *Handing on the Faith in an Age of Disbelief*. San Francisco: Ignatius Press, 2006.

Salkeld, Brett. *Educating for Eternity: A Teacher's Companion for Making Every Class Catholic*. Huntington, Ind.: Our Sunday Visitor Press, 2023.

Sasse, Ben. *The Vanishing American Adult: Our Coming-of-Age Crisis—and How to Rebuild a Culture of Self-Reliance*. New York: St. Martin's, 2017.

Sax, Leonard. *The Collapse of Parenting: How We Hurt Our Kids When We Treat Them like Grown-Ups*. New York: Basic Books, 2016.

Schultz, Bob. *Created for Work: Practical Insights for Young Men*. Eugene, Ore.: Great Expectations Book Co., 2006.

Second Vatican Council. *Lumen gentium (Dogmatic Constitution on the Church)*. November 21, 1964. https://www.vatican.va/archive/hist_councils/ii_vatican_council/documents/vat-ii_const_19641121_lumen-gentium_en.html.

———. *Gravissimum Educationis* (Declaration on Christian Education). October 28, 1965. https://www.vatican.va/archive/hist_councils/

ii_vatican_council/documents/vat-ii_decl_19651028_gravissimum-educationis_en.html.

Senior, John. *The Restoration of Christian Culture*. Norfolk, Va.: IHS Press, 2008.

Simmons, Tracy Lee. *Climbing Parnassus: A New Apologia for Greek and Latin*. Wilmington, Del.: ISI Books, 2002.

Smith, Christian. *Young Catholic America: Emerging Adults in, out of, and Gone from the Church*. New York: Oxford University Press, 2014.

Smith, Christian, and Adam Adamczyk. *Handing Down the Faith: How Parents Pass Their Religion to the Next Generation*. New York: Oxford University Press, 2021.

Smith, Christian, and Justin Bartkus, *A Report on American Catholic Religious Parenting*. Notre Dame, Ind.: University of Notre Dame, 2018. https://churchlife-info.nd.edu/a-report-on-american-catholic-religious-parenting.

Staudt, R. Jared. *How the Eucharist Can Save Civilization*. Charlotte, N.C.: TAN Books, 2023.

Staudt, R. Jared, ed. *Renewing Catholic Schools: How to Regain a Catholic Vision in a Secular Age*. Washington, D.C.: Catholic Education Press, 2020.

Stenson, James. *Successful Fathers: The Subtle but Powerful Ways Fathers Mold Their Children's Characters*. Princeton, N.J.: Scepter Press, 2001.

Stuart, Janet Erskine. *The Education of Catholic Girls*. Charlotte, N.C.: TAN Books, 2011.

Taylor, James. *Poetic Knowledge: The Recovery of Education*. New York: State University of New York Press, 1998.

Trueman, Carl R. *Strange New World: How Thinkers and Activists Redefined Identity and Sparked the Sexual Revolution*. Wheaton, Ill.: Crossway, 2022.

Twenge, Jean. *iGen: Why Today's Super-Connected Kids Are Growing Up Less Rebellious, More Tolerant, Less Happy—and Completely Unprepared for Adulthood*. New York: Atria, 2017.

University of Mary. *From Christendom to Apostolic Mission: Pastoral Strategies for an Apostolic Age*. Bismarck, N.D.: University of Mary Press, 2020.

Weil, Simone. *Waiting for God*. New York: Harper Perennial, 2009.

# Index